A PASSION FOR BREAD

LIONEL VATINET

A PASSION FOR BREAD

Lessons from a Master Baker

7 Steps to Making Great Bread

PHOTOGRAPHY BY GORDON MUNRO

LITTLE, BROWN AND COMPANY

NEW YORK   BOSTON   LONDON

To all the bakers I have taught—

and who have taught me so much

Little, Brown and Company
Hachette Book Group
237 Park Avenue, New York, NY 10017
littlebrown.com

First Edition: November 2013

Little, Brown and Company is a division of Hachette Book Group, Inc. The Little, Brown
name and logo are trademarks of Hachette Book Group, Inc.

The publisher is not responsible for websites (or their content) that are not owned by the
publisher.

The Hachette Speakers Bureau provides a wide range of authors for speaking events. To find
out more, go to hachettespeakersbureau.com or call (866) 376-6591.

Designed by Laura Lindgren

ISBN 978-0-316-20062-2
LCCN 2013935273

10 9 8 7 6 5 4 3 2 1

IM

Printed in China

CONTENTS

INTRODUCTION

Where does passion come from? Beginning in my early teens, I discovered a passion for bread making—a passion that has continued to deepen through the years that I've worked at the bread oven. Of course, my French heritage may have had something to do with it. I grew up in Montrouge, a suburb of Paris, with the aroma of baking bread permeating the early morning. Was it this deeply ingrained experience that sealed my fate, or was it the bread at the center of the family table that

The making of bread remains my life's consuming passion.

infused me with a sense of its importance to daily life? I still can't answer that question. However my passion arose and wherever it has taken me, the making of bread remains my life's consuming passion.

There are so many traditions associated with dining in France, and many of them revolve around bread. For instance, the loaf is always placed at the center of the table: directly on it, never on a plate. And never upside down; this would indicate that you didn't earn your bread, and also questions your work ethic, something one should never do in the presence of a

Our parents, who helped build our dream

1

Frenchman, particularly after his three-hour lunch. (I sometimes say that the French eat like babies, every three hours.) The crusty heel of a baguette is given to teething babies, a custom that seems to lay the groundwork for a lifelong fight over the end of the loaf. Before a meal begins and the loaf is broken open, often someone blesses the bread by making the sign of a cross over it, as my grandfather did throughout his life. And,

There was never a meal without laughter—or bread!

table manners aside, a piece of bread is still the best tool to push and absorb any food remaining on the plate. All of these rituals were part of my childhood, but it wasn't until much later in life that I realized the cultural impact of bread and the place it holds in history: the lack of it has started revolutions; in the smallest amounts it has kept communities from starvation; religious miracles have sprung from it; and for most people, memories, history, and family traditions center around the table where bread is broken.

Dad's favorite: baguette, bitter semi-sweet chocolate, and red wine

Although I grew up loving to eat and always enjoyed a good piece of bread to wipe the plate clean, I never thought about bread baking as a career. In hindsight, it makes sense—bread was at the heart of our family table. Mornings brought the smell of my dad toasting a slice of *pain de campagne*, warm and oozing with salty butter and honey or homemade jam; an afternoon snack was a crumbly slice of brioche, thickly buttered and topped with a wedge of chocolate (a favorite snack of my father's as it is now mine); and there was (and still is) nothing quite as satisfying as the last bit of dinner's pan *jus* wiped up with a bit of crust. Even a visit to my grandparents in Vendée was highlighted with a favored loaf of the local orange-scented brioche *vendéenne*. There was never a meal without laughter—or bread! But, until I came of age and started to contemplate my career options, cooking and baking unquestionably remained my mom's job.

I was not much of a student (although I did score high marks in classroom comedy), and my parents, who ran a small café in La Rochelle, a town north of Bordeaux, urged me to explore the various trades practiced by their many customers. I tried my hand at quite a few—auto mechanic, plumber, electrician—but none sparked a desire to spend my life working at them. After a day or two in each job, I was bored and ready to move on. But, from the moment I stood by the ovens in a local bakery, I knew I had found my calling. I had to learn how to make bread.

At first, I wasn't sure how to realize my passion. I knew that I would have to apprentice in a bakery, but I had no idea how to go about it. My parents had heard of a centuries-old guild of artisans, Les Compagnons du Devoir, where young men could be initiated into a specific craft. Participation was by invitation only, but as luck would have it, a distant relative who was a Les Compagnons-trained *tapissier* (upholsterer) agreed to be my sponsor.

I was sent to Bordeaux for a week to determine whether I was an acceptable candidate. I took the required tests and was observed by other Compagnons, who would judge whether I had the motivation, aptitude, and potential to honor the guild. I returned to my family and, after a brief period of anxious waiting, was accepted into the program and went off to the city of Tours to begin my new life as an apprentice baker. Once I was "adopted" into the guild, I became known as "Île-de-France," based on a tradition that goes back to the early days of the guild, when men of the lower classes were known by the area or community from which they came, as surnames were rare until well into the thirteenth century. This name would stay with me until I was initiated into my corporation at the end of my tour.

Les Compagnons du Devoir is an extraordinary guild through which young men (and now young women) are trained by apprenticing with experts to become highly accomplished craftsmen in their chosen fields. The bakers' division of the guild was formed in the seventeenth century,

Les Compagnons du Devoir, a centuries old-guild traced back to the building of Solomon's temple

The chaîne d'alliance, *symbolizing community*

and the guild itself can be traced back to the building of Solomon's temple. I find it fascinating that the word *compagnon* comes from an ancient Latin word that translates to "one with whom a person breaks bread"—indeed, baking is the only food-related craft taught at the guild. This method of intensive training is slowly dying the world over, which is a shame. It allows a young person to achieve greatness through absorbing the lessons of the masters while in the constant practice of his craft. It was at the guild that I learned how to work and got a glimpse of the man I would become.

For the first two years of my apprenticeship with a local baker in Tours, I lived in a guild house with other young men, watched over and cared for by *la Mère*. While it was the job of the craftsmen to teach each of us the basics of our chosen trade, it was her job to ensure that we became young men of character and accomplishment who would serve as positive representatives of the guild throughout our careers. This is a central philosophy of Les Compagnons: that you embrace the responsibility to give back to your chosen trade from the beginning to the end of your career. This sense of community is symbolized through the *chaîne d'alliance* (chain of alliance), a tradition that is carried out whenever we are gathered for ceremonies or events, happy or sad, in which we place our arms across our chests and link hands in comradeship with the people on either side of us. It was the two years in the guild house that instilled this sense of community in me and fully prepared me for the Tour de France, the next phase of my training, and for the future that awaited me.

The guild-sponsored Tour de France is not the famous French bicycle race, although it is similar in that you get to visit many areas of the country. The Compagnons Tour is a seven- to ten-year period spent traveling around the country, and sometimes around the world, working under the tutelage of the masters of your chosen trade. This tradition goes back to the guild's founding, fostered by the belief that travel is life-changing, character-building, and essential to the personal, professional, and cultural education of a young person. It was during this time that I refined my craft, learned techniques that had been passed down through the ages, met extraordinary people (many of whom became lifelong friends), and discovered the core of the person I wanted to be. I baked in neighborhood bakeries, huge supermarket kitchens, mass-market commercial bakeries—anywhere a guild master could teach me something new or reinforce the secrets of the past. I still value every minute of this guild-sponsored adventure; I now welcome young guild travelers into my own bakery, far away from France: La Farm Bakery in Cary, North Carolina.

As the final step before induction into the guild, each apprentice must create a masterpiece (in French, a *chef d'oeuvre*) under the watchful eye of their teacher. Each craft demands its own skill. A jeweler might design and execute an intricate piece mixing gold and gems, while a woodworker

My "masterpiece"

might create a hand-carved, hand-chiseled furniture suite. Whatever craft, the masterpiece must show that the apprentice has gained full comprehension and mastery of the most difficult aspects of their chosen field. Since bread has been made for over 30,000 years and is honored as the "staff of life," the creation of my *chef d'oeuvre* had enormous meaning to me. It was a challenge bestowed upon me by an exclusive group of bakers that had gone before me.

My masterpiece was a five-pound *boule* (ball) of light whole-wheat sourdough bread, quite similar to the loaves that, for centuries, were baked in community ovens throughout France. To me, the *boule* represented the passage of the art of traditional baking through the hands of generations of bakers directly into mine. My masterpiece paid homage to the camaraderie that flourished in communities all over France, as the townspeople waited for their weekly loaves to be pulled, golden and aromatic, from the central town oven. The oversized loaves would remain at the center of the family table for a week, gradually diminishing in size but continuing to retain their moisture and freshness all week long.

From my perspective, this substantial loaf is emblematic of the importance of bread at the table—of how bread is at the heart of French culture, as conversations ebb and flow and relationships form and fade. My *boule* was my artistic interpretation of the soul of French cuisine. It is this same bread that I still bake daily, now known as "La Farm Bread," my signature loaf named for our bakery, and offer to my adopted community in honor of the trade that has been passed down to me. After all these years, the aroma, the crust, the crumb, and the complex flavor still excite me. And, once you begin making your own, I guarantee that it will be your favorite as well.

I value the traditions of Les Compagnons du Devoir and I carry with me all the trappings of investiture in it. I treasure the beautiful bakers-only beige silk sash stamped with the symbols of accomplishment that only another guild member will recognize. I'm not averse to using the traditional ceremonial cane that comes up to my heart and is inscribed with my bespoke guild name, *La Persévérance*, given to me by fellow Compagnons to acknowledge my dedication and determination. With pride I wear small gold hoop earrings, a traditional adornment that dates back to the long-ago

era when workers weren't allowed to leave their "owners" or work for others without permission; Compagnons were the only exception to this rule, and wearing the earrings signified this freedom. My "guild godfather," Eric Kayser, now one of the world's preeminent bakers, remains my closest friend and confidant. The guild instilled in me a lifelong commitment to my trade, with work, family, and spirituality at the core.

I have found that it is often difficult for people to understand the importance I attach to guild membership and my years of training, the debt I feel to the Maîtres Boulangers (Master Bakers) of the past, and my commitment to the masters of the future. I am not alone in my appreciation of the guild. All members take their obligations very seriously. Through centuries, bakers in my guild strove to achieve quality and perfection and selflessly transfer their knowledge to others. It is those who taught me, and those who taught them, whom I honor each time I teach, passing along hundreds of years of learning. Teaching

The traditional Guild ceremony attire

and sharing my experience with others is as rewarding to me as filling my ovens with the beautifully formed loaves that become crusty, aromatic breads for my customers.

I have, perhaps, gone on too long about my early training, but without it I would not have come so far, learned so much, or met so many wonderful people, including my wife and business partner, Missy. Because I was able to mature under the training of so many Master Bakers, and, with their support, earn the title of Master Baker myself, by the time I was ready to go out on my own I possessed the skills and confidence to take on the world. I had pledged to devote my life to teaching, sharing, preserving, and demystifying the ancient art and science of bread baking, and I was eager to begin my journey, paying tribute to all of the extraordinary bakers behind the baker that I had become.

I roamed the world teaching and working with both novice and experienced bakers.

For a number of years, I roamed the world teaching and working with both novice and experienced bakers, giving them the techniques

LA FARM BREAD

Although I hadn't yet gained the experience to formulate my Seven Steps to Making Great Bread (see page 39), I simply followed the rules and techniques of the Master Bakers who had come before me as I created my *chef d'oeuvre*. After years of working with many types of dough, I still consider this bread a true masterpiece. We sell many, many pounds of it, whole or by the half or quarter, daily. Following are the ingredients I use to make a five-pound loaf of La Farm Bread. (Most home ovens do not have the capacity to bake such a large loaf, so you will find a home-oven-friendly recipe for La Farm Bread on page 177 that will enable you to create your own masterpiece.)

MAKES ONE 5-POUND *BOULE*

2 pounds plus 5.6 ounces	1066 grams	7⅓ cups unbleached, unbromated white bread flour
4.8 ounces	136 grams	1¼ cups unbromated whole-wheat bread flour
0.96 ounce	27 grams	1½ tablespoons fine sea salt
1 pound plus 12.16 ounces	799 grams	3½ cups water
9.28 ounces	263 grams	1 cup plus 1½ tablespoons liquid *levain* (see page 20)

necessary to bring their loaves to perfection. I spent a year in Vancouver, British Columbia, while shorter periods found me in New Zealand, Mexico, Martinique, Thailand, Brazil, Peru, and the United States (among other countries), both teaching and continuing to expand my own knowledge of the craft of fine bread baking. As I traveled, I was rewarded with the knowledge of the experiences and styles of baking of other cultures. In the end, I could see that we all have many things in common. No matter where I found myself, I discovered that bread, built from the same basic ingredients, was a fundamental part of the meal. In America, I loved the confident imagination and creativity that took these basics and developed combinations and styles that never seemed to end. I feel deeply that bread making is something to be shared, that there are no secrets to it. It was my

Coaching the American team for the World Cup of Baking competition

quest to reach as many bakers as possible, passing down centuries of knowledge about bread making and helping them adapt this knowledge to the modern world. With immersion in the past, young bakers have the fundamental tools to find their own creativity.

Through part of the 1990s I was associated with the San Francisco Baking Institute, the first and only school of its kind in the United States. Under the direction of Michel Suas, I had the rewarding experience of working with other bakers in the development of the curriculum, teaching both commercial and home bakers the elements of fine bread making. Artisanal bread baking in the States was really taking off at the time, and the interest from bakers across the country was almost overwhelming. During this period, I had the honor to work beside great bakers and innovative companies such as Acme Bread Company, La Brea Bakery, and Panera Bread as they instituted artisanal bread-baking programs and did research and development on existing bread programs. Each project brought a new set of bakers determined to make great breads and, for me, the opportunity to make lifelong friends. From small start-up bakeries to large parbaked commercial projects, artisanal breads were taking the States by storm, and it was exciting to be a part of it. My real reward came when I would return to the individual businesses and find them not only pursuing their own style of bread baking, while adhering to the fundamentals, but also growing financially. American skill and artistry developed to the point that in 1999 a team of bakers (for whom I had the honor of being one of the coaches) earned an undreamed-of first place in La Coupe du Monde de la Boulangerie (the World Cup of Baking) in Paris.

During my time at the San Francisco Baking Institute, I met my future wife at a trade show. It was my bread, not my personality, that got Missy's attention, and it was some time before she noticed that I had more interest in her than in improving her company's bread program. Our friendship grew over a couple of years as I consulted with the company she worked for. Then I called on Missy to help a small company I was advising to understand the complexities of running a food-based business.

We figured if we could bake bread together daily, we could probably handle marriage.

I had seen that Missy understood the intricacies of commerce in the United States and would bring a great business sense to the project. Working together daily, we discovered that we just might have a partnership that could work—in business and in life. We figured that if we could bake bread together daily, we could probably handle marriage. And so La Farm Bakery was born.

Today, we are still working at building the bakery and our family, with the added help of our two adorable daughters, Emilie and Léa. And, as with all things in life, some days it works beautifully and some days it doesn't, but we always support each other and find a way to have some fun.

At the bakery, Missy's business skills allow me the freedom to do what I do best and to continue to travel and teach around the world, meeting my obligations to the guild. Her wonderful design sense has created a space

La Farm's bread

at La Farm that hints of France but is built with American ingenuity. I love that our customers can look right into our production kitchen and watch as the breads are being formed and baked. From its early days as a small bread-only bakery, we have expanded to include a café that sells select desserts as well as sandwiches, soups, and salads. I can sit with our customers, enjoy a glass of wine, and explain just what it is that makes our breads so delicious and healthful; loaves are frequently broken open so we can demonstrate the full sense of the aroma, crumb, and crust. I offer monthly classes right in the bread kitchen that introduce customers and friends to my Seven Steps to Making Great Bread (see page 39), the skill set that I teach through my consulting in the professional and commercial baking community. And every day I bake the classic breads of my apprenticeship along with innovative loaves that reveal the influence

of my travels, incorporating new techniques, ingredients, and flavor combinations.

La Farm started with just eight varieties of bread and cinnamon buns. We have grown day by day, helped by the amazing loyalty of our customers. We are on such familiar terms with many of them that they don't hesitate to yell into the kitchen to the bakers—usually with their appreciation. We frequently have new product meetings, where our staff can share baking ideas of their own or pass along those they receive from customers. Some of the breads in this book evolved from suggestions presented in this way; we are particularly grateful for the many new ideas and recipes that come from the cultural traditions of others.

Although our fans have helped us build, it is the great team of bakers, sales associates, and office personnel that has ensured our success. From the beginning, the sense of ownership, hard work, and dedication of our team has been an inspiration for Missy and me. We have a saying at the bakery: "We sell energy—it just happens to be in the form of bread."

La Farm Bakery is, I think, a showcase for America's ingenuity and caring and for its openhearted welcome to immigrants. (My French-inflected, Southern-drawl of "Hi, y'all" lets customers know that I have settled in for the long haul, with my accent and my sense of humor intact.) We try to make it a home away from home for both our employees and our customers. At the end of every day, our associates are encouraged to take a

Lionel teaching home bakers

loaf of bread home to their families. It is how the bakers say "thank you" to the staff for the care and pride they take in their work, whether selling and sharing the breads with the community or washing the dishes. At closing, all remaining breads and pastries are donated to a local food pantry and to migrant workers, the force behind North Carolina's agricultural business.

I have no secrets. My goal as a baker has been to demystify baking for professional and home bakers.

As for me, I have no secrets. My goal as a baker has been to demystify baking for professional and home bakers, and to mentor as many as I can so everyone can enjoy high-quality, handcrafted breads. I work with a few basic ingredients and let my passion lead. I still find making bread magical—the feeling of the dough in my hands, the aroma of the yeast, the rise of a few ingredients into a magnificent baked loaf. It's mysterious and endlessly alluring.

Building on the classic recipes of my training, I have embraced America's spirit of invention to arrive at original combinations and techniques that I love to share. As I have instructed bakers in the craft of artisanal bread around the world, I have learned just as much as I have taught. As the saying goes, to teach is truly to learn twice. I hope that the lessons you find within the pages of this book will lead you to discover your own passion for baking great bread and that you, in turn, will pass along your passion to others.

—Lionel Vatinet

PILGRIMAGE:
A Baker's Journey through Life

During my time as a young baker in Les Compagnons du Devoir, I was encouraged to take a solo walking pilgrimage—at some point in my career—to bring a spiritual perspective to my life's work. In 2004, with La Farm Bakery a reality and a family on the way, I chose to make a five-week

pilgrimage from the French Pyrenees to the Basque region of Spain, a famous route called El Camino Santiago de Compostela (the Way of St. James) that has served as a path for religious pilgrims for centuries.

Starting out, I was given a *carnet de pèlerin* (a passport-like booklet) to be stamped at the churches or information centers at various points along the way, as well as at the hundreds of monasteries and *albergues* (hostels) on the route that welcome pilgrims. Some of these places have been welcoming pilgrims for centuries. Each stamp has a unique and quite beautiful mark, many of them including a scallop shell, the symbol of St. James. The stamps signify each stage of the pilgrim's accomplishment.

Traveling by foot I was able to share meals, conversation, and meditations with guild members, Master and community bakers, religious seekers, mystics, and ordinary people along the route. The way was often very difficult, with bloody feet and aching muscles urging me to give up my quest. A twisted ankle pressed me to throw in the towel, but a Spanish priest encouraged me to push on through my pain as a way to discover my own resilience. His encouragement and advice still resonates with me. I discovered how much teaching others had meant to me and vowed to continue to guide bakers through the rest of my life.

Most of the time I was walking along with only my thoughts as my companions. I came to appreciate how much I had and how little I needed for happiness. I have been a traveler all of my life, and I came to understand that you carry who you are and what is important with you. This journey brought a new perspective to my life and, more than anything else, showed me what it means to live well. I learned that life can be quite simple when you carry your house on your shoulders. I no longer yearn for material things. What matters in life comes down to who you are and how you honor your obligations, and, of course, having great bread to quell the pangs of hunger.

INGREDIENTS FOR FINE BREAD BAKING

How is it that four very simple ingredients—flour, yeast, salt, and water—come together to make extraordinary bread? Of course, some breads contain more than the basic four, but it is these essential ingredients that, in the hands of a baker, join forces to create the "staff of life." Given the simplicity of the ingredients, it should come as no surprise that at La Farm Bakery, I use only the highest-quality ingredients. You should abide by these same high standards at home. Superb products are now readily available at many supermarkets, farmers' markets, almost all specialty food stores, and, of course, online.

Flour, yeast, salt, and water create the "staff of life."

Although bread is composed of only four simple ingredients, baking does not occur in a vacuum. No matter the quality of your ingredients, you have to adapt to the weather. You shouldn't wait for the perfect day to make bread, but you do need to be aware of the elements because they can create magic—or mischief—in your dough. If it is a very hot day, you will need cooler water to begin the process, or you might also lower the amount of yeast or starter. If the temperature is cold, you will need to increase the beginning water temperature and yeast or starter to compensate. If it is raining or the humidity is high, the bread may have to be baked a little longer to help the crust maintain its crispness. Knowing how to work with the elements comes through practice.

These days, there is a great deal of discussion about organic products versus those grown conventionally. At La Farm I try to use flours (as well as other products) that are grown locally; frequently they are also grown organically. Just to clarify, conventionally raised produce (including wheat and other grains) is grown with the use of chemical fertilizers, herbicides, and insecticides, while only natural fertilizers and natural methods of weed and pest control (such as crop rotation and hand weeding) are used for organically grown produce. Neither of these methods takes into consideration the true cost, both financial and environmental, of bringing the product to market.

In bread baking, you use four simple ingredients, one unpredictable element (weather), and all of your senses to create great dough. Over the years you build a store of knowledge on how to use your senses: touch—

the memory of the texture of the dough; sight—proofing, the liveliness of the starter, the golden crust, and texture in the cuts on top of the bread; sound—the melody of the bread "singing" as it bakes; smell—fermentation, the aroma of the baked loaf; taste—the crunchiness of the crust and tender interior crumb. We bakers believe that there is a sixth sense—intuition—that tells you when to catch the right moment in the fermentation and baking that will produce a masterpiece.

One could write an entire book on the ingredients that go into bread, but I don't want to make baking sound more complicated than it is. I would rather keep the focus on making great bread. However, to help you better understand the quality you should look for, I will briefly explore each of the basic ingredients required to create a delicious loaf.

FLOUR

Without a doubt, flour quality is the most important element in creating perfect dough. Wheat flour is the most familiar variety, but there are many different types of flour available to the artisanal bread baker, all of which create their own identifiable notes. Different flours not only affect the structure and texture of baked bread, they also provide nutrients, heighten flavor, and dictate the incorporation of liquid into the dough. Each class of flour produces a specific result, so it is essential that the baker understand the properties of the flour being used. There are many excellent technical books that delve into the science of flour, but, for our purposes, I will cover only the essentials of the flours that I use to make my signature La Farm breads.

In North Carolina we are fortunate to have a regional grain initiative called the North Carolina Organic Bread Flour Project, which has launched a micro-milling facility dedicated to grains grown in the Carolinas and to cold-stone milling. The goal is to allow growers to keep food dollars in the state as well as to improve our daily breads by using locally grown and milled wheat. I feel extremely lucky to be able to work with local wheat farmers; I so appreciate their skill and dedication to bringing a superb product to market. It is a simple fact that without hard-working wheat farmers there would be no bread, for wheat is the essence of all great breads.

Bread Flours Used at La Farm Bakery

Most of the flours that I use in creating my signature breads are milled from wheat. Wheat flour is milled from hard or soft white or red wheat, or from durum wheat. No matter the type, all wheat flours are composed of

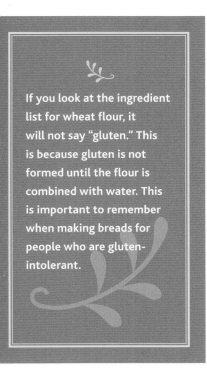

If you look at the ingredient list for wheat flour, it will not say "gluten." This is because gluten is not formed until the flour is combined with water. This is important to remember when making breads for people who are gluten-intolerant.

carbohydrates, proteins, enzymes, lipids, vitamins, and minerals, each of which has a particular job to do in creating the perfect bread. Hard wheats have a high protein and low starch content, while white wheats are the exact opposite.

To create a user-friendly flour that gives consistent results, flour must be aged or oxidized. In commercial operations in the United States and some other countries, speed is prioritized, so this is generally done chemically through the addition of azodicarbonamide (a chemical that speeds the maturing process without affecting the color) to freshly milled flour. Many pastry flours are also bleached with chlorine dioxide, while white bread flours are bleached with benzoyl peroxide. The use of bromates, which age the flour, has been banned in Europe for a number of years, as there is evidence that they may cause cancer in rats . I prefer to use unbleached, unbromated flour—organic when available—and strongly recommend that home bakers follow suit.

For a bread baker, the most important element is the protein; the baker must know not only the protein content of the flour, but also its quality and its ability to form gluten (the element that gives the dough its elasticity and ability to extend). Hard wheat flours result in a high-quality, elastic-gluten dough, producing an excellent crust and crumb when baked, while soft wheat flours produce a slack dough, resulting in a baked bread that is dense and wet, with minimum rise. Spring wheat has a higher protein content but is generally of lower quality. Winter wheat has less protein but is of higher quality because it stays in the ground longer. The more porous the wheat, the less it is able to hold strong fermentation, so I strongly recommend using hard wheat whenever possible. I use primarily the following wheat flours:

WHITE BREAD FLOUR: Generally milled from hard red or white winter wheat, white bread flour is a robust flour with a high protein content. Classically, it is used to create yeast-based bread and pastry doughs. It may be bleached or unbleached, bromated or unbromated. At La Farm I use only unbleached, unbromated white bread flour in my breads.

WHOLE-WHEAT BREAD FLOUR: This flour is milled from either hard or soft whole-grain wheat, which results in an unbleached flour with higher nutrients and more fat and fiber than white. It can be milled in either a coarse or fine grind. It is often mixed with white wheat or other flours. At La Farm I use only unbromated whole-wheat bread flour.

ALL-PURPOSE FLOUR: This everyday flour is made from a combination of flour types, yielding a medium-protein flour that can be used in all areas of baking, including artisanal bread making. It is available bleached or unbleached, bromated or unbromated. When using all-purpose flour in bread baking, it is important to remember that its gluten-producing qualities are somewhat less than desirable, as the lower protein content makes it more difficult to produce the desired results. At La Farm, all-purpose flour is used only for some breakfast pastries.

PATENT DURUM FLOUR: This high-protein, unbleached, fine, pale yellow flour is milled from durum wheat. Traditionally used in many Italian breads, it can be used in my Sesame Semolina Bread (see page 201), which is based on the breads sold in the Italian markets of my hometown.

SEMOLINA FLOUR: Semolina is a high-protein, high-gluten, hard-granule flour milled from durum wheat. It is used primarily to make pasta and noodles, but is also found in Italian-style breads and pastries. I use it in my Sesame Semolina Bread (see page 201). Semolina flour is also combined with bread flour to dust our *couche* (linen divider), as it creates a more absorbent mix that prevents the breads from sticking to the fabric.

SPELT FLOUR: Made from an ancient cereal grain, spelt flour has a low protein content and very mild flavor. It is frequently used to make breads for those who suffer from wheat allergies.

RYE FLOUR: Rye flour is an extremely low-gluten flour made from a cereal grass. Unlike wheat flour, it does not form gluten, so it is usually mixed with a bread flour to create a reliable dough. However, in some European countries, traditional breads are made from straight rye flour as it was, at one point, the only flour available. It also ferments more quickly than wheat flour and, therefore, cannot stand long fermentation periods. In the bakery, we control this by proofing rye loaves on racks placed in the coolest part of the refrigerator so that we can achieve the same proofing times as all of our breads. Rye flour comes in a variety of colors and styles ranging from light tan to dark pumpernickel. Breads containing a large amount of rye often have a long shelf life thanks to the flour's absorption of moisture.

Ancient Grains Used in La Farm Breads

At La Farm I incorporate a number of ancient grains into many of my more substantial breads. I use the whole grain, which is soaked in water overnight before being added to the dough. The soaking hydrates and tenderizes the grain, and the moist grains then lend flavor, texture, fiber, and earthiness to the baked bread. Frequently I combine the grains with seeds, such as sunflower or sesame (which are not presoaked). With the more earthy-tasting grains, I always add a touch of honey to the mix to give a complex nutty flavor to the baked bread. Among the grains I use are:

AMARANTH: An ancient grain of the Aztecs, amaranth has been cultivated for more than eight thousand years. It is high in protein and easy to grow, and adds a wonderful earthy flavor to whole-grain breads. It can also be milled into a highly nutritious and gluten-free flour.

BUCKWHEAT: Grown throughout Asia since long before the time of Christ, buckwheat has a deep, earthy flavor that some compare to molasses, provides excellent nutritional value, and adds texture and flavor to whole-grain breads. It can be milled into a gluten-free flour, which I use to make crêpes.

MILLET: A food staple in many impoverished areas in India, Africa, and elsewhere, millet is a high-protein, highly nutritional cereal grass that thrives in semi-arid regions. It adds a slightly bittersweet, deeply aromatic flavor to whole-grain breads.

YEAST

The main function of yeast in any dough is to leaven it; the action occurs when the yeast produces carbon dioxide, the element that lightens and mellows the baked product. Yeast is a living organism that is found wild in the air, in soil, and on vegetation, and it is these wild yeasts that develop when you make a natural starter. These same yeasts have been contained and cultivated for commercial use in compressed and dry yeasts. The average ratio of yeast to flour in a bread recipe is between 0.1 percent and 1.5 percent by weight.

Four types of yeasts may be used when baking bread: commercially produced compressed fresh yeast, active dry yeast, instant dry yeast, and natural starters (also called *levains*) made from captured wild yeast spores. At La Farm, I use either instant dry yeast or a natural starter for all of my breads.

For generations, home bakers have been told that to test the viability of any yeast, it should be dissolved in warm water to which a pinch of sugar has been added and then set aside in a warm place for about 10 minutes. At this point, if the liquid begins to bubble and grow, the yeast would be deemed usable. I disagree with this advice, as it leaves the temperature of the water, and subsequently the dough, too high and unreliable for proper fermentation. When too warm, your dough will be overproofed and unusable. In the bakery we call this "running after your dough." If you are careful about the yeast you buy and your method of storage, its viability should not come into question. Remember this, and you should have absolutely no problem making great bread.

In North Carolina we are fortunate to have Carolina Ground, a micro-milling facility dedicated to connecting Carolina grain growers with Carolina bakers, and to producing the highest quality artisanal flours via a process known as cold-stone milling. Carolina Ground enables growers to keep food dollars in the state, while improving our daily breads by offering locally grown, stone-ground wheat and rye flours, whole grain and sifted. I feel extremely lucky to be able to work with local wheat farmers and millers; I so appreciate their skills and dedication to bringing a superb product to market. It is a simple fact that without their hard work there would be no bread.

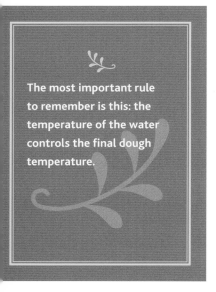

> The most important rule to remember is this: the temperature of the water controls the final dough temperature.

COMPRESSED FRESH YEAST: This refrigerated, perishable yeast has a high moisture content. It comes in a block, is easy to weigh, and can be added directly to a dry mix. Fresh yeast can be substituted for instant dry yeast by using two parts fresh yeast for one part instant dry.

ACTIVE DRY YEAST: Dry, dormant yeast granules are coated with dead yeast cells that are activated only when mixed with warm liquid, which washes away the dead cells. Active dry yeast comes as either regular or quick-rise, with the quick taking about half the time to leaven, but they can be used interchangeably. Both should be stored in a cool, dry spot or refrigerated. If refrigerated, bring to room temperature before using. Active dry yeast can be substituted for fresh yeast by using one part dry to two parts fresh. However, I *do not recommend* this readily available yeast—mainly because it requires a higher water temperature, which will affect the final dough temperature.

INSTANT DRY YEAST: This is a relatively new commercial yeast that was developed in Europe to speed production time in commercial bakeries. It is the yeast now used most frequently by artisanal bread bakers and, if not using a natural starter, the one I use both in the bakery and at home. Since it requires no initial proofing, it can be mixed directly into dry ingredients. It has a long shelf life and a low moisture content. Instant dry yeast is available to home bakers usually under the name "rapid-rise" or "quick-rise." All of the recipes in this book calling for instant dry yeast are referring to this type; in general, instant dry yeast can be substituted for fresh yeast by using 40 percent of the amount of fresh yeast called for in the recipe.

LIQUID *LEVAIN* (ALSO KNOWN AS NATURAL SOURDOUGH OR NATURAL STARTER): Flour and water, and sometimes honey, are mixed together and left to rest for a prolonged period whereby the mix captures and cultivates wild yeast spores. The spores grow on the surface, and once the collection begins, the starter is fed and watered to feed the yeast and nurture the spores. Over a period of days, a large amount of starter will be produced. The specific amount called for in a recipe can then be taken out and added to a dough as the leavening agent, and the remaining starter can be fed and watered for ongoing use. Some starters began life many, many years ago and have been handed down from one generation of baker to the next. When I first came to the States from France I traveled with my starter, and still do when I consult for bakeries around the world.

The amount of natural starter added to a dough produces a bread with a specific level of sourness. Since the baker controls this taste, the resulting bread carries the baker's "signature flavor." While most bread has a degree of sourness, it should always have an inviting taste and aroma. For example, the flavor profile of a San Francisco sourdough bread is at the high end

of sourness, while my La Farm signature bread, and my bread in general, is made with less sour *levain* because I want the grains to push their intensity forward.

You will find my method of making a liquid *levain* on page 24. I use organic flour to increase the success of the starter; chemical herbicides and insecticides may inhibit the productivity of the yeast spores. This starter is called the "mother" of La Farm Bakery. To keep her alive we carefully nurture her needs—giving her the flour she needs for her "sugar fix" and water to keep her hydrated and full of oxygen; this is called "feeding the mother" at the bakery.

POOLISH: Made from yeast, flour, and water, poolish is a traditional French pre-ferment, a mixture of dough ingredients that is allowed to ferment and is then added to the final dough during mixing. It was originally used by Polish bakers, for whom the French named it. You can add poolish in addition to instant dry yeast to any yeasted bread to add a nutty flavor profile and increase the shelf life, a technique we often use when making white-flour breads that don't have many flavor-enhancing ingredients. Poolish is something I would encourage advanced bakers to explore, adding it, for instance, when making my baguette recipe.

SALT

Salt is essential to bread making; it retards yeast activity, contributes to crust color, strengthens the gluten, and enhances the final flavor of the baked product. The ratio of salt to flour in most bread doughs is about 1.75 percent to 2 percent based on flour weight. Although some bakers use table salt or kosher salt, I use only fine-grain sea salt in all of my breads. I like the natural drying process used to create it and the mineral flavor it imparts. Sea salt comes in many colors ranging from pale cream to black, but only a natural, pale color should be used when making bread dough.

In France, salt has recently become a no-no due to concerns about high blood pressure. The government has initiated a campaign to control the levels of salt consumed by its population; in fact, a proposed law would regulate the percentage of salt that bakers can add to bread dough. At La Farm Bakery, we are conscientious about the amount of salt we use in all of our products.

WATER

The primary use for water in bread making is hydration. Once mixed with flour, water causes the formation of gluten and aids in the activation of starches, enzymes, and yeast function. The ratio of water to flour will determine both the texture of the dough and the quality of the baked result. I use only tap water processed through a carbon-filter system. The system helps control chlorine and heavy metals in the water, elements we want to keep out of our diets as much as possible. Distilled water does not have the right balance of alkalines, minerals, and hardness. Most municipal waters have a variance in their alkalinity, but it usually will not affect the dough. If you live in an area where the water is highly chlorinated and you wish to make a natural starter, the water should be refrigerated, uncovered, for 24 hours before use to allow the chlorine gas to dissipate; otherwise the chlorine will destroy the friendly bacteria that the wild yeast needs to grow. If you have hard water, increase the fermentation time to assist in the rise. If you have soft water, the addition of salt will generally ensure an even bake.

The temperature of the water used is extremely important; every bread recipe in this book will specify the correct water temperature required. When mixing by hand, water that is between 82°F and 84°F will yield a dough that will fall between the desired 72°F and 80°F no matter the time of year. If you are using a stand mixer, the friction created by the mixer heats the dough as it kneads, so it is more challenging until you know your mixer's heat-generating capabilities. In addition, the time of year and the temperature of your kitchen will have a greater impact on the result, so it is difficult to provide a range for water temperature because each environment requires a specific adaptation. It can start in the range of 65°F to 70°F but can also be as low as 50°F.

SWEETENERS

Many sweeteners can be added to bread doughs. The one that I use most often is honey, particularly one from a local beekeeper. (I prefer to use local honey when I can, both for its flavor and for the health benefits to our customers.) I prefer the flavor profile that honey offers, plus it gives me another chance to support local agriculture. Sweeteners are generally added to artisanal bread doughs in very small amounts; somewhere between 0 percent and 12 percent in ratio to flour weight, with the higher amount obviously used in sweet doughs, such as brioche. Sugar is often used because it enhances the baked product's sugary profile, adds defined flavor, color, texture, and tenderness to the baked loaf, and helps retain moisture, thereby extending shelf life. Both sugar and honey assist the yeast during the fermentation process.

You might have heard the baker's term "Maillard reaction" in reference to a finished golden brown loaf. This is the heat-activated chemical process that occurs when sugar and the amino acids in proteins react. The heat of the oven triggers this sugar reaction, which contributes to the beautiful, crisp, golden-brown exterior of a properly baked loaf of bread. This crisp exterior in turn helps the bread retain moisture.

DAIRY AND FATS

Sturdy artisanal breads, such as sourdoughs or mixed grains, rarely require the addition of any dairy products or fats other than a small amount of extra-virgin olive oil in some cases. Enriched breads, such as brioche, require butter and/or milk as well as eggs to add the richness that so defines them. The fats in these products add flavor as well as rich creaminess, while the sugars they contain help feed the yeast and assist in the creation of that wonderful golden color of a properly baked loaf. When called for in a specific recipe, butter and other fats will help create a fine crumb, smooth texture, and increased volume in the baked loaf.

When I use olive oils, I use the finest quality I can find, those with clean, light, fruity flavor. You do not want an oil that adds a strong, grassy note to the dough. The flavor should heighten the ultimate flavor you are seeking, not overpower it. Just as with wine, if you enjoy the flavor when you drink it alone, it is fine to cook with!

When it comes to butter, I use a high-butterfat, unsalted butter that is commonly referred to as "European style." These butters contain 85 percent fat versus an American butter, which contains 76 percent to 80 percent. The butter I use is more expensive than ordinary butter, but it is worth it because it adds an identifiable richness to enriched dough.

FLAVORINGS

We use the highest quality ingredients when enhancing flavor. For example, I choose Belgian chocolate, both dark and white, for its consistent high quality and high cocoa butter content. Other flavors we use regularly include fresh herbs; fresh chilies; citrus zest; spices such as nutmeg, cinnamon, and fennel seed; nuts and raisins; and wine and liqueurs.

LIQUID *LEVAIN*

(Natural Sourdough or Natural Starter)

Liquid *levain* is known as both a natural sourdough and a natural starter. In the bakery I generally refer to it as the latter. For centuries, natural starters were the only method of leavening bread doughs, and I would bet that almost every bread baker in the world still maintains a natural starter in his kitchen. I certainly do, and I think that home cooks should, too. Without a natural starter, the "mother" of our bakery, many La Farm breads would not have the extraordinary flavor and texture that make them distinctive artisanal breads. Experienced bakers will often share their starter with novice bakers. If you are lucky enough to have an artisanal bakery nearby, ask and you might receive. One cup is all you will need to take you to Day 4 in the chart on page 29.

Making and maintaining a natural sourdough starter is quite simple, but it does require some attention, because it must be fed and watered regularly, rather like having a pet. It is also important that it be kept in a warm environment, preferably one about 75°F to 80°F. If you follow these directions, you will have an active, viable, and flavor-producing starter that will live forever.

You will need a narrow, one-quart clear glass or plastic upright container with a wide mouth and cover. Although you can use other types and shapes of containers, I prefer a transparent one so I can observe the starter as the yeast cells grow. In addition, a narrow container gives the yeast room to multiply, as yeast cells are happiest and most productive when they are on top of one another rather than spread out in a shallow

container. The wide mouth allows you to feed the starter easily.

A natural sourdough starter is simply a combination of flour and water. Wild yeasts in the flour and in the environment begin to activate once the mixture is allowed to rest. Stronger than other leavening agents, a natural starter is also stable and resistant to excess acidity. A long period of development is essential because the wild yeasts do not begin to propagate until about the third day, and acidity development begins sometime between the sixth and tenth days. This acidity is particularly important as it inhibits the growth of bad bacteria.

It is important to use unbleached, unbromated flour as it contains the highest amount of the "good" bacteria that help the yeast cells grow. Begin the starter with organic whole-wheat or rye flour and then switch to unbleached, unbromated white bread flour on the fourth day. (Rye flour contains more wild yeast spores, so it will activate more quickly; it is responsible for the deep, sweet-sour flavor exhibited by many artisanal breads.) A combination of unbleached, unbromated white flour and unbromated whole-wheat flour is used when you need to bring back a starter that is left unfed in the refrigerator for a couple of days or when the starter is weak; the whole-wheat flour helps nourish the starter and brings its boost back. Honey, added only on the first day, helps activate the yeast.

Once the natural sourdough has finished developing, cover it and let it stand in a warm (75°F to 80°F), draft-free spot until the starter has increased substantially in volume, about 24 hours. Thereafter, you must feed it daily with water and unbleached, unbromated flour. Before each feeding, stir the starter with a wooden spoon. Once stirred, remove and discard all but 2.5 ounces/70 grams (¼ cup) of the mix. (The smaller the amount of starter at each feeding, the quicker the yeast will reproduce.) Then add the flour and 85°F water as directed

in the chart. At each feeding, you will want to see a foamy, slightly bubbling mixture that has increased in volume. A soft, slightly sour aroma will indicate that the yeast development is progressing nicely. If there is no foam, bubbles, or increased volume, or if the aroma is pungent rather than inviting, the starter should be discarded.

Throughout the process it is essential that you keep a log of the progression of days and times so that you adhere to the feeding schedule. You can do this by keeping a paper trail or by writing directly on the container with an indelible marker.

Always use your hands to incorporate the water into the flour, mixing until the combination is thick and smooth. At La Farm Bakery, before working with our natural sourdough, I require all staff to wash their hands and arms thoroughly and then rinse completely to be sure no contaminates, soaps, or perfumes remain on their skin. Any of these could potentially "poison" the mother or, to the devastation of our bread production, "kill" her.

It is always a good idea to plan ahead, noting the amount of starter your recipe requires, and doubling or tripling everything as needed. Make sure you have enough starter remaining to maintain the base starter.

Note: You can use 3.5 ounces/100 grams (½ cup) liquid *levain* (see page 20) in addition to instant dry yeast when making Country French Bread (see page 75) or Ciabatta (see page 131) to increase the flavor profile as well as the shelf life.

POOLISH

For any yeasted bread, you can add poolish (see page 21) in addition
to instant dry yeast to enhance the flavor profile of the baked bread,
adding a rather nutty taste. It is easy to make, but you do have to plan in
advance, as it must be made 8 to 12 hours before being added to a dough.

1.75 ounces	50 grams	⅓ cup plus 1 tablespoon 70°F water
1.75 ounces	50 grams	¼ cup plus 1 teaspoon unbromated whole-wheat flour

¹⁄₁₆ teaspoon instant dry yeast

Combine the water with the flour and yeast, using your hands to mix
thoroughly. Set aside in a warm (75°F to 80°F), draft-free place for 8 to 12
hours. The poolish is ready when it starts to collapse in the center.

LIQUID *LEVAIN* (Natural Sourdough or Natural Starter) Schedule

DAY/TIME	FLOUR	WATER (85°F)	TIME BETWEEN FEEDINGS
Start with unbromated whole-wheat flour.			
DAY 1: 8 a.m.	2.5 oz./70 grams (½ cup)	2.5 oz./70 grams (⅓ cup)	24 hours
	0.02 oz./7 grams honey (1 teaspoon)		
DAY 2: 8 a.m.	Stir, then discard all but 2.5 oz./70 grams (¼ cup) of the starter and add:		
	2.5 oz./70 grams (½ cup)	2.5 oz./70 grams (⅓ cup)	6 to 8 hours
DAY 2: 4 p.m.	Stir, then discard all but 2.5oz/70 grams (¼ cup) of the starter and add:		
	2.5 oz./70 grams (½ cup)	2.5 oz./70 grams (⅓ cup)	16 hours
DAY 3: 8 a.m.	Stir, then discard all but 2.5 oz./70 grams (¼ cup) of the starter and add:		
	2.5 oz./70 grams (½ cup)	2.5 oz./70 grams (⅓ cup)	6 to 8 hours
DAY 3: 4 p.m.	Stir, then discard all but 2.5 oz./70 grams (¼ cup) of the starter and add:		
	2.5 oz./70 grams (½ cup)	2.5 oz./70 grams (⅓ cup)	16 hours
Now, switch to unbleached, unbromated white flour.			
DAY 4: 8 a.m.	Stir, then discard all but 2.5 oz./70 grams (¼ cup) of the starter and add:		
	2.5 oz./70 grams (½ cup)	2.5 oz./70 grams (⅓ cup)	6 to 8 hours
DAY 4: 4 p.m.	Stir, then discard all but 2.5 oz./70 grams (¼ cup) of the starter and add:		
	2.5 oz./70 gram (½ cup)	2.5 oz./70 gram (⅓ cup)	16 hours
DAY 5: 8 a.m.	Stir, then discard all but 2.5 oz./70 grams (¼ cup) of the starter and add:		
	2.5 oz./70 grams (½ cup)	2.5 oz./70 grams (⅓ cup)	6 to 8 hours
DAY 5: 4 p.m.	Stir, then discard all but 2.5 oz./70 grams (¼ cup) of the starter and add:		
	2.5 oz./70 grams (½ cup)	2.5 oz./70 grams (⅓ cup)	16 hours

In five to ten days, the *levain* will be strong enough to make bread. Look for bubbly activity and a tart, nicely sour aroma.

For Days 6 through 10 (or until the starter is mature), continue following the same feeding schedule as for Days 4 and 5, then cover and refrigerate as directed.

EQUIPMENT FOR FINE BREAD MAKING

Although a few kitchen tools are used specifically for bread making, most of the equipment required is found in the everyday kitchen. The following equipment list should be taken simply as a guide; most bakers are ingenious and can make do with very basic tools, such as turning a rimless baking sheet into a bread peel. But, like everything in life, the better prepared you are, the easier the job.

The best tools for bread making are the ones you always have with you—your hands. Your hands are your memory. They provide the first sense you'll use to understand the dough. Later you will use other senses, but your hands are the starting point. Other kitchen tools will support you, but your hands impart your spirit into the dough.

BAKING PANS, BAKING SHEETS, AND SHEET PANS: There are many pans made for baking specific types of bread, ranging from baguette trough pans to ornate, fluted pans used for enriched breads such as brioche or Italian panettone. A standard flat baking pan, known commercially as a sheet pan, always has rimmed sides, usually about an inch deep. This flat pan is extremely useful in bread making, as you can proof your dough directly on it and then slide it right into the oven. The best sheet pans are made of heavy-duty shiny aluminum or heavy-gauge black stainless steel and come in a variety of sizes. A full sheet pan (18 by 26 inches) does not easily fit in most home ovens, but a half sheet (18 by 13 inches) will. A standard jelly roll pan, which is usually about 11 inches by 17 inches, can be used as a substitute. Commercial bakers also use quarter and three-quarter sheet pans.

BAKING STONE OR UNGLAZED TILE: A baking stone or unglazed tile is an oven-proof circle or square made from unglazed clay. It is placed in the oven at least 30 minutes prior to baking so the heat it absorbs and radiates will provide an even flow of indirect heat to baking bread. Both stones and tiles are commercially made for this purpose, but unglazed pottery tiles from a home improvement

store can effectively be used as a replacement. I have done this many times on consulting jobs when a commercial kitchen did not have a stone-lined hearth oven.

BANNETON: Although not a necessity, many bakers use a *banneton*, a shallow muslin-lined willow basket to hold bread dough during its final rise. The shape of the basket determines the shape of the baked bread and also leaves an imprint

on the crust. An unlined willow basket used for the same purpose is known as a *brotformen*. Breads are not baked in either of these baskets.

BENCH BRUSH: This small, handy tool is used to brush flour and other light ingredients from the work surface. The bristles should be very soft and pliable. It is one of my recommended tools.

BENCH SCRAPER: A bench scraper, also known as a bench knife, bench chopper, or dough scraper, is a straight-sided, slightly flexible stainless-steel blade with a curled handle that is used for cleaning flour from a work surface as well as for lifting, turning, and dividing bread dough. A bench scraper is indispensible for keeping a work surface clean. If you don't own one, I suggest you buy one before beginning to develop your passion for bread making.

BOWL SCRAPER: This small, rounded, flexible rubber or plastic tool is used to scrape dough cleanly from the mixing bowl. If you learn to use it well, your mixing bowl will be almost perfectly clean when you have scraped the last bit of dough from it. A bowl scraper is another indispensible and inexpensive tool for a bread baker.

BREAD PEEL: A peel is a wooden or aluminum tool with a short handle and a large, flat, almost round front that is used to slide breads into and out of the oven. It is also known as a baker's or transfer peel. A rimless baking sheet can be used in the same manner.

BREAD KNIFE: A knife, usually about 10 inches long, with a serrated blade made specifically for cutting cleanly through bread is especially useful for artisanal breads with a crusty or tough exterior and a soft interior.

COOLING RACK: A metal wire or mesh rack with small feet allows cool air to circulate around cooling breads (or other items) to keep the exterior dry and crisp. Cooling racks come in a wide variety of sizes.

COUCHE: A *couche* is a linen cloth used to separate unbaked loaves during the final rising, when the loaves are too large for a *banneton* or when their size or shape does not conform to the basket. The cloth is used as a divider between loaves to ensure that the soft dough keeps its shape and the loaves do not touch and stick together during this crucial rise. We import our *couche*s from France; it is a special linen made specifically to not impede fermentation. It is washed as infrequently as possible, because a yeasty environment—not a chemically cleaned one—is required to coddle proofing breads.

CUTTING BOARD: Every kitchen should have a hardwood or heavy plastic board on which doughs can be divided and breads can be safely cut. You may also use a maple butcher's block for the final fermentation of dough. It offers a fairly consistent temperature and the dough seems to stick less than it does on other surfaces. A cutting board will also provide some insulation from a cool granite or marble counter that could significantly chill the dough. Cutting boards should be constantly maintained to prevent bacterial contamination, and they should be discarded once cracked, splintered, or in other ways badly worn.

DIGITAL KITCHEN SCALE: Kitchen scales are programmed to measure a number of different weights and ingredients accurately. Since accurate measurements are essential to bread (and pastry) making, a solidly built, reliable kitchen scale is an absolute necessity. Some digital scales are fitted with a tare button, which makes it possible to weigh one item, tare the scale (return it to zero), and then add another ingredient for continuous accurate weighing. In addition, the tare button allows you to place a mixing bowl or other container directly on the scale, tare it, and continue to measure ingredients right into the container. I have a standard joke about scales to break the ice when teaching—"Don't be afraid to get out your scale. You don't have to get on it, just put your flour on it."

DIGITAL THERMOMETER: A digital thermometer is another indispensible tool for any baker, to draw an instant and precise reading of dough and water temperatures. A high-end digital thermometer can register temperatures ranging from -40°F to 450°F, but in bread baking, one ranging up to only 350°F is suitable. Some digital thermometers are also equipped with an infrared beam to instantly read the surface temperature of a dough; this type is quite expensive.

DOUGH LOG: An essential tool to keep track of water and final dough temperatures as well as time required in baking steps. See pages 127, 173, 215, and 255.

DUTCH OVEN: A Dutch oven is a large, deep, heavy-duty kettle, often made of cast iron or enameled cast iron, with a tight-fitting lid that prevents steam from escaping. Although traditionally used for braising or stewing, it can also serve as a vessel in which a home baker can bake crusty bread, thanks to its ability to hold heat and create internal steam.

HEAVY-DUTY ELECTRIC STAND MIXER: Although I prefer mixing by hand, a heavy-duty stand mixer with a powerful motor does an excellent job of mixing dense artisanal bread doughs. A hand-held or portable mixer cannot be used for the same jobs. Most heavy-duty mixers come with a selection of attachments, such as a dough hook and a wire whisk.

HOTEL PANS: I don't need hotel pans (also known as steam-table pans) in the bakery, but at home I use a 20¾-by-12¾-by-4-inch pan to cover longer breads such as baguettes during baking, because it is long enough to fit over an almost standard-size loaf. I cover the corners, or any other open areas, with aluminum foil to create a stronger seal.

LA CLOCHE: La Cloche is the trade name of an unglazed clay baking dish with a domed lid that, when used to bake bread, creates an environment similar to a

hearth or brick oven, resulting in a classic artisanal loaf with a crisp, golden crust and a perfect crumb. It is an excellent baking tool made by Sassafras Enterprises, available through many online sources (see page 290). Some local potters also make this style of bread dome.

LAMÉ: This traditional baker's tool is a very sharp curved blade that is used to mark the tops of signature loaves before baking. It may also have a razor attached. A single-edged razor may be used in the same way.

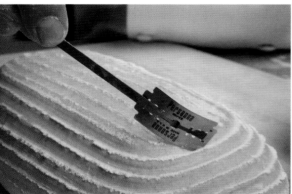

LAVA ROCKS: These are basalt rocks formed when hot lava from erupting volcanoes cools on the surface of the earth. They are available in garden supply stores and generally used in garden decoration or to line a natural barbecue. I use them to recreate the atmosphere of a commercial steam bread oven in my home oven.

MEASURING CUPS: Made of metal, plastic, or glass, measuring cups are marked in designated amounts, usually from 1/4 cup to 4 cups. Individual-measure cups are generally used for measuring dry ingredients, while multiple-measure cups are used for liquid. I rarely use measuring cups when making bread as I think it essential that ingredients be weighed for accuracy.

MEASURING SPOONS: Metal or plastic spoons in designated amounts—usually from 1/8 teaspoon to 1 tablespoon—are necessary for measuring amounts of ingredients that are too small to register on a scale.

MIXING BOWLS: High-quality mixing bowls are essential to the baker's kitchen. Metal mixing bowls are made from heavy-gauge 18/10 stainless steel. They are multipurpose, almost indestructible, and extremely easy to clean. They are nonreactive to acidic ingredients and impervious to heat and cold. Metal mixing bowls are available in many different sizes, generally with rolled rims for ease of handling. Some also have handles as well as pour spouts. They are perfect for mixing, rising, and creating a steam chamber when baking doughs.

PARCHMENT PAPER: Parchment paper is opaque paper that has been chemically treated to make it nonstick and heat resistant. Some supermarkets now carry rolls and sheets of natural-colored parchment paper similar to the type we use in the bakery. Since its main purpose is as a baking pan liner, it is also known as pan-liner paper.

PLASTIC WRAP: A thin, transparent sheet that clings to hard surfaces is indispensable for making an almost airtight cover for fermenting doughs.

SILICONE BAKING SHEET: Reusable nonstick silicone pan liners were originally created to line either half or full sheet pans but are now made in a number of sizes for home use. Made of woven fiberglass injected with food-grade silicone, these sheets cannot be cut or trimmed, as the damage caused will render them unsafe for use.

TIMER: This small, inexpensive tool allows accurate measure of fermenting and/or baking times. At La Farm our team would be lost without timers, and our products would certainly be in jeopardy.

Many larger cities have a restaurant supply house that will sell commercial equipment to the public. This is a very cost-effective way to purchase heavy-duty, long-lasting kitchen supplies. Some large warehouse-type discount stores have sections dedicated to restaurant kitchenware and small equipment that is less expensive; however, be sure to check for the highest quality. Even more fun, and one of my favorite things to do, is to go to a used restaurant equipment shop or auction. You can find lots of treasures there. Should you find yourself in the First Arrondissement in Paris, stop by my favorite professional kitchen supply house, Mora. They carry a huge selection of top-quality professional European kitchen and baking equipment, and they are open to the public.

SEVEN STEPS TO MAKING GREAT BREAD

At La Farm Bakery, I use all of the knowledge I have accumulated though my years as a professional baker to create breads that are delicious and that I am proud to serve. To ensure quality results, I use only unbleached and unbromated flours, no preservatives, and a natural starter (see page 20). My signature La Farm bread is handcrafted using a three-day process; one day to build the natural starter, one day to form the loaves, and one day to allow the slow fermentation necessary to achieve maximum flavor. The bread is baked in a formidable steam-injected hearth oven, which produces the desired crisp, crunchy crust and interior crumb that I look for. However, even if you don't take the time that I do or use the equipment that I have, you can make great artisanal bread at home by following my Seven Steps to Making Great Bread.

Throughout my career, as both baker and teacher, I have always tried to simplify and demystify bread baking. Even if it is not your passion, it should be a joy, as there is nothing more rewarding than watching the dough make its way from a soft, slightly wet mass to a beautifully golden-brown loaf. Like any artist, once you have respect for the basics, you will have the canvas upon which you can create incredible artwork.

After years and years of baking, I have devised seven easy steps to follow to make great bread. Once you master the basics behind bread baking, your imagination and creativity will be reflected in your own breads. There is nothing complex about these steps. Once you learn them, bread making will become second nature to you and, perhaps, even a passion.

From my early lessons with Master Bakers, I would say that the summation of centuries of baking knowledge comes down to this: *The essence of great bread baking is in proper fermentation.* I have spent my career teaching professionals and home bakers this simple lesson. There are two periods of fermentation: the first "bulk" fermentation develops the flavor, and the second and final "proofing" stage develops the volume. Whether you are baking a rustic no-knead bread or a complex-grained sourdough, you will be baking fine artisanal bread if you take the time to fully understand the standards of fermentation. You will find that making great

Lionel loads loaves.

Mise en place

bread doesn't take much work, but it does take time—time to ferment to perfection while you busy yourself with other things.

Yeast is a living entity. By making sure that its basic needs are met, you optimize the happiness of the yeast and allow it to support your work. It is like any living thing—a baby, a flower, wheat—if you don't feed it, it will eventually die; if you overfeed it, it will collapse due to an "overdose." If the temperature of the air or the dough is too high, the yeast will overeat, and if too low, its metabolism will not develop as it should. Again, the secret of great bread baking revolves around fermentation and temperature. *Dough is a living entity.*

Before you begin to make bread, it is important that you have a nicely organized preparation space. There is a cooking term from classic French cuisine that describes this—*mise en place*—which simply translates to "putting in place." This means that before you begin to cook or bake, read the recipe thoroughly so that you completely understand it. Then, be sure that all of the ingredients that are required for the completion of the recipe are measured, laid out in an orderly fashion, checked off on the ingredient list, and ready to use. Following this procedure guarantees fewer mistakes and no omissions. Furthermore, *mise en place* should also cover the organization of your baking tools, equipment, and pans. This includes extra batteries for your scale if it requires them, unmarred measuring utensils and pans, and a clean, ready-to-work space. If you get used to doing

this, you will be amazed at how much time you save and how easy putting together a recipe becomes. If you organize your ingredients and tools, you will never again put a pan in the oven and then remember that you left out the salt or sugar, or get halfway through a recipe and realize that you are out of vanilla.

There are just a few unfamiliar words and concepts that you will need to get comfortable with when making bread at home. The first is fermentation. Fermentation is a baker's term for what home bakers often call "rising." Simply replace "allow the dough to rise" with "allow the dough a fermentation period." It is good to learn the proper term as it accurately describes what the dough does—it ferments as it goes through the chemical changes that give the baked bread its depth of flavor. The first fermentation period, also known as bulk fermentation, develops the bread's flavor profile, while the second, referred to as proofing, is done after the loaf is shaped and creates the volume of the baked loaf. As long as you measure correctly and mix properly, the dough will do the rest of the work for you during fermentation.

It is in the final fermentation period (the "proofing" or "second rise") that the final crumb (the interior texture) of the baked bread is set. Following my instructions, you will find that it is only a matter of time and patience that will produce the best results.

Another expression familiar to most bread bakers, novice or Master, is to place the dough in a "warm, draft-free spot." What exactly does warm and draft-free mean, and why is it important? "Warm" is a comfortable temperature between 75°F and 80°F. If there is more than a slight breeze moving through your kitchen, it will impact the proper fermentation of the dough by creating a thin skin on the exterior, which will then slow down the process. An open window or door or even an air-conditioning vent can have this effect. The preferred spot would be a closed oven; however, if it

Shaping dough

A tight, firm shape

Scoring

has a pilot light, it could then be too hot for the dough to rise properly. Generally any enclosed space in your kitchen—a closet, a pantry, a cupboard—will serve as a warm, draft-free spot.

The final shaping of the dough is an important stage, and I'd like to share a baker's tip with you. After the first fermentation, when the dough is ready to be turned into a loaf, it is absolutely essential that it be formed into a tight, firm shape. If not shaped correctly, the final fermentation will not occur properly, and the dough will deflate when you move it to the baking surface. In addition, shaping is often the only distinguishing note for a loaf of bread, since many different styles are created using the same base dough. Remember, dough is not as fragile as it might seem; don't beat it up, but don't handle it like a newborn baby. I like to say, "Love the dough."

And finally, there is scoring. This is the term used to describe the act of cutting a design in the top of a properly fermented and shaped piece of dough. Scoring gives the dough a directed path for gases to expand during baking and serves as the baker's identifying or signature mark for a specific type of bread. Scoring is done with a lamé (see page 36) or a single-edged razor blade just prior to putting the bread in the oven. The cuts are done in a series of single, quick slashes, barely marking the dough. A baker will say, "Cut through the skin of the dough, but don't create a trench."

Beautiful loaves

If you commit these steps to memory, along with the techniques they require, your hands will automatically find the tempo to create the perfect loaf. I suggest that you practice with my recipe for basic Country French Bread (see page 75). Your first loaf may not be perfect, but I guarantee that it will be tasty. Just as the answer to the old joke "How do you get to Carnegie Hall?" is "Practice, practice, practice!" the same answer applies to "How do you make great bread?"

STEP 1: MEASURING AND PREPARING INGREDIENTS

Quick tips for measuring and preparing ingredients:

* Always use a scale to measure ingredients.
* Keep the salt and yeast separate prior to mixing.
* The water (or other liquid) temperature controls the final dough temperature; for hand mixing start with 82°F to 84°F and for mixing with a heavy-duty electric stand mixer start at 65°F to 70°F.
* Always place the salt and yeast in separate piles on top of the flour prior to mixing.
* When using ingredients such as cheese, remember to bring them to room temperature before adding to the dough or they will adversely affect the desired final dough temperature of 72°F to 80°F and negatively impact the fermentation.

To create a desirable rise, a bread baker "scales" all ingredients precisely by weight, not by volume. Accurate measurement on a scale is your insurance for achieving active fermentation and a perfect loaf of bread.

When measuring small quantities of ingredients, do not place them on top of the larger amounts on the scale. Weigh these small amounts separately, directly on the scale or in small cups, and set them aside. Then

Add yeast and salt.

Do not allow contact between the yeast and the salt.

Tare the scale.

Weigh flour.

place the mixing bowl on the scale, tare it off (bring it to zero), and weigh out the flour and any other ingredients that call for a large amount. After scaling the larger amounts into the bowl, remove it from the scale and place the weighed smaller amounts on top of the larger amounts. When adding the yeast and salt, place them in separate piles on top of the flour, taking care that they do not touch each other. If they do come in contact, a chemical reaction will occur that will decrease the yeast's ability to develop.

Tare the scale.

Take water temperature.

Add water, tare, and then add levain.

Weigh out your water, then check its temperature and record it in your Dough Log just prior to adding it to the dry ingredients. The temperature of the water controls the final dough temperature; it should be between 82°F to 84°F when mixing by hand and between 65°F and 70°F when using a heavy-duty stand mixer. (See page 23 for more detailed water temperature information.) To cool water, toss in a couple of ice cubes and take the temperature frequently. As soon as it reaches the desired temperature, remove the ice cubes, measure again, and proceed with the recipe.

Similarly, when using ingredients such as cheese, bring them to room temperature before adding them to the dough or they will adversely affect

To avoid clogging your sink drain when cleaning excess dough from your hands, place your hands in a bowl of flour, coating them well. Then, vigorously rub them together over a waste basket until all of the dough has been removed. Save the flour in a container marked "For Hand Cleaning Only" and set aside for use on other bread baking days.

Cleaning hands with flour

the desired final dough temperature of 72°F to 80°F and negatively impact the fermentation.

If using a liquid *levain* (see page 20), first scale the correct temperature water. Pour about half of the water into a small bowl, tare the scale, and add the proper amount of *levain* to the water. Mix gently until the *levain* is fully blended into the water, which will keep it from sticking to the sides of the measuring tool. This way you will not lose any precious yeast, the "spirit of the bakery."

Although I strongly urge you always to measure by weight with a scale, if you have to measure by volume, many home cooks have found the following system to be relatively successful. First, aerate the flour—you don't have to sift it, just lift it up and fluff it a bit with a fork or spoon to make sure that it is not densely packed. Then, dip a 1-cup dry measuring cup into the flour and scoop it out. Smooth the top with the straight edge of a kitchen knife but do not tap the cup on the counter! Repeat as necessary for the total amount of flour required. (It is not recommended that you use a measuring cup larger than 1 cup because it will become too packed.) For amounts less than 1 cup, simply use the dry measuring cup in the designated amount to get an accurate measurement.

When you use a cup versus a scale for measuring, each measurement will be different, giving extremely inconsistent results. The above instruction is the best I can do to standardize cup measurements. In the end, if you use volume rather than weight to measure your ingredients, you will have to adjust the recipe by feel, adding more water or flour as needed to achieve the desired result.

STEP 2: MIXING AND KNEADING

Quick mixing tips:

- ❊ Never let salt and yeast touch until ready to mix.
- ❊ Water temperature controls the final dough temperature.
- ❊ Always taste the dough to be sure salt has been added.
- ❊ Bring additional ingredients such as cheese to room temperature before adding.
- ❊ The final dough temperature should range from 72°F to 80°F.

Blend dry ingredients by hand.

MIXING BY HAND: Hand mixing is my preference, especially for new bakers. Mixing by hand helps build your feeling for gluten development and the desired consistency of the dough and, crucially, develops your "sixth sense" (see page 16). After learning these sensations, you can move to an electric mixer with this "historical" knowledge at your fingertips.

The first step in mixing is to gently bring the dry ingredients together using your hands. This is done immediately before you begin the entire mixing and kneading process to ensure that the instant dry yeast (if using) and salt do not stay in contact. Once blended, quickly form a well in the center of the mix.

Now, gradually add the 82°F to 84°F water (or liquid *levain* mixture and remaining water) into the well, rotating the bowl with one hand while simultaneously mixing the liquid into the dry ingredients with your other hand. The dough will be soft, slightly wet, and extremely sticky. Stop often as you work to scrape the bowl and your fingers with your bowl scraper, taking care that all of the ingredients have been gathered into the dough mass. The bowl should be quite clean. Pinch off a bit of dough and taste it— this is a simple way to check whether you have forgotten the salt, a frequent mistake of even experienced bakers. If the salt is missing, add it now and mix for another minute or so to fully incorporate it into the dough.

Add water and tare the scale.

Add levain *into water.*

Add levain *and water into well.*

Rotate the bowl while mixing.

Stop often to scrape bowl and fingers.

Taste dough for salt.

When the dough begins to come together, turn it out onto a clean work surface, using your bowl scraper to ensure that no dough is left behind. It is important that you not add any flour to the work surface or to the dough mass, no matter how sticky the dough feels, as this will change the consistency of the dough. I like to say that the baker should work *with* the flour not *in* the flour. It is good to keep this in mind when the dough is at its stickiest.

Place dough on nonfloured work surface.

Instructions for Kneading by Hand

Quick kneading tips:

❉ Your fingers are your memory.
❉ Pinch, do not tear the dough.

KNEADING BY HAND: This is the way to really learn how dough feels, and it is something I strongly suggest that all home bakers practice. When you work with your hands, you can almost memorize the feel of the dough and learn exactly how it comes together. I often say that "your fingers are your memory."

Unlike most bakers, I use my fingers and thumbs rather than my palms to knead bread dough. With this technique your fingers learn to "recognize" thoroughly kneaded dough and sufficiently developed gluten so that you can achieve the desired consistency and texture. I believe that when you knead using the palms of your hands, you tear and shred the dough as you fold and push it away from you. Using my technique, you use the area between the base of your thumb and the index finger to feel the consistency as it moves toward the final texture. My method of kneading does take some practice, but the payoff is well worth the effort.

Here goes! Hold your hands, palms facing up, at opposite sides of the dough mass closest to your body. Slide your fingers, still facing up, under the dough and lift the dough an inch or so from the work surface. Squeeze your thumbs and index fingers together to form a tight "OK" sign, then continue to curl your thumbs and index fingers tightly together to pinch off a portion of dough. Working as quickly and smoothly as you can, continue lifting and pinching the dough mass using the same technique, moving up

It's sticky; keep with it.

Use "OK" sign.

Pinch the dough.

Pinch through the dough.

Lift.

Fold.

Repeat as needed.

Keep incorporating dough.

Lift.

the dough mass in approximately 1-inch to 1½-inch increments until you have gone through the entire mass. You should begin to feel the dough coming together.

Turn the dough a quarter turn and continue lifting, pinching, and turning the dough until it begins to take on an identifiable shape and is less and less sticky. This can take anywhere from 5 to 15 minutes. Remember, do not add any flour to speed the process. Use

Confirm that the dough is not sticky with the back of your hand.

your scraper to keep incorporating all of the dough into the mass. Lastly, fold the dough onto itself, four to six times, and touch the dough with the back of your hand to confirm that it is no longer sticky. If it is sticky, continue to knead. You do not want a stiff, dry dough; you want a soft, pliable mass that still holds its shape.

If you are adding ingredients, as for *Pain aux Lardons* (see page 93), add them here. Just make certain that all ingredients are at room temperature

Add ingredients.

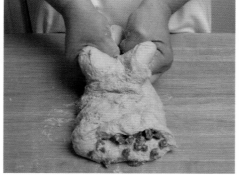

Use "OK" sign.

Pinch through the dough.

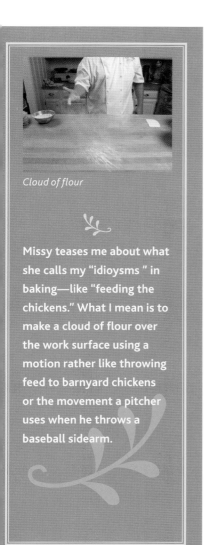

Cloud of flour

Missy teases me about what she calls my "idioysms " in baking—like "feeding the chickens." What I mean is to make a cloud of flour over the work surface using a motion rather like throwing feed to barnyard chickens or the movement a pitcher uses when he throws a baseball sidearm.

so they do not negatively impact the overall temperature of the dough. Using the palms of your hands, lightly flatten the dough and place the ingredients down the middle of the dough. Fold each side up and over the ingredients, lightly press down, and begin to pinch up the length of the dough, turning a quarter turn and repeating a few times until the ingredients are well enclosed. Lastly, fold the dough onto itself four to six times, and, with the back of your hand, touch the dough to make sure that it is no longer sticky.

Using your instant-read thermometer, take the temperature of your dough and record it in your Dough Log. The temperature should be between 72°F and 80°F. If it is not, immediately make the necessary adjustments to either increase or lower the temperature for the first fermentation as directed on page 52. It is important that you record the time you finish this step, as you will need to note the time required for the first fermentation.

Take final dough temperature.

Although kneading takes some time and practice, it can be extremely relaxing and rewarding, almost therapeutic, to feel the dough come together in your hands. Remember that it is very unlikely that you will overwork the dough. And if you do, sometimes a baker has to fail to learn!

MIXING AND KNEADING WITH A HEAVY-DUTY ELECTRIC STAND MIXER:
The stand mixer both mixes and kneads the dough, so when using an electric mixer you will not have to knead by hand. This is not necessarily a bad thing if you are a skilled baker, but if you're a novice, the time spent kneading the dough is when you learn how to "feel" and "understand" it.

Weigh your dry ingredients as instructed on page 43, then place them in a mixing bowl—not the bowl of the electric mixer—and set it aside.

Measure the water, check that it is between 65°F and 70°F, and pour about half of it into the bowl of the electric mixer. (Adding the water first keeps the dry ingredients from sticking to the bottom of the bowl.) Add the dry ingredients, place the bowl on the mixer, and then attach the dough hook. Begin mixing on low speed ("1" on most mixers) and add the remaining water quickly so that the dough is not allowed to firm up, as mixing will become impossible once this occurs. Mix until the dough becomes soft and slightly wet, and lightly sticks to the interior of the bowl (a couple minutes). Stop the mixer frequently and scrape down the sides and bottom of the bowl with your bowl scraper or a rubber spatula to ensure that all of the ingredients are incorporated into the dough.

Once the dough is soft and moist, set your timer and continue to mix the dough on the lowest speed for 5 minutes. Again, frequently stop the mixer and scrape down the sides and the bottom of your bowl to ensure that all of the ingredients are evenly blended. Right after the dough comes together, feel it to familiarize yourself with the consistency. The dough should begin to be pliable.

Yeast and salt should not touch.

Add water first.

Add dry ingredients.

Add remaining water on low speed.

Scrape down sides and bottom.

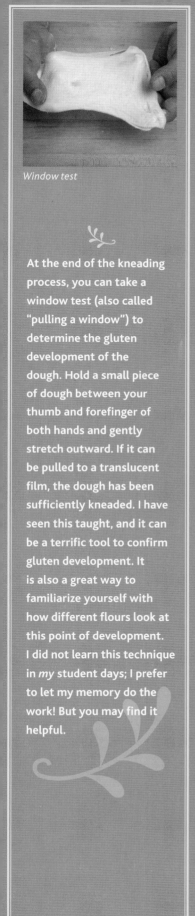

Window test

At the end of the kneading process, you can take a window test (also called "pulling a window") to determine the gluten development of the dough. Hold a small piece of dough between your thumb and forefinger of both hands and gently stretch outward. If it can be pulled to a translucent film, the dough has been sufficiently kneaded. I have seen this taught, and it can be a terrific tool to confirm gluten development. It is also a great way to familiarize yourself with how different flours look at this point of development. I did not learn this technique in *my* student days; I prefer to let my memory do the work! But you may find it helpful.

Stop the mixer and lift the dough hook so that you can easily get down into the bowl. Using your bowl scraper, scrape down the sides and lift up from the bottom of the bowl to loosen the dough from the bowl. Continuing to use the bowl scraper, clean off the dough hook. Pinch off a bit of dough and taste it—one more chance to see if you have forgotten the salt. If so, add it now.

Place the dough hook back down into the bowl. Increase the speed to medium-low ("2" on most mixers) and mix until the dough is soft and smooth with a slightly tacky, moist surface, an additional 2 to 4 minutes (depending on the specific recipe). If you are adding ingredients, make certain that they are at room temperature and add them at this point, mixing on the lowest speed for about 1 minute or just until they are incorporated.

Lightly toss a thin film of flour into the bowl you are going to use for the first fermentation. You need just enough of a dusting to keep the dough from sticking to the bowl.

Using your bowl scraper, scrape the dough out into the floured bowl. Take the temperature of the dough using an instant-read thermometer and record it in your Dough Log. The temperature should be between 72°F and 80°F. If it is not, make the necessary adjustments described below. It is also

Clean off dough hook.

Taste dough for salt.

Add ingredients.

Mix on low speed until incorporated.

important that you record the time you finish this step, as you will need to note the time required for the first (bulk) fermentation step.

If the temperature is under 72°F, allow the dough to ferment for an additional 10 minutes past the first fermentation period for every 2 degrees below that number. For example: If the first fermentation time is 3 hours, and the dough temperature is 70°F (2°F below the desired temperature), the new fermentation period will increase to 3 hours and 10 minutes. This allows you to build back fermentation to the desired point so that you can resume the process.

If the temperature is higher than 80°F, place the dough in the refrigerator for 15 minutes. Remove it from the refrigerator and check the temperature. If it remains too high, refrigerate for an additional 15 minutes. Continue to refrigerate in 15-minute increments until the temperature is between 72°F and 80°F. In this scenario, you are trying to slow down fermentation. These 15-minute periods are deducted from the first fermentation time. For example: If the first fermentation time is 3 hours, and the dough temperature is 82°F (2°F above the desired temperature), immediately refrigerate the dough for the first 15 minutes of the fermentation period. Confirm the correct temperature and then continue with the remaining fermentation period of 2¾ additional hours. Do not add any additional time to the total fermentation period.

Take dough temperature.

Dough log

STEP 3: FIRST (BULK) FERMENTATION

Quick tips for first (bulk) fermentation:

✤ Lightly cover the dough and place in a warm (75°F to 80°F), draft-free spot.

✤ Keep a skin from forming on the fermenting dough.

✤ Make corrections to the dough temperature, if necessary.

When mixing by machine, you are creating friction that, in turn, creates heat, and the longer you mix on higher speeds, the more heat you will create. Do not be tempted to continue mixing to achieve the desired dough temperature (between 72°F and 80°F), as this will overdevelop the gluten and render the dough unusable. Instead, you can adjust by following my directions to either lower or increase the temperature during the first fermentation.

The first fermentation is where the baker develops the flavor profile and shelf life of the bread. Very lightly dust a large bowl (preferably glass to allow observation of the process) with flour. The bowl should be large enough to allow the dough to rise without coming in contact with the plastic wrap that will cover it. Transfer the dough ball to the bowl, smooth side up, taking care that the dough holds its round shape. To keep a thin skin from forming on the dough while it rises, loosely cover the bowl with plastic wrap. For proper fermentation, the plastic wrap must not touch the dough.

Place the bowl in a warm (75°F to 80°F), draft-free place until the dough has doubled in volume or reached whatever stage is directed in a specific recipe, usually about 1 hour. Each dough will differ, and the specific times will be given in each recipe.

If a recipe calls for folds, lightly dust a clean work surface with flour. Uncover the dough and, using cupped hands, pat the dough into a thick square. Lift the right corners up and fold into the center of the square, lightly patting the seam down. Lift the left corners up and fold them into the center of the square, again lightly patting the seam down. Repeat this process with the two top and two bottom corners, meeting in the middle of the square and lightly patting down the seams.

Lightly dust bowl.

Cover with plastic wrap.

FIRST FOLD

Lightly flour top of dough.

Scrape dough onto lightly floured surface.

Pat dough into thick square.

Folding technique

Return to lightly floured bowl.

Cover with plastic wrap.

Lightly flour the bowl again and return the dough to it, seam side down. Cover loosely with plastic wrap and return to a warm (75°F to 80°F), draft-free place. Record the time in your Dough Log.

If the recipe calls for repeated folds, do so as directed. If the dough feels too soft, not supple and pliable, you can give it strength by "overfolding." To do this, overlap the folds completely rather than just having them meet in the middle.

Because ciabatta dough sits in oil in the bowl, you do not remove the dough from the bowl; you do the folds directly in the bowl.

CIABATTA FOLD

Dough in bowl with olive oil.

Pull dough into center.

Rotate bowl and continue pulling.

SECOND AND THIRD FOLDS

The ideal temperature for proofing dough is 77°F, but it is difficult to maintain this temperature in any setting, no matter the effectiveness of the heating and cooling system. The absolute best way to control dough temperature is by making sure that your water is the proper temperature before mixing.

Lightly pat into square.

Fold bottom to center.

Fold top to center.

Fold side to center.

Make last overlapping fold.

Roll seam side down.

Cut through the dough.

Continue to divide if needed.

STEP 4: DIVIDING

If the recipe calls for the dough to be divided, as for rolls, use a bench scraper to divide the dough into the amounts required for shaping in the given recipe. You slice through the top of the dough completely down to the bottom, gently moving the scraper back and forth to avoid tearing the dough. When the dough is divided, let it rest for a minimum of 10 minutes (directly on a lightly floured work surface is fine) before shaping. Many recipes do not call for dividing, in which case you can jump straight from Step 3 to Step 5!

STEP 5: SHAPING

Very lightly flour a clean work surface. Uncover the dough and, using your bowl scraper, scrape the dough onto the lightly floured work surface. Let the dough rest for 30 seconds.

Holding the palm of your hand flat down, lightly press on the dough. If the dough is very sticky, lightly flour your hands, but do not add more flour to the dough. Then, using your hands, gently pick up the dough to make sure it is not sticking to the work surface. If it is, use your bench scraper to loosen it and, if needed, coat the work surface with another light dusting of flour. Do not pull or stretch the dough.

To make the standard *boule* (ball) shape:

Pick up a corner of the dough and pull it to the center. Using the heel of your hand, press it down very lightly. Repeat this process for the other three corners, taking care to stretch the dough gently, without pulling or tearing it. When you have gone all around the dough, gently pick up the dough with your hands to make sure that it is not sticking to the work surface. The dough should now be a fairly smooth, almost round shape.

Turn the dough over so that the smooth side is facing up. Then, lay the dough so it is leaning slightly to one side to create tension on the round.

Pull corner to center.

Continue pulling each corner to center.

Press down with heel of hand.

Dough seam side down and smooth side up

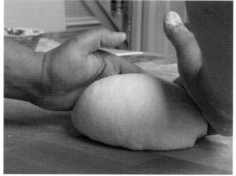

Place hands in triangle shape.

Pull dough toward your body.

Round up the dough, pushing to the right side.

Continue in circular motion.

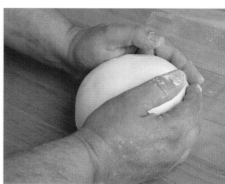

Repeat process until the dough is a tight ball.

Round, smooth ball sealed on the bottom

Fine, firm skin; finished shape

Moved onto couche

Place your hands behind the dough in a triangle shape with your fingertips touching over the back side of the dough and the sides of your hands touching the work surface.

Gently pull the ball-shaped dough toward your body, in the process pressing the ball into an oval shape. In one quick motion, move your hands to the left side of the oval and round up the shape by pushing to the right side. Continue with this motion, rotating the dough a quarter-turn, until each side of the dough has been pushed in a circular motion moving to the right.

Pick up the dough and repeat all of the above process until the dough has become a tight, round, smooth ball that is sealed on the bottom. The ball should have a bit of a spring to it and the exterior should feel as though it is covered in a fine, firm skin or, as I like to say, "smooth as a baby's bottom."

To make the standard baguette shape:

Turn the dough so that the longer side is facing you and press down lightly with your palm. Using both hands, pick up the side of the dough closest to you at the corners and, with a light pull, fold the dough up and over to the center of the rectangle. Using the heels of your hands, press down firmly to seal the seam. Then, using a light pull, pick up the corners of the far side of the dough and fold it up and halfway over the first fold. Using the heels of your hands, press down firmly to seal the fold.

Roll the top of the dough toward your body until the seam is on its side. With the tips of your thumbs touching and your fingers outstretched, roll the dough away from you again, tightening it. Then, roll the dough back toward you until the seam is facing down on the work surface.

Place the heel and fingertips of one hand on the work surface with the center of the dough cupped in between. Begin rolling the dough and tightening it in a back-and-forth motion. The dough will begin to form a shape rather like a doggie bone.

Pick up the dough to make sure that it is not sticking to the work surface. Place your hands together in the center of the dough and, using the same back-and-forth motion, continue rolling, gently pulling the dough to elongate it. It is important that the motion comes from the strength of your shoulders or you will create a thinner edge along the side of your strongest hand. The baguette should be no more than 20 inches long so that it can fit under the hotel pan that I recommend (see page 35). If you are using a stainless-steel bowl or another style of baking vessel, curl the loaf slightly at the ends so that it can fit completely. Carefully pick up the dough to check that the bottom is well sealed.

Longer side of dough facing you

Fold dough into center of rectangle.

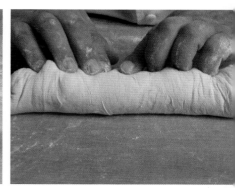

Fold to meet the other seam.

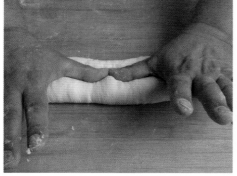

Roll dough away with tips of thumbs.

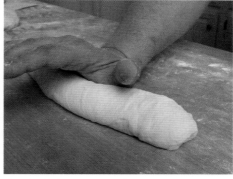

Place heel of your hand on the work surface.

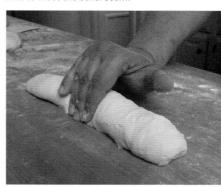

Place your fingertips on the work surface.

Tighten with back-and-forth motion.

Doggie-bone shape

Hands together in center of dough

Gently roll back and forth to elongate.

Finished shape

Baguette on couche

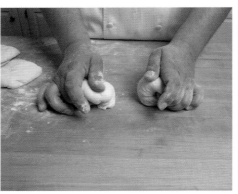

Fold short side of dough in half.   *Turn and repeat, using thumbs to rotate.*   *Final ball with smooth outer skin*

To make the standard roll shape:

Place a piece of the dough (which you already cut in Step 4) on the work surface. Fold the shorter side of the dough in half, from front to back. Turn the dough a quarter turn and fold in half again. Repeat this four more times, lifting up the dough between each turn, until a small ball has formed. Place the ball, seam side down, on the work surface and shape it into a round using your thumb and the side of your hand to rotate the ball against the surface. Using a wheel-like motion and keeping the seam side down, firmly pull the sides in without tearing the dough. The final ball should feel as though it has a smooth outer skin.

To make the standard *bâtard* shape:

Turn the dough so that the short side is facing you and press down lightly with your palm. Using both hands, pick up the edge of the dough closest to you at the corners and, with a light pull, fold the dough up and over to the center of the rectangle. Using the heels of your hands, press down firmly to seal the seam. Then, using a light pull, pick up the corners of the far side of the dough and fold it up and halfway over the first fold. Using the heels of your hands, press down firmly to seal the fold.

Gently pick up the dough and turn it so that the seam is on its side. Using the heels of your hands, with the tips of your thumbs touching and your fingers pointing up, press down hard, keeping your thumbs against the seam and pushing away from your body to flatten and create tension in the dough. Repeat two more times until the dough is firmly shaped. Gently pick up the dough and turn it over, with the smooth side facing up. Roll the seam on its side one last time and seal the seam and ends by pressing firmly with the heel of your hand.

Transfer the shaped dough to its final fermentation spot—a *banneton* (see page 32), a *couche* (see page 34), or a rimless baking sheet (see page 31)—and record the time in your Dough Log.

Fold bottom to center.

Fold top to center.

Turn dough so the seam is on its side.

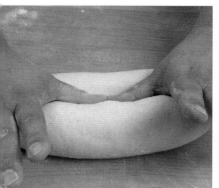

Use tips of thumbs to push away and tighten.

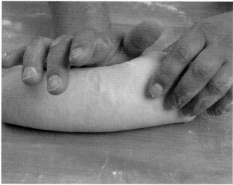

Seal seam and ends with the heel of your hand.

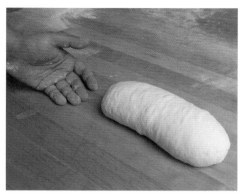

Finished shape

If using a *banneton*, flour it lightly and evenly so that the dough does not stick to it when you remove it after the final proof. Carefully place the dough into the *banneton*, smooth side down. Lightly dust the top with flour so that when covered with plastic wrap, the dough will not stick to it. Once the bread is baked, the flour dusting will present a rustic look and create a nice contrast of the white flour against the dark crust. Cover with plastic wrap.

Lightly flour banneton.

Place dough seam side up.

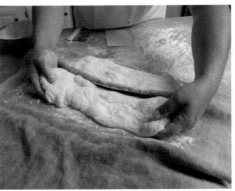

Lightly flour couche.

Fold couche *up to hold shape.*

Couche *provides gentle support.*

If using a *couche*, lightly dust it with flour. Fold the cloth near one edge to make a vertical ridge and place the dough into the *couche* so that it leans against the ridge. It can be either seam side up or down. Pull the flat part of the *couche* up snugly against the opposite side of the dough and fold it over the top of dough. This provides the dough with gentle support throughout the final proofing.

If using a rimless baking sheet, lightly dust it with flour. Turn the dough onto it with the seam side up. Lightly dust the top with flour so that when covered with plastic wrap the dough will not stick to it. Cover with plastic wrap.

STEP 6: FINAL FERMENTATION (PROOFING)

Quick tip for final fermentation:

❀ Your finger is the only tool you need to determine whether bread is ready to bake.

The final fermentation, often called "proofing" by home bakers, is when the bread takes on volume. Whether the dough is in a *banneton*, in a *couche*, or on a baking sheet, transfer it to a warm (75˚F to 80˚F), draft-free place.

Dough is ready when indentation disappears.

Record the time in your Dough Log, as well as the exact time required for the final fermentation, and set your timer. It will usually take about 1 hour for the final proofing, although some recipes may take less or more time. You should keep a close eye on the dough, since it will be unusable if it is overproofed.

To determine whether the dough is ready to be baked, remove the plastic wrap and gently make a small indentation in the center of the dough with your fingertip. If the indentation slowly and evenly disappears, the bread is ready to bake.

If the indentation quickly pops back up, the bread is not yet ready to bake. Again, cover loosely with plastic wrap and let ferment for an additional 15 minutes. Check again, making another small indentation in the center. If it still pops back up, cover and continue to ferment for another 15 minutes. If still not ready, cover and continue to ferment, checking every 5 minutes until the indentation disappears slowly and evenly.

If, on the other hand, the indentation causes the entire shape to completely deflate, the dough is overproofed. This means that it has been allowed to rest for too long. It is now unusable and would yield an unpleasant texture and flavor if baked.

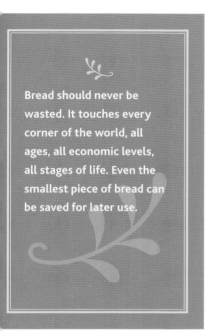

Bread should never be wasted. It touches every corner of the world, all ages, all economic levels, all stages of life. Even the smallest piece of bread can be saved for later use.

STEP 7: BAKING

Quick tips for baking:

* If you want the top of the bread coated with flour when baked, lightly flour first, then score.
* Scoring is the baker's signature on the bread.
* If not using a stainless-steel bowl, La Cloche, or an enameled cast-iron pot to bake, add steam to your oven.
* The bread is done when the interior of the score is lightly browned and you hear a hollow sound when you tap on the bottom of the loaf.

Cinnamon Raisin Bread

La Cloche

Getting Ready to Bake

STAINLESS-STEEL BOWL METHOD: One of the least expensive and most effective methods of achieving a crisp crust on your artisanal bread is by using a stainless-steel mixing bowl (about 12 inches in diameter and 5 inches deep) as the insulator. This works for almost all breads except the baguette shape. For a baguette, use a commercial hotel pan (see page 35), which is long enough to fit over an almost standard-size loaf. I cover the corners, or anywhere else air could escape from, with aluminum foil to create a stronger seal. Move one oven rack to the lowest rung and remove the other. When the dough begins its final fermentation, place a large baking stone on the rack and preheat the oven to 450°F.

ALL OTHER METHODS: When the dough begins its final fermentation, place one oven rack on the bottom rung and the other rack one rung below the center. Preheat the oven to 450°F.

If using La Cloche, place the bottom part in the oven 30 minutes before you are ready to bake. Fifteen minutes before baking, place the lid upside down in a bowl (so it will remain level) in the sink and fill the lid with cold water. Allow the lid to soak until ready to use. (You can also use a German Römertopf or any other clay cooker with a lid in the same way.)

If using an enameled cast-iron Dutch oven with a lid, place the bottom in the oven 30 minutes before you are ready to bake. You do not need to soak the lid.

If you are not using any of these vessels, you will need to add steam to the oven during the initial baking process to achieve the desired crusty, artisanal-style loaf. I have had great luck, as have our home recipe testers, creating steam through the use of lava rocks (see page 36). To do this when using a baking stone in a home oven, fill the base of a broiler pan or a disposable aluminum baking pan with a single layer of clean (washed and dried) lava rocks. Place the pan in the oven to preheat for about 30 minutes before you are ready to bake. You will add the necessary water later in the process.

SCORING CHART

This is the traditional chart used to identify many of the scoring patterns for classic bread shapes. Scoring is done with a lamé (see page 36) or a single-edged razor blade just prior to baking the bread. Although many breads do call for defined markings, you can score in any way you like— diagonal slashes, crisscross markings, or whatever you would like your signature look to be. Cut in quick, decisive slashes, marking into the dough by no more than $^1/_8$ inch. The most important thing to remember is that much as a musician uses a metronome to keep an even, measured pace, you want to keep moving in steady, even, measured movements as you score.

For centuries, in community ovens all across France, the score mark identified each family's bread so that everyone returned home with the correct loaf. The mark was as distinguishing as a family crest.

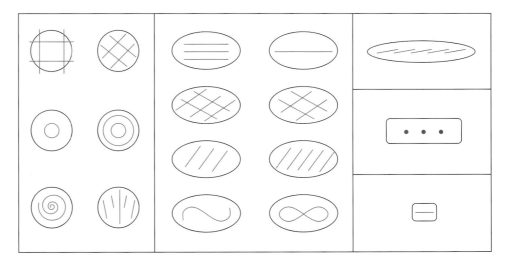

IT'S TIME TO BAKE

Remove the dough from whatever it has been proofed in or on—a *banneton*, a *couche*, or a baking sheet. Place the dough, seam side down, on a cornmeal-dusted bread peel or the back of a sheet pan lightly coated with cornmeal. For a rustic look, lightly dust the top of the loaf with flour, then score the top (see page 65). When scoring a *boule*, cut no more than 4 slashes across the top. If your dough is particularly shiny, the slashes may stick together a bit.

STAINLESS-STEEL BOWL METHOD

Quickly but carefully slide the shaped dough from the peel to the hot baking stone and cover with the stainless-steel mixing bowl. Immediately close the oven door. Bake for 10 minutes; then, lift the edge of the bowl with the tip of a sharp knife and use oven mitts to carefully remove the hot bowl. Continue to bake until the bread is deep golden brown with a crisp crust and sounds hollow when tapped on the bottom, another 25 to 30 minutes (or as noted in the recipe).

Place loaf on hot baking stone.

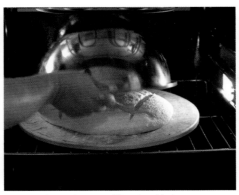

Cover with stainless-steel bowl and bake.

Pop hot bowl up with tip of knife.

Remove hot bowl with oven mitts.

Continue baking per recipe.

ALL OTHER METHODS

For La Cloche or an enameled cast-iron Dutch oven, carefully slide the dough, top side up, from the peel into the base, or use your hands to gently lift it and place it into the base. Either way, take care that you do not touch the hot surface. Immediately cover the loaf with the lid (wet if using La Cloche) and place it in the preheated oven. Set your timer and bake for 10 minutes. Carefully remove the lid, reset your timer, and continue to bake

Transfer loaf to bottom of La Cloche.

Place lid on for 10 minutes, then remove.

Gently pick up dough.

Transfer dough to Dutch oven.

Score loaf.

Place in oven, cover for 10 minutes.

until the loaf is a deep golden-brown, about 35 more minutes (or as directed in a specific recipe).

If using a baking stone combined with lava rocks, put on oven mitts and quickly pour 2 cups of cool water over the preheated lava rocks. The rocks will immediately begin to emit hot steam, so quickly close the oven door and leave it closed for 5 seconds. Then, open the door and, using a cornmeal-dusted bread peel or the back of a sheet pan lightly coated with cornmeal, swiftly transfer the scored dough to the hot stone in the preheated oven. Set your timer and bake until the bread is a deep golden-brown or as directed in a specific recipe, about 35 minutes.

WHEN IS IT DONE?

Over the years I have learned that color is the first indication of a perfectly baked loaf. It should be a rich, golden-brown with a fine network of visible cracking running over it. The color inside of the scoring marks should be a lighter brown. To further check for perfection, remove the bread from the oven and, using your knuckles, lightly tap on the bottom. The bread should

Pour water over hot lava rocks.

reply with a hollow thumping sound. You can do this even if the bread has been baked in a loaf pan; just pop it out, give a tap, and, if necessary, return it to the pan for more baking.

If you are still concerned about the bread's doneness, insert an instant-read thermometer from the bottom of the bread into the center. If it reads 185°F to 210°F, the bread is fully baked.

Once baked, transfer the loaf to a cooling rack and allow it to cool for at least 1 hour before cutting into it with a serrated knife or wrapping it for storage.

Lightly tap the bottom of the loaf.

WHAT IF YOU ARE MAKING MORE THAN ONE LOAF?

If your oven (or baking stone) is too small to hold more than one loaf and you have made more, cover the unscored loaves with plastic wrap and refrigerate until ready to bake. If the refrigeration period is kept short (less than 2 hours), the dough will not have to be brought back to room temperature before baking. Simply remove it from the refrigerator, unwrap, score, and place in the hot oven immediately after the first loaf is done.

EATING AND ENJOYING: HOW TO TASTE AND STORE BREAD

I grew up knowing that enjoying the fruits of my labors is as important as baking the product itself. Much as a wine connoisseur tastes and experiences each bottle, a baker fully experiences the loaves that he bakes. When the bread has cooled a bit, I hold it up to my ear to listen to it "sing"—soft crackling sounds. I admire its warm, golden color. I slice it and deeply inhale its aroma. I listen as the crust crackles and snaps in my hands. I admire the crumb—the shiny holes, the color, the textures—and look to see whether the air pockets are the correct size for the type of bread. I touch the surfaces to determine whether the crust and crumb are of the right consistency. I shut my eyes, and *Ah!* The aroma embraces me. Then, and only then, do I taste.

Lionel tasting bread

What a joy to acknowledge the generations of bakers whose artistry I sense as I chew. So many flavors explode in my mouth—sour ones, sweet ones, buttery and nutty ones. I hope you will pay homage to your baking skills in the same way as you discover your passion in every bite.

When you purchase artisanal breads, how do you determine the quality? Let your senses tell you. Is the crust a good color, is it crackling and crisp? When you cut into the bread, does the crumb (the interior structure) present an uneven pattern of shiny holes indicating good fermentation and correct hydration? When you squeeze the bread, does a wonderful aroma arise or is there a yeasty odor, indicating that too much yeast was used to hasten the process? And, please, don't eat your bread warm. While I respect that some cultures love a warm loaf of bread, to get the optimum flavor profile, it should be enjoyed at room temperature, so the complexities or flavors that identify a fine artisanal bread can be experienced.

Uncut artisanal breads should be stored at room temperature, away from direct sunlight, in a linen or paper bag or in a bread box (as my mom does). In our house, there is never any bread left at the end of the meal, but if there is in yours there are some simple rules to keep it fresh. Store bread unwrapped and cut side down on a cutting board. Do not store in a plastic bag (the crust will soften) or in the refrigerator (it will dry out the entire loaf). To recrisp, wrap the bread in aluminum foil and place in a preheated 375°F oven for about 5 minutes.

TO FREEZE: Place the unwrapped loaf directly in the freezer. When solidly frozen, remove it and wrap it tightly in aluminum foil. Then, wrap the foil-covered loaf in plastic wrap, or place it in a heavy-duty resealable plastic bag and press all of the air out. The foil will help protect the bread from freezer burn and the plastic helps keep the packet airtight. Fresh bread will keep, frozen, for about three months. For ease of storage and future use, cut a large loaf into usable amounts before freezing. This allows you to thaw just the amount you need.

TO THAW: Remove the bread from the freezer. Remove and discard the plastic, but leave the aluminum foil on, as it will capture moisture molecules and keep them from adhering to the bread. Allow the bread to come to room temperature slowly.

TO REHEAT: Place the thawed, foil-wrapped loaf in a preheated 375°F oven for 8 to 15 minutes, depending upon the size of the loaf. The foil will act like a steam chamber to recrisp the crust.

TO SLICE: Always use a serrated knife made for bread slicing. Slice quickly and evenly, crosswise, into slices of whatever thickness you like. Once sliced, bread will begin to lose its freshness very quickly.

QUESTIONS FROM HOME BAKERS

Although it is almost impossible to answer queries without seeing the bread in question, here are some common exchanges I have had with home bakers.

Q: Everything looked fine until I baked my bread. It was flat when I pulled it from the oven. What did I do wrong?

A: Your dough was either too cool (under 72°F) during mixing, or it was overproofed (see page 63.)

Q: The holes in the crumb were almost nonexistent; the bread was dense. Why?

A: Your dough may have been handled too much, bursting the cell structure and releasing gas. Or maybe there was not enough hydration, or too much flour was incorporated, or too much yeast was added, causing the fermentation to move too quickly and lowering the fermentation period. Or maybe the dough was overproofed.

Q: My dough was too sticky to handle easily. How can I fix this next time?

A: Stickiness is the nature of great dough. Although the inclination is to add flour, resist doing so—it will cause your dough to be dry and dense. Just stick to it (pun intended), and you will learn how to take the dough from stickiness to a smooth ball. One of my favorite quotations from a home baker testing recipes for this book is, "At first the dough was sticky, but I stuck to it and when I saw the quality of the baked loaf I felt like a rock star."

Q: Can I knead as my grandmother taught me by pushing and pulling at the dough?

A: There is nothing wrong with your grandmother's technique, as it allows your hands to come in contact with the dough without tearing it. However, when the dough goes between your thumb and index finger, as I teach, you get a deeper sensory perception of the dough, much as a chef may use the fleshy part of his hand to determine the degree of doneness of a steak.

Q: What type of flour do you recommend that I use?

A: Unbleached, unbromated bread flour. It does not have to be labeled "high gluten," but it should be 10 percent to 12 percent protein.

Q: Since there are so few ingredients to making bread, do you ever forget one?

A: Salt! In baking we have a saying: If an experienced baker tells you that he never forgets the salt, don't trust him!

CLASSIC FRENCH BREADS

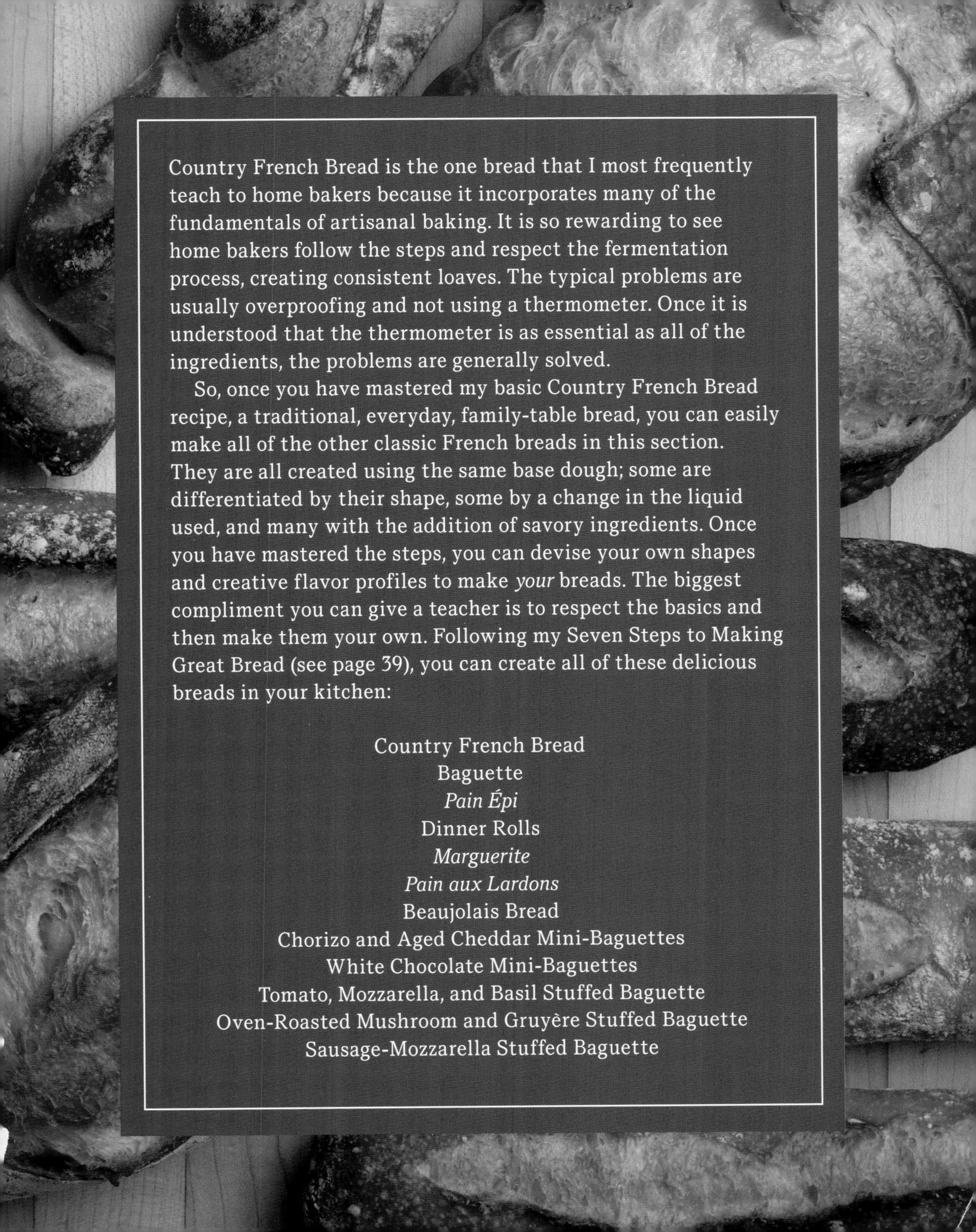

Country French Bread is the one bread that I most frequently teach to home bakers because it incorporates many of the fundamentals of artisanal baking. It is so rewarding to see home bakers follow the steps and respect the fermentation process, creating consistent loaves. The typical problems are usually overproofing and not using a thermometer. Once it is understood that the thermometer is as essential as all of the ingredients, the problems are generally solved.

So, once you have mastered my basic Country French Bread recipe, a traditional, everyday, family-table bread, you can easily make all of the other classic French breads in this section. They are all created using the same base dough; some are differentiated by their shape, some by a change in the liquid used, and many with the addition of savory ingredients. Once you have mastered the steps, you can devise your own shapes and creative flavor profiles to make *your* breads. The biggest compliment you can give a teacher is to respect the basics and then make them your own. Following my Seven Steps to Making Great Bread (see page 39), you can create all of these delicious breads in your kitchen:

Country French Bread
Baguette
Pain Épi
Dinner Rolls
Marguerite
Pain aux Lardons
Beaujolais Bread
Chorizo and Aged Cheddar Mini-Baguettes
White Chocolate Mini-Baguettes
Tomato, Mozzarella, and Basil Stuffed Baguette
Oven-Roasted Mushroom and Gruyère Stuffed Baguette
Sausage-Mozzarella Stuffed Baguette

COUNTRY FRENCH BREAD
QUICK REFERENCE

Once you have learned to make a basic Country French Bread, you can follow this Quick Reference guide for a reminder of the steps involved. It will also work for other breads created from the same basic dough.

* Scale all ingredients.
* Measure the temperature of the water (82°F to 84°F if mixing by hand) and note it in your Dough Log (see page 127).
* Mix by hand for 5 to 15 minutes, or with a heavy-duty electric stand mixer for 5 minutes on low speed ("1" on most mixers) and 2 minutes on medium-low speed ("2" on most mixers).
* Measure the dough temperature (72°F to 80°F) and record it in your Dough Log.
* Set aside for the first fermentation for 45 minutes to 1 hour.
* Divide and shape.
* Proof for 1 hour.
* Bake at 450°F on a baker's stone using the stainless-steel bowl method for 25 minutes.
* Cool and eat, or store at room temperature for 1 day.

❧ Country French Bread ❧

MAKES 1 BOULE

Country French Bread is a classic all-purpose bread—great for sandwiches, delicious for morning toast, and a wonderful loaf to set at the center of the table. This is the style of bread that appeared on the table throughout my childhood, and it has never lost its appeal. It is frequently used to make croutons and breadcrumbs and also as a thickener for soups, sauces, and dressings. It has a crisp, crackling crust with a firm crumb that doesn't fall apart when buttered or covered with a sandwich filling. For the home baker, it is best baked on a stone under a stainless-steel bowl, as are most of my recipes.

Although I recommend mixing and kneading by hand, Country French Bread can also be made in a heavy-duty electric stand mixer (see page 49).

16 ounces	454 grams	3½ cups unbleached, unbromated white bread flour
0.31 ounce	9 grams	1½ teaspoons fine sea salt
0.18 ounce	5 grams	1½ teaspoons instant dry yeast
11.28 ounces	320 grams	1¼ cups plus 2 tablespoons water

Cornmeal for dusting

1 MEASURING

Scale all of the ingredients.

Place the flour in a large mixing bowl. Add the salt and yeast, making sure that they do not touch each other.

2 MIXING AND KNEADING

Using your hands, bring the dry ingredients together. Once blended, quickly form a well in the center of the mix.

Take the temperature of the water (it should be 82°F to 84°F for hand mixing, or 65°F to 70°F for an electric mixer) and record it in your Dough Log. Immediately begin adding the water to the well in a slow, steady stream, rotating the bowl with one hand while simultaneously mixing the water into the dry ingredients with your other hand. Stop often as you work to scrape the bowl and your fingers with your bowl scraper, making sure that all of the ingredients have been gathered into the dough mass. The bowl should be quite clean. The dough will be soft, slightly wet, and extremely sticky.

Pinch off a bit of dough and taste to see whether you have forgotten the salt. If so, add it now and mix for another minute or so to fully incorporate it into the dough. The dough should just be beginning to come together.

This dough can also be baked in a loaf pan to create a traditional *pain de mie*. Toasted nuts or chopped dried fruit can be added at the end of the mixing to make a terrific pairing for cheese.

When the dough begins to come together, use your bowl scraper to scrape the dough out onto your work surface, taking care not to leave any dough behind. The dough will still be very, very sticky. Do not give in to your temptation to add more flour, since that will alter the flour ratio of the dough. Stick with it; you can do it. The end result will prove it.

Hold your hands, palms facing up, at opposite sides of the dough mass that are closest to your body. Slide your fingers, still facing up, under the dough and lift the dough an inch or so from the work surface. Squeeze your thumbs and index fingers together to form a tight "OK" sign through the dough. While holding the "OK" sign, continue to curl your thumbs and index fingers tightly together to pinch off a portion of dough. Working as quickly and smoothly as you can, continue lifting and pinching the dough mass using the same technique, moving up the dough mass in approximately 1-inch to 1½-inch increments, approximately 5 to 7 times, until you have gone through the entire mass. You should begin to feel the dough coming together. Remember, your hands are your memory—really get the feel of the dough as it comes together.

Turn the dough a quarter turn and continue lifting, pinching, and turning the dough until it begins to take on an identifiable shape and is less and less sticky. Don't give up; keep working the dough without adding additional flour, and it will begin to take shape. This can take anywhere from 5 to 15 minutes. Remember, do not add any flour to speed the process. Use your scraper to keep incorporating all of the dough into the mass. The dough is sufficiently kneaded when it can be formed into a ball. You do not want a stiff, dry dough; you want a soft, pliable mass that still holds its shape.

To form the dough into a ball, using both hands, lift it up from the front and fold it over and onto itself in one swift motion, quickly dropping it down on the work surface. Repeat this process 4 to 5 times until a ball forms. At all times, use the scraper to ensure that you are gathering all of the dough.

Touch the dough with the back of your hand to make sure that it is no longer sticky. If it is sticky, use the OK-sign pinching method to knead up and down the dough once or twice more, quickly folding the dough over itself 4 to 5 times. Touch the top of the dough again to ensure that it is no longer sticky. If it is, repeat the folding process until it is no longer sticky.

3 FIRST FERMENTATION

At this point, you should take the dough temperature and record it, along with the time, in your Dough Log. It should be between 72°F and 80°F. If it is not, make the necessary adjustments (see page 52). It is particularly important that you record the time you finish this step as you will need to note the time required for the first (bulk) fermentation, in this case about 1 hour.

Lightly dust a large bowl (preferably glass to allow observation of the process) with flour. The bowl should be large enough to allow the dough to rise without coming in contact with the plastic wrap that will cover it. Transfer the dough ball to the bowl, smooth side up, taking care to retain the round shape of the dough. Cover the bowl loosely with plastic wrap.

Place the bowl in a warm (75°F to 80°F), draft-free place until the dough has doubled in volume, about 1 hour.

4 DIVIDING

Since you are making just 1 loaf, skip to Step 5!

5 SHAPING

If the dough is very sticky, lightly flour your hands, but do not add more flour to the dough. If the dough adheres to the table, use your bench scraper to lift it up; do not pull and stretch the dough. You can, at this point, give a light dusting of flour to the work surface. With the palm of your hand, lightly press the dough into a rectangle. Then, using your hands, gently pick up the dough to make sure it is not sticking to the work surface.

Carefully form the dough into a *boule* (see page 56).

6 FINAL FERMENTATION

Place the shaped dough in its final fermentation spot—a *banneton* (see page 61), a *couche* (see page 62), or a rimless baking sheet (see page 62), carefully following the directions for the appropriate preparation of whatever vessel you are using. Lightly flour the top of the dough to ensure that the plastic wrap does not stick to it.

Transfer to a warm (75°F to 80°F), draft-free place. Record the time in your Dough Log, as well as the exact time required for the final fermentation in your Dough Log, and set your timer. It should take about 1 hour for the final proofing; however, you should keep a close eye on the dough, because if it is overproofed it will be unusable.

If you are using the stainless-steel bowl method for baking (see page 64), about 30 minutes before you are ready to bake, move one oven rack to the lowest rung and remove the other. Place a large baking stone on the rack, and preheat the oven to 450°F. (For all other baking methods, follow the directions on page 64)

To determine whether the dough is ready to be baked, uncover it and gently make a small indentation in the center of the dough with your fingertip. If the indentation slowly and evenly disappears, the bread is ready to bake. If not, follow the instructions on page 63 for additional fermentation.

7 BAKING

Place the dough, seam side down, on a cornmeal-dusted bread peel or the back of a sheet pan lightly coated with cornmeal. For a rustic look, lightly dust the top of the loaf with flour.

The baguette is the classic shape you see everywhere in France, peeking out of a burlap shopping bag or carried under the arm of a shopper in those iconic photos of Parisian life. Although not officially called a "baguette" until the early part of the last century, long, thin loaves were made in France for generations but did not supplant the huge, round loaf of the village bakery (see La Farm Bread, page 7) until after World War I.

Working quickly with a lamé or single-edged razor blade, score the top of the loaf (see page 65) in a traditional manner or use your own signature score. Cut in quick decisive slashes, marking into the dough by no more than ⅛ inch.

Carefully slide the loaf, top side up, onto the center of the stone, taking care to not touch the hot surface.

Quickly cover the dough with the stainless-steel mixing bowl. Immediately close the oven door. Bake for 10 minutes; then, lift the edge of the bowl with the tip of a small knife and use oven mitts to carefully remove the hot bowl. Continue to bake until the bread is a deep golden brown with a crisp crust and sounds hollow when tapped on the bottom, another 25 to 30 minutes. (It is a good idea to check after the bread has been baking for about 20 minutes to make sure it is browning evenly. If not, rotate the bread.) If you are concerned about the bread's doneness, insert an instant-read thermometer from the bottom of the bread into the center. If it reads 185°F to 210°F, the bread is fully baked.

Transfer the bread to a cooling rack. Let cool for at least 1 hour before cutting with a serrated knife or wrapping for storage.

Baguette

MAKES 2 LOAVES

The baguette was the household bread of my youth, the most popular bread in France. We ate it with every meal—breakfast toast, sandwiches, or to wipe up our sauces from the dinner plate. One of my favorite guilty memories, and a story my mom still tells with annoyance, was being sent with my brother to buy baguettes for a celebration meal and arriving home empty handed, as we had eaten both loaves as we walked. Our guests had no bread to enjoy with their meal, a sacrilege at a French table.

Although a baguette can be made in almost any length and in any diameter, it is traditionally about 2 feet long and 2½ inches in diameter, with tapered ends. This bread is made from my Country French Bread recipe and is distinguished only by its shape. To keep the classic shape, when baking at home I use a 20¾-by-12¾-by-4-inch hotel pan (see page 35) rather than a large stainless-steel bowl, because it is long enough to fit over an almost standard-size loaf. If you are going to include baguettes in your regular baking routine, I suggest that you purchase this pan.

1 recipe Country French Bread (page 75)

Cornmeal for dusting

1–3 MEASURING, MIXING AND KNEADING, AND FIRST FERMENTATION

Make the dough according to the directions for Country French Bread through the first fermentation stage, mixing either by hand or with an electric mixer.

4 DIVIDING

Very lightly dust a clean work surface with flour. Uncover the dough and, using your bowl scraper, scrape the dough onto the lightly floured work surface. Let the dough rest for 30 seconds.

If the dough is very sticky, lightly flour your hands, but do not add more flour to the dough. If the dough sticks to the table, use your bench scraper to lift it up; do not pull and stretch the dough. With the palm of your hand, lightly press down on the dough to form it into a rectangle. Then, using your bench scraper, cut the dough into 2 rectangles of equal size. Again, using your hands, gently pick up the dough to make sure it is not sticking to the work surface.

5 SHAPING

Carefully shape each piece into a baguette (see page 58).

Place the first baguette in a lightly floured *couche* (or a strong linen towel) as directed on page 62. It does not matter whether you have the smooth side up or down for the final proofing as long as you bake it smooth side up. Make a second ridge next to the first loaf and place the second loaf against it. Fold the remaining *couche* over the top.

6 FINAL FERMENTATION

Set the *couche* in a warm (75°F to 80°F), draft-free place. Record the time in your Dough Log, as well as the exact time required for the final fermentation, and set your timer. It should take about 1 hour for the final proofing; however, you should keep a close eye on the dough, because if it is overproofed it will be unusable.

If you are using the hotel pan or stainless-steel bowl method to bake the bread (see page 64), about 30 minutes before you are ready to bake, move one oven rack to the lowest rung and remove the other. Place a large baking stone on the rack and preheat the oven to 450°F. (For all other baking methods, follow the directions on page 64.)

To determine whether the dough is ready to be baked, gently make a small indentation in the center of the dough with your fingertip. If the indentation slowly and evenly disappears, the bread is ready to bake. If not, follow the instructions on page 63 for additional fermentation.

7   **BAKING**

Uncover the dough and carefully transfer the loaves, smooth side up, to a cornmeal-coated bread peel or the back of a sheet pan lightly coated with cornmeal. If your oven is too small to hold more than one loaf, cover one loaf with plastic wrap and refrigerate until ready to bake. (Since the refrigeration period is short, the dough will not have to be brought back to room temperature before baking. Simply remove it from the refrigerator, unwrap, score, and place immediately in the hot oven as directed for the first loaf.)

Using a lamé or single-edged razor blade at a 45-degree angle and with a quick, decisive movement, cut one 3-inch-long line down the center of the loaf, just barely breaking through the skin and cutting about 1/8 inch into the dough. Then, overlapping the scoring by one-third, cut a second line in the center. Then, repeat the pattern down the length of the loaf. A baguette is always scored in this defined pattern.

Carefully slide the baguette(s), smooth side up, onto the center of the stone, taking care not to touch the hot surface.

Quickly cover the stone with the stainless-steel hotel pan or mixing bowl. If using a hotel pan, I use aluminum foil on the corners to assure an even seal against the stone. Immediately close the oven door. Bake for 10 minutes; then, lift the edge of the bowl with the tip of a small knife and use oven mitts to carefully remove the hot bowl. Continue to bake until the bread is a deep golden brown with a crisp crust and sounds hollow when tapped on the bottom, another 25 to 30 minutes. The color inside of the scoring marks should be a lighter brown. If you are concerned about the bread's doneness, insert an instant-read thermometer from the bottom of the bread into the center. If it reads 185°F to 210°F the bread is fully baked.

Transfer to a cooling rack. Let cool for at least 1 hour before cutting into it with a serrated knife or wrapping it for storage.

Scoring a baguette

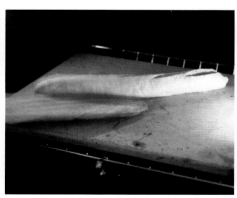

Slide onto baking stone.

Quickly cover and bake for 10 minutes.

Pain Épi

MAKES 2 LOAVES

In French, *épi* is the word used to describe the kernels that make up the spike at the end of a wheat stalk. A *pain épi* is a loaf of bread formed by connecting a group of small, slightly pointed rolls so that, when baked, the loaf resembles the spike of a wheat stalk. The individual "rolls" can be easily pulled off without making a mess of the entire loaf. Again, made from Country French Bread dough, this is an easy-to-form yet interesting shape to place at the center of the table or to take along to a picnic to make little sandwiches. Don't hesitate to make the rolls in any shape you find interesting or to roll the loaf in seeds—sesame, poppy, or sunflower—for added flavor and dimension.

To keep the classic shape, when baking at home I use a 20³⁄₄-by-12³⁄₄-by-4-inch hotel pan (see page 35).

1 recipe Country French Bread (page 75)

Cornmeal for dusting

1–3 MEASURING, MIXING AND KNEADING, AND FIRST FERMENTATION

Make the dough according to the directions for Country French Bread through the first fermentation stage, mixing either by hand or with an electric mixer.

4 DIVIDING

Very lightly dust a clean work surface with flour. Uncover the dough and, using a bowl scraper, scrape the dough onto the lightly floured work surface. Let the dough rest for 30 seconds.

If the dough is very sticky, lightly flour your hands, but do not add more flour to the dough. If the dough sticks to the table, use your bench scraper to lift it up; do not pull and stretch the dough. With the palm of your hand, lightly press the dough into a rectangle. Then, using your bench scraper, cut the dough into 2 rectangles of equal size. Again, using your hands, gently pick up the dough to make sure it is not sticking to the work surface.

5 SHAPING

Carefully shape each piece into a baguette (see page 58).

If you want to roll the dough in seeds, do it now. Place the first baguette in a lightly floured *couche* (or a strong linen towel) as directed on page 62. It does not matter whether you have the smooth side up or down for the final proofing as long as you bake it smooth side up. Make a second ridge next to the first loaf and place the second loaf against it. Fold the remaining *couche* over the top.

Choose your seed toppings.

Roll gently in seeds.

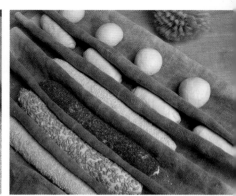

Place seam side down on couche.

6 FINAL FERMENTATION

Set the *couche* in a warm (75°F to 80°F), draft-free place. Record the time in your Dough Log, as well as the exact time required for the final fermentation, and set your timer. It should take about 1 hour for the final proofing; however, you should keep a close eye on the dough, because if it is overproofed it will be unusable.

If you are using the hotel pan or stainless-steel bowl method to bake the bread (see page 64), about 30 minutes before you are ready to bake, move one oven rack to the lowest rung and remove the other. Place a large baking stone on the rack and preheat the oven to 450°F. (For all other baking methods, follow the directions on page 64.)

To determine whether the dough is ready to be baked, gently make a small indentation in the center of the dough with your fingertip. If the indentation slowly and evenly disappears, the bread is ready to bake. If not, follow the instructions on page 63 for additional fermentation.

7 BAKING

Carefully transfer the loaves, smooth side up, to a cornmeal-dusted bread peel or the back of a sheet pan lightly coated with cornmeal. If your oven or stone is too small to hold more than one loaf, cover one loaf with plastic wrap and refrigerate until ready to bake. (Since the refrigeration period is short, the dough will not have to be brought back to room temperature before baking. Simply remove it from the refrigerator, unwrap, cut into the *épi* shape as described below, and place immediately in the hot oven as directed for the first loaf.)

Instead of scoring, you will cut the dough into the *épi* shape. Starting about 2 inches from the end of one loaf, use kitchen shears at a 45-degree angle above the loaf to cut into the top of the dough. Snip about three-quarters of the way into the top of the dough. Gently move the cut piece of dough from the center to one side of the baguette. Move down another 2 inches and make another cut, this time moving the cut piece to the other

Cut at a 45-degree angle.

Gently turn cut dough from center.

Continue cutting and turning down loaf.

Different styles of pain épi *and baguette*

Épi rolled in poppy seeds and cut

Different styles of épi

side of the baguette. It is very important to hold the kitchen shears at the same angle for every cut. Continue moving down 2 inches, snipping into the dough, and gently moving the dough to alternate sides of the baguette until you reach the other end of the loaf. You want to create the shape of a row of wheat kernels on each side of the loaf.

Carefully slide the loaf onto the center of the stone, taking care not to touch the hot surface. (Bake one at a time if they don't both fit.)

Quickly cover the stone with the stainless-steel hotel pan or mixing bowl. Immediately close the oven door. Bake for 10 minutes; then, lift the edge of the bowl with the tip of a small knife and use oven mitts to carefully remove the hot bowl. Continue to bake until the bread is a deep golden brown with a crisp crust and sounds hollow when tapped on the bottom, another 25 to 30 minutes. (It is a good idea to check after the bread has been baking for about 20 minutes to make sure it is browning evenly. If not, rotate the bread.) If you are concerned about the bread's doneness, insert an instant-read thermometer from the bottom of the bread into the center. If it reads 185°F to 210°F the bread is fully baked.

Transfer to a cooling rack. Let cool for at least 1 hour before pulling apart, cutting with a serrated knife, or wrapping for storage.

Finished épi

Dinner Rolls

MAKES 8 ROLLS

I've found that most Americans think of a dinner roll as a small, soft, almost squishy, slightly sweet bread. At La Farm Bakery, our dinner rolls are more in the European tradition—crusty, with a hint of salt and a moist, chewy interior. We call them "hard rolls" because our customers have always referred to them in this way. They are a customer favorite served with European butter and jam or made into a breakfast sandwich with scrambled eggs and applewood-smoked bacon. These are elegant rolls to be placed on the bread plate when entertaining.

1 recipe Country French Bread (page 75)

Cornmeal for dusting

1–3 MEASURING, MIXING AND KNEADING, AND FIRST FERMENTATION

Make the dough according to the directions for Country French Bread through the first fermentation stage, mixing either by hand or with an electric mixer.

4 DIVIDING

Very lightly dust a clean work surface with flour. Uncover the dough and, using your bowl scraper, scrape the dough onto the lightly floured work surface. Let the dough rest for 30 seconds.

    If the dough is very sticky, lightly flour your hands, but do not add more flour to the dough. If the dough sticks to the table, use your bench scraper to lift it up; do not pull and stretch the dough. With the palm of your hand,

Cut dough into four equal pieces.

Divide each piece again.

Place rolls on couche.

lightly press down on the dough. Then, using your hands, gently pick up the dough to make sure it is not sticking to the work surface. Using your bench scraper, cut the dough into 8 equal pieces. .

5 SHAPING

Carefully form each piece into a small roll (see page 60). Place 4 rolls in a lightly floured *couche* (or a strong linen towel) as directed on page 62. Make a second ridge next to them and place the 4 remaining rolls against it. Fold the remaining *couche* over top of dough.

6 FINAL FERMENTATION

Set the *couche* in a warm (75°F to 80°F), draft-free place. Record the time in your Dough Log, as well as the time required for the final fermentation, and set your timer. It should take about 1 hour for the final proofing.

If you are using the stainless-steel bowl method to bake the rolls (see page 64), about 30 minutes before you are ready to bake, move one oven rack to the lowest rung and remove the other. Place a large baking stone on the rack and preheat the oven to 450°F. (For all other baking methods, follow the directions on page 64.)

To determine whether the dough is ready to be baked, uncover and gently make a small indentation in the center of the dough with your fingertip. If the indentation slowly and evenly disappears, the rolls are ready to bake. If not, follow the instructions on page 63 for additional fermentation.

7 BAKING

Uncover the dough and carefully transfer the rolls, smooth side up, to a cornmeal-coated bread peel or the back of a sheet pan lightly coated with cornmeal.

Using a lamé or single-edged razor blade and with quick, decisive movements, cut a couple of small slashes into each roll, just barely breaking through the skin and cutting about 1/8 inch into the dough.

Carefully slide the rolls onto the center of the stone, taking care not to touch the hot surface.

Quickly cover the stone with the stainless-steel mixing bowl. Immediately close the oven door. Bake for 5 minutes; then, lift the edge of the bowl with the tip of a small knife and use oven mitts to carefully remove the hot bowl. Continue to bake until the rolls are a deep golden brown with a crisp crust and sound hollow when tapped on the bottom, about 15 minutes more. If you are concerned about doneness, insert an instant-read thermometer from the bottom of the roll into the center. If it reads 185°F to 210°F the bread is fully baked.

Transfer to a cooling rack. Let cool for at least 1 hour before eating.

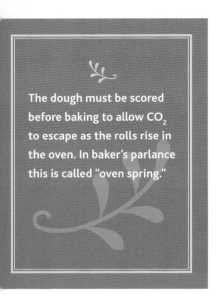

The dough must be scored before baking to allow CO_2 to escape as the rolls rise in the oven. In baker's parlance this is called "oven spring."

Marguerite

MAKES 7 ROLLS

This is simply a pull-apart bread that looks a bit like a flower—*marguerite* being the name of a daisy. It has a raised center surrounded by six "petals," which are served much as you would dinner rolls. It is a great bread to place at the center of a luncheon table since it is as decorative as it is delicious! This style is particularly popular in northern France, in those regions bordering Germany, where breads are often baked with various toppings.

1 recipe Country French Bread (page 75)

¼ cup sesame seeds

¼ cup poppy seeds

1–3 MEASURING, MIXING AND KNEADING, AND FIRST FERMENTATION

Make the dough according to the directions for Country French Bread through the first fermentation stage, mixing either by hand or with an electric mixer.

4 DIVIDING

Very lightly dust a clean work surface with flour. Uncover the dough and, using your bowl scraper, scrape the dough onto the lightly floured work surface. Let the dough rest for 30 seconds.

If the dough is very sticky, lightly flour your hands, but do not add more flour to the dough. If the dough sticks to the table, use your bench scraper to lift it up; do not pull and stretch the dough. With the palm of your hand, lightly press the dough into a rectangle. Then, using your bench scraper, cut the dough into 7 equal pieces. Again using your hands, gently pick up the dough pieces to make sure they are not sticking to the work surface.

5 SHAPING

Place the sesame seeds in one shallow bowl and the poppy seeds in another. Line a baking sheet with parchment paper.

Carefully form each piece into a small roll (see page 60). Place one unseeded roll, smooth side up, in the center of the parchment-lined baking sheet.

Dip another roll, smooth side down, into the sesame seeds and place it, seeded side up, against the center roll so that they are touching. Then dip another ball, smooth side down, into the poppy seeds and place it, seeded

Dip roll in seeds smooth side down.

Rolls after being dipped in seeds

Place a plain roll in the center.

Alternate seed rolls.

side up, next to the sesame-seed-covered ball up against the center ball. Continue dipping and alternating seeds until you have used all of the balls and formed a flower shape with an unseeded center and 6 alternately seeded "petals."

Cover the dough with a clean linen towel followed by plastic wrap.

6 FINAL FERMENTATION

Set the baking sheet in a warm (75°F to 80°F), draft-free place. Record the time in your Dough Log, as well as the exact time required for the final fermentation, and set your timer. It should take about 1 hour for the final proofing; however, you should keep a close eye on the dough, because if it is overproofed it will be unusable.

About 30 minutes before you are ready to bake, move one oven rack to the lowest rung and remove the other. Place a large baking stone on the rack and preheat the oven to 450°F.

To determine whether the dough is ready to be baked, uncover and gently make a small indentation in the center of the dough with your fingertip. If the indentation slowly and evenly disappears, the bread is ready to bake. If not, follow the instructions on page 63 for additional fermentation.

7 BAKING

Uncover the dough and carefully transfer the parchment paper with the *marguerite* on it onto the center of the stone, taking care not to touch the hot surface. This bread does not require scoring.

Quickly cover the stone with the stainless-steel mixing bowl. Immediately close the oven door. Bake for 10 minutes; then, lift the edge of the bowl with the tip of a small knife and use oven mitts to carefully remove the hot bowl. Continue to bake until the bread is a deep golden brown with a crisp crust and sounds hollow when tapped on the bottom, about 15 minutes more. If you are concerned about the bread's doneness, insert an instant-read thermometer from the bottom of the bread into the center. If it reads 185°F to 210°F the bread is fully baked.

Transfer to a cooling rack. Let cool for at least 1 hour before pulling apart, cutting with a serrated knife, or wrapping for storage.

Pain aux Lardons

When I was still a student, I spent a year in Nîmes in southern France, where bread baked with bits of ham or bacon and fresh herbs was a local favorite. It is often served with olives and charcuterie, and perhaps some aged cheese, along with a pre-dinner apéritif. This is my version, which is essentially Country French Bread dough enhanced with wonderfully aromatic applewood-smoked bacon. I created this recipe for the tenth anniversary of La Farm Bakery, celebrating my French heritage and the wonderful pork products of North Carolina.

16 ounces	454 grams	3½ cups unbleached, unbromated white bread flour
0.24 ounce	7 grams	1⅛ teaspoons fine sea salt
0.18 ounce	5 grams	1½ teaspoons instant dry yeast
11.26 ounces	320 grams	1¼ cups plus 2 tablespoons water
3 ounces		85 grams cooked lardons, at room temperature (approx. ¾ cups or 7 slices slab applewood-smoked bacon, rind discarded, bacon cut crosswise into ¼-inch-thick strips, sautéed until nearly crisp)
0.04 ounce	1 gram	1½ teaspoons chopped fresh thyme

1 tablespoon extra-virgin olive oil for brushing

1 MEASURING

Scale all of the ingredients. Place the flour in a large mixing bowl. Add the salt and yeast, making sure that they do not touch each other.

2 MIXING AND KNEADING

Using your hands, bring the dry ingredients together. Once blended, quickly form a well in the center of the mix.

Take the temperature of the water (it should be 82°F to 84°F for hand mixing, or 65°F to 70°F for an electric mixer) and record it in your Dough Log. Immediately start adding the water to the well in a slow, steady stream, rotating the bowl with one hand while simultaneously mixing the water into the dry ingredients with your other hand. Stop often as you work to scrape the bowl and your fingers with your bowl scraper, making sure that all of the ingredients have been gathered into the dough mass. The bowl should be quite clean. The dough will be soft, slightly wet, and extremely sticky.

Pinch off a bit of dough and taste to see whether you have forgotten the salt, a frequent mistake of even skilled bakers. If so, add it now and mix for another minute or so to fully incorporate it into the dough. The dough should just be beginning to come together.

When the dough begins to come together, use your bowl scraper to scrape the dough out onto your work surface, taking care not to leave any dough behind. The dough will still be very, very sticky. Do not give in to your temptation to add more flour, since that will alter the flour ratio of the dough. Stick with it; you can do it. The end result will prove it.

Hold your hands, palms facing up, at opposite sides of the dough mass. Slide your fingers under the dough and lift the dough an inch or so from the work surface. Squeeze your thumbs and index fingers together to form a tight "OK" sign through the dough. While holding the "OK" sign, continue to curl your thumbs and index fingers tightly together to pinch off a portion of dough. Working as quickly and smoothly as you can, continue lifting and pinching the dough mass using the same technique, moving up the dough mass in approximately 1-inch to 1½-inch increments, until you have gone through the entire mass. You should begin to feel the dough coming together. Remember, your hands are your memory—pay attention to the feel of the dough as it comes together.

Turn the dough a quarter turn and continue lifting, pinching, and turning the dough until it begins to take on an identifiable shape and is less and less sticky. Don't give up; keep working the dough without adding additional flour and it will begin to take shape. This can take anywhere from 5 to 15 minutes. Remember, do not add any flour to speed the process. Use your scraper to keep incorporating all of the dough into the mass. The dough is sufficiently kneaded when it can be formed into a ball. You do not want a stiff, dry dough; you want a soft, pliable mass that still holds its shape.

To form the dough into a ball, using both hands, lift it up from the front and fold it over and onto itself in one swift motion, quickly dropping it down on the work surface. Repeat this process 4 to 5 times until a ball forms. At all times, use the scraper to ensure that you are gathering all of the dough.

When the dough is sufficiently kneaded, use the palms of your hands to flatten it out into a rectangle. Scatter the lardons and fresh thyme evenly down the middle. Wrap the sides of the dough up and over the lardons and thyme and pinch and turn the dough until they are completely incorporated.

Again, form the dough into a ball. Using both hands, lift it up from the front and fold it over and onto itself in one swift movement, quickly dropping it down on the work surface. Repeat this process 4 to 5 times until a ball forms. At all times, use the scraper to be sure that you are gathering all of the dough.

With the back of your hand, touch the dough to confirm that it is no longer sticky. If it is sticky, knead once or twice more, each time folding the dough over itself 4 to 5 times. Touch the top of the dough again to be sure that it is no longer sticky. If it is, repeat the folding process until it is no longer sticky.

3 FIRST FERMENTATION

At this point, you should take the temperature of the dough and record it, along with the time, in your Dough Log. It should be between 72°F and 80°F. If it is not, make the necessary adjustments (see page 52). It is particularly important that you record the time you finish this step, since you will need to note the time required for the first (bulk) fermentation, in this case about 1 hour.

Very lightly dust a large bowl (preferably glass to allow observation of the process) with flour. The bowl should be large enough to allow the dough to rise without coming in contact with the plastic wrap that will cover it. Transfer the dough ball to the bowl, smooth side up, taking care to retain the round shape of the dough. Loosely cover the bowl with plastic wrap.

Place the bowl in a warm (75°F to 80°F), draft-free place until the dough has doubled in volume, about 1 hour.

4 DIVIDING

Very lightly dust a clean work surface with flour. Uncover the dough and, using your bowl scraper, scrape the dough onto the work surface. Let the dough rest for 30 seconds.

If the dough is very sticky, lightly flour your hands, but do not add more flour to the dough. If the dough sticks to the table, use your bench scraper to lift it up; do not pull and stretch the dough. With the palm of your hand, lightly press the dough into a rectangle. Then, using your hands, gently pick up the dough to make sure it is not sticking to the work surface.

Using your bench scraper, cut the dough into two equal pieces.

Cut dough into 2 equal pieces.

Cut 3 diagonal slices on each side.

Transfer dough to parchment.

Gently pull apart cut areas.

5 SHAPING

Line two baking sheets with parchment paper.

Working with one piece at a time and again using the bench scraper, cut two columns of three diagonal slices about 1 inch wide and an equal distance apart into each piece. Make sure that you cut completely through the dough to the work surface. Again, use the bench scraper to cut about ½ inch into the center edge of the dough closest to you. Gently pull on the dough to separate the cut areas away from the dough.

Transfer the dough pieces to the baking sheets. Cover with a clean linen towel followed by plastic wrap.

6 FINAL FERMENTATION

Set the baking sheets in a warm (75°F to 80°F), draft-free place. Record the time in your Dough Log, as well as the exact time required for the final fermentation, and set your timer. It should take about 1 hour for the final proofing.

About 30 minutes before you are ready to bake, arrange the oven racks to fit two baking sheets. Preheat the oven to 450°F.

To determine whether the dough is ready to be baked, uncover and gently make a small indentation in the center of the dough with your fingertip. If the indentation slowly and evenly disappears, the bread is ready to bake.

7 BAKING

Uncover the dough and place the baking sheets in the preheated oven. Bake until the bread is deep golden brown with a crisp crust, 20 to 25 minutes.

If you are concerned about the bread's doneness, insert an instant-read thermometer from the bottom of the bread into the center. If it reads 185°F to 210°F the bread is fully baked.

Transfer the *pains aux lardons* to a cooling rack. Using a pastry brush, lightly coat the top of each bread with extra-virgin olive oil.

Beaujolais Bread

MAKES 1 LARGE "GRAPE CLUSTER" OR 16 ROLLS

I spent much of my youth at my grandparents' beautiful stone house, which is surrounded by a vineyard in the Rhône region of France. This bread pays homage to the first grape harvest of the year. Once again, this recipe uses the basic Country French Bread (see page 75) and then, with just a little sleight of hand, turns it into something unusual and spectacular. Using wine as the liquid slows the fermentation process, so you have to allow extra time. Since the bread is shaped into a grape cluster, it is the perfect centerpiece for an appetizer buffet to celebrate the arrival of November's *Beaujolais Nouveau*. Guests are encouraged to pull off a "grape" to enjoy with their glass of wine. A wonderful way to celebrate the harvest!

16 ounces	454 grams	3½ cups unbleached, unbromated white bread flour
0.24 ounce	7 grams	1⅛ teaspoons fine sea salt
0.18 ounce	5 grams	1½ teaspoons instant dry yeast
0.75 ounce	21 grams	1 tablespoon honey
11.26 ounces	320 grams	1¼ cups plus 2 tablespoons Beaujolais wine (see Note)
4 ounces	113 grams salami, cut into ¼-inch cubes (about 1 cup), at room temperature	

Mise en place

Add honey to dry ingredients.

1 MEASURING

Scale all of the ingredients.

Place the flour in a large mixing bowl. Add the salt and yeast, making sure that they do not touch each other. Add the honey to the dry ingredients.

2 MIXING AND KNEADING

Using your hands, bring the dry ingredients together. Once blended, quickly form a well in the center of the mix.

Take the temperature of the wine—it should be 82°F to 84°F—and record it in your Dough Log. Immediately start adding the wine to the well in a slow, steady stream, rotating the bowl with one hand while simultaneously mixing the wine into the dry ingredients with your other hand. Stop often as you work to scrape the bowl and your fingers with your bowl scraper, making sure that all of the ingredients have been gathered into the dough mass. The bowl should be quite clean. The dough will be soft, slightly wet, and extremely sticky.

Pinch off a bit of dough and taste to see whether you have forgotten the salt. If so, add it now and mix for another minute or so to fully

Add wine at 82°F to 84°F.

Rotate bowl while mixing.

Stop often to scrape bowl and fingers.

Form "OK" sign.

Curl thumbs and pinch dough.

incorporate it into the dough. The dough should just be beginning to come together.

When the dough begins to come together, use your bowl scraper to scrape the dough out onto your work surface, taking care not to leave any dough behind. The dough will still be very, very sticky. Do not give in to your temptation to add more flour to the surface, since that will alter the flour ratio of the dough. Stick with it; you can do it. The end result will prove it.

Hold your hands, palms facing up, at opposite sides of the dough mass. Slide your fingers under the dough and lift the dough an inch or so from the work surface. Squeeze your thumbs and index fingers together to form a tight "OK" sign through the dough. While holding the "OK" sign, continue to curl your thumbs and index fingers tightly together to pinch off a portion of dough. Working as quickly and smoothly as you can, continue lifting and pinching the dough mass using the same technique, moving up the dough mass in approximately 1-inch to 1½-inch increments, until you have gone through the entire mass. You should begin to feel the dough coming together. Remember, your hands are your memory—pay attention to the feel of the dough as it comes together.

Pinch through the dough.

Lift dough from front.

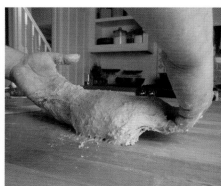

Quickly fold dough over.

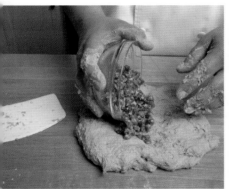

Flatten dough and add salami.

Wrap sides of dough over salami.

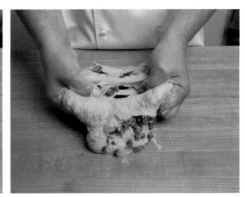

Pinch through the dough to mix.

Lift dough up from front.

Quickly fold over 4 to 5 times.

Final dough formed into ball

Take final dough temperature.

Cover with plastic wrap.

Turn the dough a quarter turn and continue lifting, pinching, and turning the dough until it begins to take on an identifiable shape and is less and less sticky. This can take anywhere from 5 to 15 minutes. Remember, do not add any flour to speed the process. Use your scraper to keep incorporating all of the dough into the mass. The dough is sufficiently kneaded when it can be formed into a ball. You do not want a stiff, dry dough; you want a soft, pliable mass that still holds its shape.

To form the dough into a ball, using both hands, lift it up from the front and fold it over and onto itself in one swift motion, quickly dropping it down on the work surface. Repeat this process 4 to 5 times until a ball forms. At all times, use the scraper to ensure that you are gathering all of the dough.

When the dough is sufficiently kneaded, use the palms of your hands to flatten it out into a rectangle. Scatter the salami evenly down the middle. Wrap the sides of the dough up and over the salami and pinch and turn the dough until the salami is completely incorporated.

Again, form the dough into a ball. Using both hands, lift it up from the front and fold it over and onto itself in one swift movement, quickly

Pat dough into a thick square.

Lift right side and fold to center.

Lift left side and fold to center.

Lift bottom to center.

Lightly pat seams after folding.

Return seam side down to bowl.

dropping it down on the work surface. Repeat this process 4 to 5 times until a ball forms. At all times, use the scraper to be sure that you are gathering all of the dough.

With the back of your hand, touch the dough to confirm that it is no longer sticky. If it is sticky, knead once or twice more, each time folding the dough over itself 4 to 5 times. Touch the top of the dough again to be sure that it is no longer sticky. If it is, repeat the folding process until it is no longer sticky.

3 FIRST FERMENTATION

At this point, you should take the temperature of the dough and record it, along with the time, in your Dough Log. It should be between 72°F and 80°F. If it is not, make the necessary adjustments (see page 52). It is particularly important that you record the time you finish this step, since you will need to note the time required for the first (bulk) fermentation. Because of the wine, this dough will require a longer first fermentation period, 3 hours total.

Very lightly dust a large bowl (preferably glass to allow observation of the process) with flour. The bowl should be large enough to allow the dough to rise without coming in contact with the plastic wrap that will cover it. Transfer the dough ball to the bowl, smooth side up, taking care to retain the round shape of the dough. Loosely cover the bowl with plastic wrap.

Place the bowl in a warm (75°F to 80°F), draft-free place for approximately 1 hour.

Lightly dust a clean work surface with flour. Remove the plastic wrap. Using cupped hands, lift the dough from the bowl and place it on the floured work surface. With your palms, pat the dough into a thick square. Lift the right two corners and fold them into the center of the square, lightly patting the seam down. Lift the left two corners and fold them into the center of the square, again lightly patting the seam down. Repeat this process with the top two corners and then the bottom two corners, meeting in the middle of the square and lightly patting down the seams.

Return the dough to the bowl, seam side down, cover, and return to the warm, draft-free place for 1 hour. Record the time in your Dough Log.

At the end of the hour, repeat this process one more time. Record the time in your Dough Log and return the dough to the warm, draft-free place for a third hour.

4 DIVIDING

Very lightly dust a clean work surface with flour. Uncover the dough and, using your bowl scraper, scrape the dough onto the lightly floured work surface. Let the dough rest for 30 seconds.

If the dough is very sticky, lightly flour your hands, but do not add more flour to the dough. If the dough sticks to the table, use your bench scraper to lift it up; do not pull and stretch the dough. With the palm of your hand, lightly press the dough into a rectangle about 12 inches long and 4 to 5 inches wide. Then, using your hands, gently pick up the dough to make sure it is not sticking to the work surface.

Using your bench scraper, cut the dough into 16 equal pieces.

Divide dough in half.

Divide again.

Divide into 16 equal pieces.

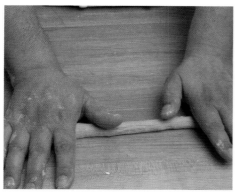
Roll remaining dough into rope.

Place dough as directed.

Final dough shape

5 SHAPING

Line a baking sheet with a silicone liner or parchment paper.

Set one dough piece aside and roll each of the remaining 15 pieces into a small ball shape as for rolls (see page 60). Then, placing the dough balls on the parchment-lined baking sheet as you work, create a triangle by setting 4 balls together in a line followed by a line of 3 balls, then 2, and finally 1 ball. Angle the remaining 4 balls to one side of the triangle so that the entire piece resembles a large cluster of grapes with a smaller one to the side.

Using your hands, roll the remaining piece of dough into a rope about 10 inches long. Then, shape the rope into a curved grapevine shape and attach it to the top of the grape cluster. Lightly flour.

Cover the baking sheet with a clean linen towel followed by plastic wrap.

6 FINAL FERMENTATION

Set the baking sheet in a warm (75°F to 80°F), draft-free place. Record the time in your Dough Log, as well as the exact time required for the final fermentation, and set your timer. It should take from 1 hour to 90 minutes for the final proofing; however, you should keep a close eye on the dough, because if it is overproofed it will be unusable.

If you are using the stainless-steel bowl method to bake the bread (see page 64), about 30 minutes before you are ready to bake, move

Lightly flour.

one oven rack to the lowest rung and remove the other. Place a large baking stone on the rack and preheat the oven to 450°F. (For all other baking methods, follow the directions on page 64.)

To determine whether the dough is ready to be baked, uncover and gently make a small indentation in the center of the dough with your fingertip. If the indentation slowly and evenly disappears, the bread is ready to bake. If not, follow the instructions on page 63 for additional fermentation.

7 BAKING

Uncover the dough and slide the parchment-lined sheet pan holding the loaf onto the center of the stone, taking care not to touch the hot surface.

Quickly cover the bread with the stainless-steel mixing bowl and immediately close the oven door. Bake for 10 minutes; then, lift the edge of the bowl with the tip of a small knife and use oven mitts to carefully remove the hot bowl. Continue to bake until the bread is a deep golden brown with a crisp crust, 15 to 20 minutes more. If you are concerned about the bread's doneness, insert an instant-read thermometer from the bottom of the bread into the center. If it reads 185°F to 210°F, the bread is fully baked.

Transfer to a cooling rack. Let cool for at least 1 hour before pulling the rolls apart or wrapping for storage.

Note: If the wine does not register the correct temperature for whichever type of mixing you are doing, place the bottle in warm water until the wine reaches the desired temperature for making the dough.

Finished baking

Chorizo and Aged Cheddar Mini-Baguettes

MAKES 4 MINI-LOAVES

This is a zesty bread made a bit spicy with the addition of chorizo sausage. During my pilgrimage through Spain I ate chorizo on the Camino every morning; this bread pays tribute to Spanish flavors in an easy-to-carry snack. Chorizo can be either fresh or dried. If using fresh chorizo, you will have to cook and cool it before adding it to the dough. I always use the more traditional European dried version. With the combination of the sausage and the cheese, you have a sandwich-like bread to eat out-of-hand for lunch. This bread is also a great accompaniment to a bowl of steaming soup.

Although in the bakery we call these baguettes, they are, technically, formed into a classic *bâtard* shape.

16 ounces	454 grams	3½ cups unbleached, unbromated white bread flour
0.24 ounce	7 grams	1⅛ teaspoons fine sea salt
0.18 ounce	5 grams	1½ teaspoons instant dry yeast
11.26 ounces	320 grams	1¼ cups plus 2 tablespoons water
4.5 ounces	128 grams	about 1 cup chopped dried cured chorizo, at room temperature
3 ounces	85 grams	¾ cup shredded sharp aged cheddar cheese, at room temperature

1 tablespoon extra-virgin olive oil for brushing

1 **MEASURING**

Scale all of the ingredients.

Place the flour in a large mixing bowl. Add the salt and yeast, making sure that they do not touch each other.

2 **MIXING AND KNEADING**

Using your hands, bring the dry ingredients together. Once blended, quickly form a well in the center of the mix.

Take the temperature of the water (it should be 82°F to 84°F for hand mixing, or 65°F to 70°F for an electric mixer) and record it in your Dough Log. Immediately start adding the water to the well in a slow, steady stream, rotating the bowl with one hand while simultaneously mixing the water into the dry ingredients with your other hand. Stop often as you work to scrape the bowl and your fingers with your bowl scraper, making sure that all of the ingredients have been gathered into the dough mass. The bowl should be quite clean. The dough will be soft, slightly wet, and extremely sticky.

Pinch off a bit of dough and taste to see whether you have forgotten the salt. If so, add it now and mix for another minute or so to fully incorporate it into the dough. The dough should just be beginning to come together.

When the dough begins to come together, use your bowl scraper to scrape the dough out onto your work surface, making sure not to leave any dough behind. The dough will still be very, very sticky. Do not give in to your temptation to add more flour to the surface, since that will alter the flour ratio of the dough. Stick with it; you can do it. The end result will prove it.

Hold your hands, palms facing up, at opposite sides of the dough mass. Slide your fingers under the dough and lift the dough an inch or so from the work surface. Squeeze your thumbs and index fingers together to form a tight "OK" sign through the dough. While holding the "OK" sign, continue to curl your thumbs and index fingers tightly together to pinch off a portion of dough. Working as quickly and smoothly as you can, continue lifting and pinching the dough mass using the same technique, moving up the dough mass in approximately 1-inch to 1½-inch increments, until you have gone through the entire mass. You should begin to feel the dough coming together. Remember, your hands are your memory—pay attention to the feel of the dough as it comes together.

Turn the dough a quarter turn and continue lifting, pinching, and turning the dough until it begins to take on an identifiable shape and is less and less sticky. This can take anywhere from 5 to 15 minutes. Remember, do not add any flour to speed the process. Use your scraper to keep incorporating all of the dough into the mass. The dough is sufficiently kneaded when it can be formed into a ball. You do not want a stiff, dry dough; you want a soft, pliable mass that still holds its shape.

To form the dough into a ball, using both hands, lift it up from the front and fold it over and onto itself in one swift motion, quickly dropping it down on the work surface. Repeat this process 4 to 5 times until a ball forms. At all times, use the scraper to ensure that you are gathering all of the dough.

When the dough is sufficiently kneaded, use the palms of your hands to flatten it out into a rectangle. Scatter the chorizo pieces evenly down the middle. Wrap the sides of the dough up and over the chorizo and pinch and turn the dough until the chorizo is completely incorporated.

Again, form the dough into a ball. Using both hands, lift it up from the front and fold it over and onto itself in one swift movement, quickly dropping it down on the work surface. Repeat this process 4 to 5 times until a ball forms. At all times, use the scraper to be sure that you are gathering all of the dough.

With the back of your hand, touch the dough to confirm that it is no longer sticky. If it is sticky, knead once or twice more, each time folding the dough over itself 4 to 5 times. Touch the top of the dough again to be sure that it is no longer sticky. If it is, repeat the folding process until it is no longer sticky.

3 FIRST FERMENTATION

At this point, you should take the temperature of the dough and record it, along with the time, in your Dough Log. It should be between 72°F and 80°F. If it is not, make the necessary adjustments (see page 52). It is particularly important that you record the time you finish this step, as you will need to note the time required for the first (bulk) fermentation, in this case about 1 hour.

Very lightly dust a large bowl (preferably glass to allow observation of the process) with flour. The bowl should be large enough to allow the dough to rise without coming in contact with the plastic wrap that will cover it. Transfer the dough ball to the bowl, smooth side up, taking care that the dough holds its round shape. Loosely cover the bowl with plastic wrap.

Place the bowl in a warm (75°F to 80°F), draft-free place until the dough has doubled in volume, about 1 hour.

4 DIVIDING

Very lightly dust a clean work surface with flour. Uncover the dough and, using your bowl scraper, scrape the dough onto the work surface. Let the dough rest for 30 seconds.

If the dough is very sticky, lightly flour your hands, but do not add more flour to the dough. If the dough sticks to the table, use your bench scraper to lift it up; do not pull and stretch the dough. With the palm of your hand, lightly press the dough into a rectangle about 12 inches long and 4 to 5 inches wide. Then, using your hands, gently pick up the dough to make sure it is not sticking to the work surface.

Using your bench scraper, cut the dough in half to form 2 rectangles. Gently pick up the dough to make sure that it is not sticking to the work surface. Then, again using the bench scraper, cut each rectangle in half to make 4 pieces of dough.

5 SHAPING

Line a baking sheet with parchment paper or a silicone liner. Working with one piece of dough at a time and using both hands, carefully form each piece into a *bâtard* (see page 60). As each loaf is shaped, place it on the baking sheet, taking care not to crowd the loaves. When all have been shaped, cover with a clean linen towel followed by plastic wrap.

6 FINAL FERMENTATION

Set the baking sheet in a warm (75°F to 80°F), draft-free place. Record the time in your Dough Log, as well as the exact time required for the final fermentation, and set your timer. It should take about 1 hour for the final proofing; however, you should keep a close eye on the dough, because if it is overproofed it will be unusable.

If you are using the stainless-steel bowl method to bake the bread (see page 64), about 30 minutes before you are ready to bake, move one oven rack to the lowest rung and remove the other. Place a large baking stone on the rack and preheat the oven to 450°F. (For all other baking methods, follow the directions on page 64.)

To determine whether the dough is ready to be baked, uncover and gently make a small indentation in the center of the dough with your fingertip. If the indentation slowly and evenly disappears, the bread is ready to bake. If not, follow the instructions on page 63 for additional fermentation. If all of the loaves won't fit under your stainless-steel bowl, cover the extras with plastic wrap and place in the refrigerator, then bake after the first loaves come out of the oven.

7 BAKING

Using a lamé or single-edged razor blade, and using a quick, decisive movement, cut one 3-inch-long line down the center of each loaf, just barely breaking through the skin and cutting about 1/8 inch into the dough. Then, cut a crisscross pattern into the top. If the dough is very shiny, the slashes may stick a bit. Then, sprinkle each loaf with an equal portion of the cheese.

Score down center of loaf.

Sprinkle loaf with cheese.

Immediately slide the loaves on the parchment paper onto the center of the stone, taking care not to touch the hot surface.

Quickly cover the loaves with the stainless-steel mixing bowl and immediately close the oven door. Bake for 10 minutes; then, lift the edge of the bowl with the tip of a small knife and use oven mitts to carefully remove the hot bowl. Continue to bake until the bread is a deep golden brown with a crisp crust, the cheese has melted, and the bread sounds hollow when tapped on the bottom, 10 to 15 minutes more. If you are concerned about the bread's doneness, insert an instant-read thermometer from the bottom of the bread into the center. If it reads 185°F to 210°F the bread is fully baked.

Transfer to a cooling rack. Let cool for at least 1 hour before cutting with a serrated knife or wrapping for storage.

Finished baking

White Chocolate Mini-Baguettes

MAKES 8 MINI-LOAVES

From time to time we are honored to receive an intern from my trade guild, Les Compagnons du Devoir (see page 3), who wants to train outside of France. It gives me such pride because it allows me to give back in the way I was trained—the older, experienced generation teaching the younger. From my years in America, I have absorbed much of the country's flair for personal expression, and I encourage my guild trainees not only to concentrate on the fundamentals but also to embrace the creative spirit of American culture.

At La Farm, we have quarterly new-product meetings, where the staff can bring fresh ideas to the table. This particular bread was developed by Kevin Neveu, a guild intern, for one of these meetings. It quickly became our most popular treat—so much so that we caution new customers that they may become addicts!

Although we call these loaves mini-baguettes, they are actually made in the traditional *bâtard* shape.

16 ounces	454 grams	3½ cups unbleached, unbromated white bread flour
0.31 ounce	9 grams	1½ teaspoons fine sea salt
0.18 ounce	5 grams	1½ teaspoons instant dry yeast
11.26 ounces	320 grams	1¼ cups plus 2 tablespoons water
5 ounces	140 grams	¾ cup white chocolate chips

1 MEASURING

Scale all of the ingredients.

Place the flour in a large mixing bowl. Add the salt and yeast, making sure that they do not touch each other.

2 MIXING AND KNEADING

Using your hands, bring the dry ingredients together. Once blended, quickly form a well in the center of the mix.

Take the temperature of the water (it should be 82°F to 84°F for hand mixing, or 65°F to 70°F for an electric mixer) and record it in your Dough Log. Immediately start adding the water to the well in a slow, steady stream, rotating the bowl with one hand while simultaneously mixing the water into the dry ingredients with your other hand. Stop often as you work to scrape the bowl and your fingers with your bowl scraper, making sure that all of the ingredients have been gathered into the dough mass. The bowl should be quite clean. The dough will be soft, slightly wet, and extremely sticky.

Pinch off a bit of dough and taste to see whether you have forgotten the salt. If so, add it now and mix for another minute or so to fully incorporate it into the dough. The dough should just be beginning to come together.

When the dough begins to come together, use your bowl scraper to scrape the dough out onto your work surface, taking care not to leave any dough behind. The dough will still be very, very sticky. Do not give in to your temptation to add more flour to the surface, since that will alter the flour ratio of the dough. Stick with it; you can do it. The end result will prove it.

Hold your hands, palms facing up, at opposite sides of the dough mass. Slide your fingers under the dough and lift the dough an inch or so from the work surface. Squeeze your thumbs and index fingers together to form a tight "OK" sign through the dough. While holding the "OK" sign, continue to curl your thumbs and index fingers tightly together to pinch off a portion of dough. Working as quickly and smoothly as you can, continue lifting and pinching the dough mass using the same technique, moving up the dough mass in approximately 1-inch to 1½-inch increments, until you have gone through the entire mass. You should begin to feel the dough coming together. Remember, your hands are your memory—pay attention to the feel of the dough as it comes together.

Turn the dough a quarter turn and continue lifting, pinching, and turning the dough until it begins to take on an identifiable shape and is less and less sticky. This can take anywhere from 5 to 15 minutes. Remember, do not add any flour to speed the process. Use your scraper to keep incorporating all of the dough into the mass. The dough is sufficiently kneaded when it can be formed into a ball. You do not want a stiff, dry dough; you want a soft, pliable mass that still holds its shape.

To form the dough into a ball, using both hands, lift it up from the front and fold it over and onto itself in one swift motion, quickly dropping it down on the work surface. Repeat this process 4 to 5 times until a ball forms. At all times, use the scraper to ensure that you are gathering all of the dough.

When the dough is sufficiently kneaded, use the palms of your hands to flatten it out into a rectangle. Scatter the white chocolate pieces evenly down the middle. Wrap the sides of the dough up and over the white chocolate and pinch and turn the dough until the chocolate is completely incorporated.

Again, form the dough into a ball. Using both hands, lift it up from the front and fold it over and onto itself in one swift movement, quickly dropping it down to the work surface. Repeat this process 4 to 5 times until a ball forms. At all times, use the scraper to be sure that you are gathering all of the dough.

With the back of your hand, touch the dough to confirm that it is no longer sticky. If it is sticky, knead once or twice more, each time folding the dough over itself 4 to 5 times. Touch the top of the dough again to be sure that it is no longer sticky. If it is, repeat the folding process until it is no longer sticky.

3 FIRST FERMENTATION

At this point, you should take the temperature of the dough and record it, along with the time, in your Dough Log. It should be between 72°F and 80°F. If it is not, immediately make the necessary adjustments (see page 52). It is particularly important that you record the time you finish this step, as you will need to note the time required for the first (bulk) fermentation, in this case about 1 hour.

Very lightly dust a large bowl (preferably glass to allow observation of the process) with flour. The bowl should be large enough to allow the dough to rise without coming in contact with the plastic wrap that will cover it. Transfer the dough ball to the bowl, smooth side up, taking care to retain the round shape of the dough. Loosely cover the bowl with plastic wrap.

Place the bowl in a warm (75°F to 80°F), draft-free place until the dough has doubled in volume, about 1 hour.

4 DIVIDING

Very lightly dust a clean work surface with flour. Uncover the dough and, using your bowl scraper, scrape the dough onto the work surface. Let the dough rest for 30 seconds.

If the dough is very sticky, lightly flour your hands, but do not add more flour to the dough. If the dough sticks to the table, use your bench scraper to lift it up; do not pull and stretch the dough. With the palm of your hand, lightly press the dough into a rectangle about 12 inches long and 4 to 5 inches wide. Then, using your hands, gently pick up the dough to make sure it is not sticking to the work surface.

Using your bench scraper, cut the dough in half to form two rectangles. Gently pick up the dough to make sure that it is not sticking to the work surface. Then, again using the bench scraper, cut each rectangle in half, and then in half again, to make 8 pieces of dough.

5 SHAPING

Line two baking sheets with parchment paper or silicone liners. Working with one piece of dough at a time and using both hands, carefully form each piece into a *bâtard* (see page 60). As each loaf is shaped, place it on a

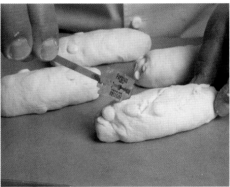

Place loaves on parchment.   Score each loaf.   Detail of score, 3 slashes

parchment-lined baking sheet, taking care not to crowd them. You should put 4 loaves on each sheet pan. When all have been shaped, cover with a clean linen towel followed by plastic wrap.

6 FINAL FERMENTATION

Set the baking sheets in a warm (75°F to 80°F), draft-free place. Record the time in your Dough Log, as well as the exact time required for the final fermentation, and set your timer. It should take about 1 hour for the final proofing; however, you should keep a close eye on the dough, because if it is overproofed it will be unusable.

If you are using the stainless-steel bowl method to bake the bread (see page 64), about 30 minutes before you are ready to bake, move one oven rack to the lowest rung and remove the other. Place a large baking stone on the rack and preheat the oven to 450°F. (For all other baking methods, follow the directions on page 64.)

To determine whether the dough is ready to be baked, uncover and gently make a small indentation in the center of the dough with your fingertip. If the indentation slowly and evenly disappears, the bread is ready to bake. If not, follow the instructions on page 63 for additional fermentation. Since only one pan will fit on the stone, cover the remaining one with plastic wrap and place in the refrigerator, then bake after the first loaves come out of the oven. Score the remaining loaves just before baking.

7 BAKING

Using a lamé or single-edged razor blade and with a quick, decisive movement, cut three 1-inch long lines in the loaf, just barely breaking through the skin and cutting about ⅛ inch into the dough. If the dough is very shiny, the slashes may stick a bit.

Immediately slide the loaves on the parchment paper onto the center of the stone, taking care not to touch the hot surface.

Quickly cover the loaves with the stainless-steel mixing bowl and immediately close the oven door. Bake for 10 minutes; then, lift the edge of the bowl with the tip of a small knife and use oven mitts to carefully remove the hot bowl. Continue to bake until the bread is a deep golden brown with a crisp crust and sounds hollow when tapped on the bottom, 10 to 15 minutes more. If you are concerned about the bread's doneness, insert an instant-read thermometer from the bottom of the bread into the center. If it reads 185°F to 210°F the bread is fully baked.

Transfer to a cooling rack. Let cool for at least 1 hour before cutting with a serrated knife or wrapping for storage.

Finished baking

Stuffed Baguettes

Stuffed baguettes are among our most popular bakery items. They are favorites both in the store and at the farmers' market. Customers treat them as a quick meal or snack and often serve them when entertaining. These are great for the home baker—you can experiment and use your creativity in the mixture of ingredients. One little bit of advice: choose dry ingredients and do not overfill or the bread will be soggy.

Following you will find just a few of the fillings I use at La Farm Bakery. Some others might be sliced brie, local honey, and toasted almonds; thinly sliced ham and Gruyère cheese; well-drained sautéed spinach with garlic and Parmesan cheese; thinly sliced salami, capicola, ham, and provolone with a touch of Italian seasoning sprinkled on the mix.

As I've said, I don't think my breads should be eaten hot from the oven or really even while still warm; however, I have to admit that most of our customers enjoy the stuffed baguettes warm.

Tomato, Mozzarella, and Basil Stuffed Baguette

MAKES 2 LOAVES

1 recipe Country French Bread (page 75)

4 ounces	120 grams	about 2 thinly sliced Roma tomatoes
1.4 ounces	40 grams	a generous handful julienned fresh basil leaves

Fine sea salt and freshly ground black pepper

1.6 ounces	50 grams	⅓ cup shredded mozzarella or Asiago cheese, at room temperature

1–3 MEASURING, MIXING AND KNEADING, AND FIRST FERMENTATION

Make the dough according to the directions for Country French Bread through the first fermentation stage, mixing either by hand or with an electric mixer.

4 DIVIDING

Very lightly dust a clean work surface with flour. Uncover the dough and, using your bowl scraper, scrape the dough onto the lightly floured work surface. Let the dough rest for 30 seconds.

If the dough is very sticky, lightly flour your hands, but do not add more flour to the dough. If the dough sticks to the table, use your bench scraper to lift it up; do not pull and stretch the dough. With the palm of your hand, lightly press the dough into a rectangle about 9 inches by 12 inches. Then, using your hands, gently pick up the dough to make sure it is not sticking to the work surface.

Using your bench scraper, cut the dough in half to form two rectangles, 6 inches by 9 inches each. Again, using your hands, gently pick up the dough to make sure it is not sticking to the work surface.

5 SHAPING

Line two baking sheets with parchment paper or silicone liners.

Working with one piece of dough at a time, turn the dough so that the longer side is facing you, and again press down lightly with your palm.

Then, place half of the tomatoes, in a slightly overlapping pattern, down the center of the dough. Sprinkle half of the basil over the tomatoes, season with salt and pepper, and top with an even layer of half of the cheese.

Using both hands, pick up each corner of the side of the dough closest to you. Very lightly pulling on the dough, fold the dough in, horizontally, to the center of the rectangle, covering the tomato stuffing. Using the heel of your hand, press down firmly to seal.

Using your fingertips, pick up the far side of the dough and fold it halfway up and over the first seam, again with a very light pull on the dough. Using the heel of your hand, again press down firmly to seal.

Gently pick up the dough and place it so the seam is on the side. Using the heel of your hand, firmly press the seam against the work surface to

Layer tomatoes.

Add fresh basil.

Top with cheese.

Fold dough to center.

Lightly pull and fold dough.

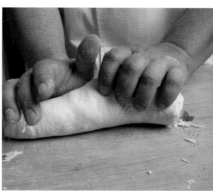

Using the heel of your hand, press to seal.

Using the heel of your hand, close end seam.

flatten and to create tension in the dough.

Transfer the shaped dough to a prepared baking sheet, seam side down.

Fill and shape the remaining piece of dough in the same way and place it on the other baking sheet, seam side down.

Cover each baking sheet with a clean linen towel followed by plastic wrap.

6 **FINAL FERMENTATION**

Set the baking sheets in a warm (75°F to 80°F), draft-free place. Record the time in your Dough Log, as well as the exact time required for the final fermentation, and set your timer. It should take about 1 hour for the final proofing; however, you should keep a close eye on the dough, because if it is overproofed it will be unusable.

If you are using the stainless-steel bowl method to bake the bread (see page 64), about 30 minutes before you are ready to bake, move one oven rack to the lowest rung and remove the other. Place a large baking stone on the rack and preheat the oven to 450°F. (For all other baking methods, follow the directions on page 64.)

To determine whether the dough is ready to be baked, uncover and gently make a small indentation in the center of the dough with your fingertip. If the indentation slowly and evenly disappears, the bread is ready to bake. If not, follow the instructions on page 63 for additional fermentation. Since only one pan will fit on the stone, cover the remaining one with plastic wrap and place in the refrigerator, then bake after the first loaf comes out of the oven. If scoring, score the remaining loaf just before baking.

7 BAKING

Although scoring is not required on this bread, I usually do so. Using a lamé or single-edged razor blade and with a quick, decisive movement, cut three 1-inch long lines on the loaf, just barely breaking through the skin and cutting about ⅛ inch into the dough. If the dough is very shiny, the slashes may stick a bit.

Immediately slide the loaf on the parchment paper onto the center of the stone, taking care not to touch the hot surface.

Quickly cover the loaf with the stainless-steel mixing bowl and immediately close the oven door. Bake for 10 minutes; then, lift the edge of the bowl with the tip of a small knife and use oven mitts to carefully remove the hot bowl. Continue to bake until the bread is a deep golden brown with a crisp crust, the cheese has melted, and the bread sounds hollow when tapped on the bottom, 10 to 15 minutes more. If you are concerned about the bread's doneness, insert an instant-read thermometer from the bottom of the bread into the center. If it reads 185°F to 210°F the bread is fully baked.

Transfer to a cooling rack. Let cool for at least 1 hour before cutting with a serrated knife or wrapping for storage. Or, as some of my customers do, enjoy as soon as it has cooled enough to be handled.

Oven-Roasted Mushroom and Gruyère Stuffed Baguette

MAKES 2 LOAVES

2.8 ounces	80 grams	½ cup balsamic vinegar
2 ounces	60 grams	⅓ cup soy sauce
10.5 ounces	300 grams	2 cups sliced cremini mushrooms
1 recipe Country French Bread (page 75)		
8.8 ounces	150 grams	1½ cups shredded Comté or Gruyère cheese, at room temperature (see Note, page 123)
Fresh thyme leaves		

1–3 MEASURING, MIXING AND KNEADING, AND FIRST FERMENTATION

Combine the vinegar and soy sauce in a large resealable plastic bag. Add the mushrooms, seal, and shake to coat evenly. Transfer to the refrigerator to marinate for at least 8 hours or overnight.

Make the dough according to the directions for Country French Bread through the first fermentation stage, mixing either by hand or with an electric mixer.

Remove the marinated mushrooms from the refrigerator and place in a fine-mesh sieve to drain well and come to room temperature.

4 DIVIDING

Very lightly dust a clean work surface with flour. Uncover the dough and, using your bowl scraper, scrape the dough onto the lightly floured work surface. Let the dough rest for 30 seconds.

If the dough is very sticky, lightly flour your hands, but do not add more flour to the dough. If the dough sticks to the table, use your bench scraper to lift it up; do not pull and stretch the dough. With the palm of your hand, lightly press the dough into a rectangle about 9 inches by 12 inches. Then, using your hands, gently pick up the dough to make sure it is not sticking to the work surface.

Using your bench scraper, cut the dough in half to form two rectangles, 6 inches by 9 inches each. Again, using your hands, gently pick up the dough to make sure it is not sticking to the work surface.

5 SHAPING

Line two baking sheets with parchment paper or silicone liners.

Working with one piece of dough at a time, turn the dough so that the longer side is facing you, and again press down lightly with your palm.

Then, layer half of the well-drained mushrooms evenly down the center of the dough. Sprinkle half of the cheese over the mushrooms in an even layer. Then, sprinkle with thyme to taste.

Using both hands, pick up each corner of the side of the dough closest to you. Very lightly pulling on the dough, fold the dough in, horizontally, to the center of the rectangle, covering the mushroom-cheese stuffing. Using the heel of your hand, press down firmly to seal.

Using your fingertips, pick up the far side of the dough and fold it halfway up and over the first fold, again with a very light pull on the dough. Using the heel of your hand, again press down firmly to seal.

Gently pick up the dough and place it so the seam is on the side. Using the heel of your hand, firmly press the seam against the work surface to flatten and to create tension in the dough.

Transfer the shaped dough to a prepared baking sheet, seam side down.

Fill and shape the remaining piece of dough in the same way and place it on the other baking sheet, seam side down.

Cover each baking sheet with a clean linen towel followed by plastic wrap.

6 FINAL FERMENTATION

Set the baking sheets in a warm (75°F to 80°F), draft-free place. Record the time in your Dough Log, as well as the exact time required for the final fermentation, and set your timer. It should take about 1 hour for the final proofing; however, you should keep a close eye on the dough, because if it is overproofed it will be unusable.

If you are using the stainless-steel bowl method to bake the bread (see page 64), about 30 minutes before you are ready to bake, move one oven rack to the lowest rung and remove the other. Place a large baking stone on the rack and preheat the oven to 450°F. (For all other baking methods, follow the directions on page 64.)

To determine whether the dough is ready to be baked, uncover and gently make a small indentation in the center of the dough with your fingertip. If the indentation slowly and evenly disappears, the bread is ready to bake. If not, follow the instructions on page 63 for additional fermentation. Since only one pan will fit on the stone, cover the remaining one with plastic wrap and place in the refrigerator, then bake after the first loaf comes out of the oven. If scoring, score the remaining loaf just before baking.

7   BAKING

Although scoring is not required on this bread, I usually do so. Using a lamé or single-edged razor blade and with a quick, decisive movement, cut three 1-inch-long lines on the loaf, just barely breaking through the skin and cutting about ⅛ inch into the dough. If the dough is very shiny, the slashes may stick a bit.

Immediately slide the loaf on the parchment paper onto the center of the stone, taking care not to touch the hot surface.

Quickly cover the loaf with the stainless-steel mixing bowl and immediately close the oven door. Bake for 10 minutes; then, lift the edge of the bowl with the tip of a small knife and use oven mitts to carefully remove the hot bowl. Continue to bake until the bread is a deep golden brown with a crisp crust and sounds hollow when tapped on the bottom, 10 to 15 minutes more. If you are concerned about the bread's doneness, insert an instant-read thermometer from the bottom of the bread into the center. If it reads 185°F to 210°F, the bread is fully baked.

Transfer to a cooling rack. Let cool for at least 1 hour before cutting with a serrated knife or wrapping for storage. Or, as some of my customers do, enjoy as soon as it has cooled enough to be handled.

Note: I suggest you go the extra distance to find Comté, a deeply flavored cheese that, in France, has its own appellation and is produced under strict guidelines. It is the most produced of all French AOC (*appellation d'origine contrôlée*) cheeses. It is a hard, creamy yellow cheese with a fat content of about 45 percent. French Gruyère is actually Comté that has not met the rigorous standards of Comté and is not the same as the highly regarded Swiss Gruyère, which would be my preference if you can't find Comté.

Sausage-Mozzarella Stuffed Baguette

MAKES 2 LOAVES

1 recipe Country French Bread (page 75)

4 ounces	120 grams	¾ cup crumbled cooked breakfast sausage, at room temperature
1.6 ounces	50 grams	⅓ cup shredded mozzarella or Asiago cheese, at room temperature

1–3 MEASURING, MIXING AND KNEADING, AND FIRST FERMENTATION

Make the dough according to the directions for Country French Bread through the first fermentation stage, mixing either by hand or with an electric mixer.

4 DIVIDING

Very lightly dust a clean work surface with flour. Uncover the dough and, using your bowl scraper, scrape the dough onto the lightly floured work surface. Let the dough rest for 30 seconds.

If the dough is very sticky, lightly flour your hands, but do not add more flour to the dough. If the dough sticks to the table, use your bench scraper to lift it up; do not pull and stretch the dough. With the palm of your hand, lightly press the dough into a rectangle about 9 inches by 12 inches.

Using your bench scraper, cut the dough in half to form two rectangles, 6 inches by 9 inches each.

5 SHAPING

Line two baking sheets with parchment paper or silicone liners.

Working with one piece of dough at a time, turn the dough so that the longer side is facing you, and again press down lightly with your palm.

Then, sprinkle half of the sausage evenly down the center of the dough, followed by an even layer of half of the cheese.

Using both hands, pick up each corner of the side of the dough closest to you. Very lightly pulling on the dough, fold the dough in, horizontally, to the center of the rectangle, covering the sausage-cheese stuffing. Using the heel of your hand, press down firmly to seal.

Using your fingertips, pick up the far side of the dough and fold it halfway up and over the first seam, again with a very light pull on the dough. Using the heel of your hand, again press down firmly to seal.

Gently pick up the dough and place it so the seam is on the side. Using the heel of your hand, firmly press the seam against the work surface to flatten and to create tension in the dough.

Transfer the shaped dough to a prepared baking sheet, seam side down.

Fill and shape the remaining piece of dough in the same way and place it on the other baking sheet, seam side down.

Cover each baking sheet with a clean linen towel followed by plastic wrap.

6 FINAL FERMENTATION

Set the baking sheets in a warm (75°F to 80°F), draft-free place. Record the time in your Dough Log, as well as the exact time required for the final fermentation, and set your timer. It should take about 1 hour for the final proofing.

If you are using the stainless-steel bowl method to bake the bread (see page 64), about 30 minutes before you are ready to bake, move one oven rack to the lowest rung and remove the other. Place a large baking stone on the rack and preheat the oven to 450°F. (For all other baking methods, follow the directions on page 64.)

To determine whether the dough is ready to be baked, uncover and gently make a small indentation in the center of the dough with your fingertip. If the indentation slowly and evenly disappears, the bread is ready to bake. If not, follow the instructions on page 63 for additional fermentation. Since only one pan will fit on the stone, cover the remaining one with plastic wrap and place in the refrigerator, then bake after the first loaf comes out of the oven. If scoring, score the remaining loaf just before baking.

7 BAKING

Although scoring is not required on this bread, I usually do so. Using a lamé or single-edged razor blade and using a quick, decisive movement, cut three 1-inch-long lines in the loaf, just barely breaking through the skin and cutting about ⅛ inch into the dough. If the dough is very shiny, the slashes may stick a bit.

Immediately slide the loaf on the parchment paper onto the center of the stone, taking care not to touch the hot surface.

Quickly cover the loaf with the stainless-steel mixing bowl and immediately close the oven door. Bake for 10 minutes; then, lift the edge of the bowl with the tip of a small knife and use oven mitts to carefully remove the hot bowl. Continue to bake until the bread is a deep golden brown with a crisp crust, the cheese has melted, and the bread sounds hollow when tapped on the bottom, 10 to 15 minutes more. If you are concerned about the bread's doneness, insert an instant-read thermometer from the bottom of the bread into the center. If it reads 185°F to 210°F the bread is fully baked.

DOUGH LOG
(Country French Bread)

beginning water temp:
hand mix 82°–84°
stand mixer 65°–70°

final dough temp:
72°–80°

Dough Type	Measure Water Temp	Mixing Dough Temp	Mixing Finish Mix Time	Rest Time	Bulk Fermentation (1st Proof) 1st Fold	Rest Time	2nd Fold	Rest Time	Divide	Rest Time	Shape	Shape Time	Final Proof Proof Time	Scoring	Baking 450°
Example: Baguette (hand mix)	82°	76°	10:00 am	1 hr					11:00 am 2 pieces	10–15 min	baguette	11:15 am	1–1.5 hr	(oval, slashed)	12:15 am
Country French Bread				1 hr						10–15 min	boule		1–1.5 hr	(round, single line)	
Baguette				1 hr					2 pieces	10–15 min	baguette		1–1.5 hr	(oval, slashed)	
Epi				1 hr					2 pieces	10–15 min	baguette		1–1.5 hr		
Dinner Rolls				1 hr					8 pieces	10–15 min	rolls		1–1.5 hr	(rounded square, line)	
Marguerite				1 hr					7 pieces	10–15 min	seeded rolls shaped into flower		1–1.5 hr		
Pain aux Lardons				1 hr					2 pieces	10–15 min	fougasse		1–1.5 hr		
Beaujolais Bread				1 hr					16 pieces	10–15 min	rolls shaped into grape cluster		1–1.5 hr		
Chorizo and Aged Cheddar Baguette				1 hr					4 pieces	10–15 min	mini batards		1–1.5 hr	(oval, line) add cheese	
White Chocolate Mini Baguette				1 hr					8 pieces	10–15 min	mini batards		1–1.5 hr	(oval, diagonal lines)	
Stuffed Baguette				1 hr					2 pieces	10–15 min	baguette with ingredients in center		1–1.5 hr		

Notes: _____

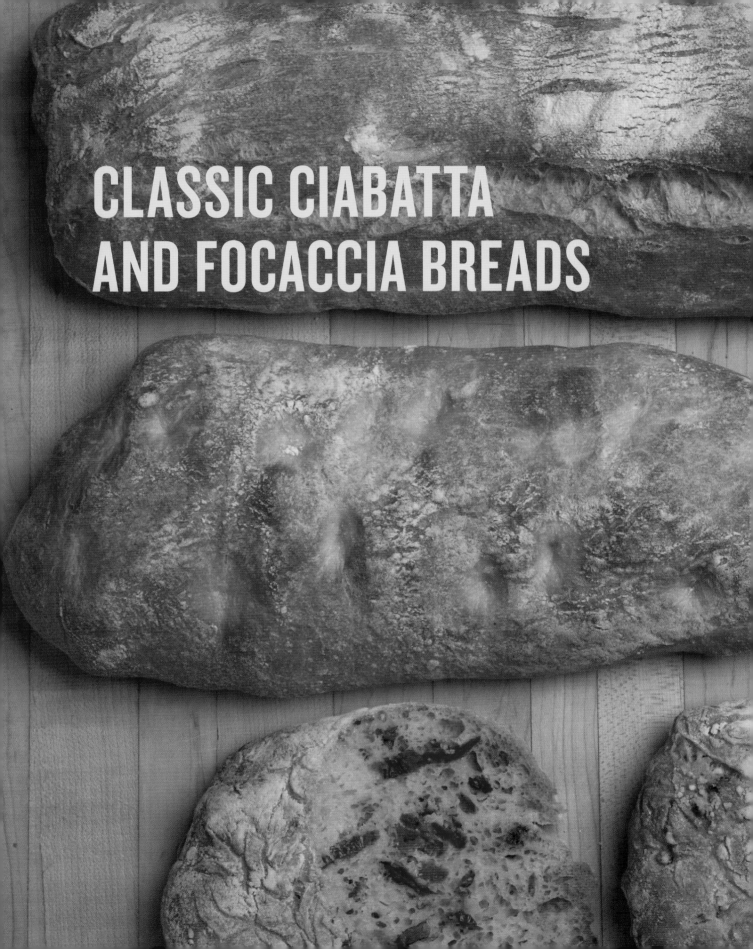

CLASSIC CIABATTA AND FOCACCIA BREADS

Ciabatta doughs allow the baker great creativity with little effort—the doughs differentiated by toppings and savory additions—and they follow the current rage for "no-knead" bread with absolutely no sacrifice to quality. Italian ciabatta doughs are much wetter than classic French bread doughs, so I encourage home bakers to use a heavy-duty electric stand mixer to make them, rather than the hand mixing and kneading that I normally prefer. (When the dough is wet, it is very sticky and quite frustrating to work with; the electric mixer eliminates the frustration and creates a wonderfully open-crumbed loaf.)

Until I came to the United States, I had not known of ciabatta. Once I tasted it, it quickly became a favorite of mine. It has large air pockets, great elasticity, and, once baked, the finished crumb is very open and silky in texture. What's more, it is thanks to ciabatta that I met my wife, Missy. Now every time I eat a slice, I think of Missy and our two beautiful girls, Léa and Emilie. As a baker, I never dreamed that a piece of bread could bring so much beauty into my life.

CLASSIC ITALIAN CIABATTA QUICK REFERENCE

Once you have learned to make Classic Italian Ciabatta, you can follow this Quick Reference guide for a reminder of the steps involved. It will also work for other breads created from the same basic dough.

* Scale all ingredients.
* Measure the temperature of the water (65°F to 70°F) and note it in your Dough Log (see page 173).
* Mix with a heavy-duty electric stand mixer for 5 minutes on low speed ("1" on most mixers) and 4 minutes on medium-low speed ("2" on most mixers).
* Measure the dough temperature (72°F to 80°F) and record it in your Dough Log.
* Set aside in an oiled bowl for the first fermentation for 3 hours, folding the dough each hour.
* Divide and shape in a free-form style.
* Proof in a *couche* for 45 minutes to 1 hour.
* Bake at 450°F on a baker's stone using the stainless-steel bowl method for 25 minutes.
* Cool and eat, or store at room temperature for 1 day.

Ciabatta holding assorted dips

Ciabatta

MAKES 2 SMALL LOAVES OR 1 LARGE LOAF

I recently learned that ciabatta was first introduced in Italy in the 1980s. This is remarkable when you think of how common ciabattas and focaccias are now throughout the world. Its name comes from its shape, with *ciabatta* translating from the Italian as "slipper," describing the flat, wide, and relatively long free-form shape of the traditional bread. I love to cut it in half horizontally, build a sandwich with the ingredients piled high, and then cut it, crosswise, into individual sandwiches. You can also cut holes in the top and fill them with different dips.

Ciabatta is most often used to make small sandwiches called *panini*. Throughout Italy, ciabatta comes in many forms, all depending upon the region in which it is made. It can be slightly crisp with a very soft, moist crumb, very crisp with a dense crumb, or extremely crisp with an open crumb. It can be flavored with herbs and olive oil, with milk, with salt, or with bits of savory ingredients. This is my version of the classic.

16 ounces	454 grams	3½ cups unbleached, unbromated white bread flour
0.31 ounce	9 grams	1½ teaspoons fine sea salt
0.12 ounce	3 grams	1 teaspoon instant dry yeast
13.76 ounces	390 grams	1½ cups plus 2 teaspoons water
0.32 ounce	10 grams	1 tablespoon extra-virgin olive oil, plus about 2 tablespoons to coat the bowl

1 MEASURING

Scale all of the ingredients.

Place the flour in a large bowl. Add the salt and yeast, making sure that they do not touch each other. If they do, it will cause a reaction that decreases the yeast's ability to develop.

Take the temperature of the water (it should be 65°F to 70°F) and record it in your Dough Log.

2 MIXING AND KNEADING

Pour half of the water into the bowl of the mixer; then, add the dry ingredients. Attach the bowl and dough hook to the mixer.

Begin mixing on low speed ("1" on most mixers), and quickly add enough of the remaining water in a slow, steady stream to make a soft, moist dough that slightly sticks to the sides of the bowl. Take care to add the remaining water immediately; if the water is added too late in the mixing process, the dough will become too firm to mix easily. Stop the mixer often and use a rubber spatula to scrape down the hook and sides of the bowl to ensure that all of the ingredients have been well incorporated.

When all of the water has been added, set a timer and mix for 5 minutes.

Placing the water in the bowl of the stand mixer first helps keep the dry ingredients from sticking to the bottom of the bowl.

Pour half of water into mixing bowl.

Mix dry ingredients.

Add dry ingredients.

On low speed, add remaining water.

Feel dough for consistency.

Add olive oil on medium speed.

Take temperature of the dough.

Stop the mixer and touch your dough; it should be soft and pliable. Taste the dough to check whether you have forgotten the salt. If so, add it now and mix for another 2 minutes.

Increase the speed to medium-low ("2" on most mixers) and mix for 4 minutes, gradually adding 1 tablespoon olive oil. Continue to mix until the oil is thoroughly incorporated, about 1 more minute. The dough should be soft and smooth, with a moist, tacky surface.

3 FIRST FERMENTATION

Using an instant-read thermometer, take the temperature of the dough. It should be between 72°F and 80°F. If it is higher or lower, make the necessary adjustments (see page 52). Record the temperature of the dough and the time you finished this step in the Dough Log, and note the time the first fermentation should be completed. This dough will be in first fermentation for 3 hours, with a fold after each hour.

Using your fingertips, coat the inside of a large bowl with the remaining 2 tablespoons olive oil.

Using a bench scraper, scrape the dough into the oil-coated bowl. Using your hands, pull one edge of the dough and fold it into the center and press

Coat bowl with olive oil.

Scrape dough into bowl.

Fold dough to center.

Turn bowl a quarter turn and repeat.

down slightly. Give the bowl a quarter turn and continue to fold the dough in and press for 4 additional turns. The dough should begin to form a ball. Roll the ball around in the bowl to coat all sides with olive oil, turning it so that the smooth side is up. The dough does not need to be covered, as the oil prevents dryness.

Place the dough in a warm (75°F to 80°F), draft-free place for 3 hours, folding as above after the first hour and again after the second hour.

4–5 DIVIDING AND SHAPING

Generously coat a clean work surface with flour.

Generously flour the top of the dough and, using a bowl scraper, scrape the dough onto the floured work surface. Lightly dust the exterior of the dough with flour and allow the dough to rest for 30 seconds.

If the dough is very sticky, lightly flour your hands and add more flour to the work surface. If the dough sticks to the table, use your bench scraper to lift it up; do not pull and stretch the dough.

If you are making two small loaves, lightly press down on the dough with a flat hand, forming the dough into a square. Using a bench scraper, cut the dough in half to form two rectangles. For one large loaf, lightly press down

Flour top of dough.

Scrape dough onto floured surface.

Flatten dough into rectangle.

Divide dough in half.

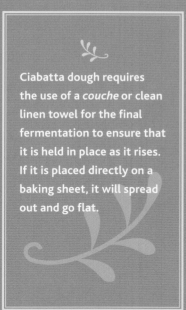

Ciabatta dough requires the use of a *couche* or clean linen towel for the final fermentation to ensure that it is held in place as it rises. If it is placed directly on a baking sheet, it will spread out and go flat.

on the dough with a flat hand, forming the dough into a large rectangle. This is a rather free-form bread, so the shape does not have to be perfect.

Place the dough in a lightly floured *couche* (or a strong linen towel) as directed on page 62. It does not matter whether you have the smooth side up or down for the final proofing as long as you bake it smooth side up. (If making 2 loaves, make a second ridge in the *couche* to separate them.) Fold the remaining *couche* over the top.

6 FINAL FERMENTATION

Place the *couche* in a warm (75°F to 80°F), draft-free place. Record the time in your Dough Log, as well as the exact time required for the final fermentation, and set your timer. It should take from 45 minutes to 1 hour for the final proofing; however, you should keep a close eye on the dough, because if it is overproofed it will be unusable.

If you are using the stainless-steel bowl method to bake the bread (see page 64), about 30 minutes before you are ready to bake, move one oven rack to the lowest rung and remove the other. Place a large baking stone on the rack and preheat the oven to 450°F. (For all other baking methods, follow the directions on page 64.)

Pull into free form.

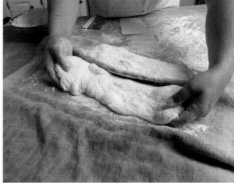

Place on couche *for proofing.*

To determine whether the dough is ready to be baked, uncover it and gently make a small indentation in the center of the dough with your fingertip. If the indentation slowly and evenly disappears, the bread is ready to bake. If not, follow the instructions on page 63 for additional fermentation.

If you are making two loaves and both won't fit under your stainless-steel bowl, cover one with plastic wrap and place in the refrigerator, then bake after the first loaf comes out of the oven.

7 BAKING

Cover a bread peel with a sheet of parchment paper. Using your hands, gently remove the loaf from the *couche* and transfer it to the peel, top side up.

Carefully slide the loaf on the parchment paper onto the center of the stone, taking care not to touch the hot surface. If you are baking two loaves together, take care that they don't "kiss" (touch and get stuck together while baking).

Quickly cover the loaf with the stainless-steel mixing bowl and immediately close the oven door. Bake for 10 minutes; then, lift the edge of the bowl with the tip of a small knife and use oven mitts to carefully remove the hot bowl. Continue to bake until the bread is a pale golden brown with a lightly floured crust, about 15 minutes more. If you are concerned about the bread's doneness, insert an instant-read thermometer from the bottom of the bread into the center. If it reads 185°F to 210°F the bread is fully baked.

Transfer the loaf to a cooling rack and let it cool for at least 1 hour before cutting with a serrated knife or wrapping for storage.

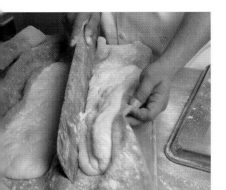

Roll gently onto peel.

Place on center of hot stone.

Finished baking

Ciabatta Rolls

MAKES 4 ROLLS

Made from the basic ciabatta dough, these little rolls are the perfect bread for overstuffed sandwiches. Although the baguette is the bread of choice for sandwiches in France, I have found through consulting with bakeries and cafés all across this country that ciabatta, with its light crust and airy interior, currently reigns as the preferred sandwich roll here in America.

Although I, personally, love a deep, dark crust, I have created rolls with different degrees of toastiness since every client has their own preference. We use them in the café at La Farm Bakery to make some of our most popular sandwiches, and our customers seem to prefer a lighter crust because it is easier to bite into without having the ingredients slip out.

1 recipe Ciabatta (page 131)

1–3   MEASURING, MIXING AND KNEADING, AND FIRST FERMENTATION

Make the dough according to the directions for Ciabatta through the first fermentation stage.

4–5   DIVIDING AND SHAPING

Generously coat a clean work surface with flour.

Generously flour the top of the dough and, using a bowl scraper, scrape the dough onto the floured work surface. Lightly dust the exterior of the dough with flour and allow the dough to rest for 30 seconds.

If the dough is very sticky, lightly flour your hands and add more flour to the work surface. If the dough sticks to the table, use your bench scraper to lift it up; do not pull and stretch the dough.

Lightly press down on the dough with a flat hand, forming the dough into a rectangle. Using a bench scraper, cut the dough into 4 equal-sized squares.

Place 2 rolls in a lightly floured *couche* (or strong linen towel) as directed on page 62. Make a second ridge next to them and place the 2 remaining rolls against it. Fold the remaining *couche* over the top of the dough.

Dividing rolls

Dividing rolls

6   FINAL FERMENTATION

Place the *couche* in a warm (75°F to 80°F), draft-free place. Record the time in your Dough Log, as well as the exact time required for the final fermentation, and set your timer. It should take from 45 minutes to 1 hour for the final proofing; however, you should keep a close eye on the dough, because if it is overproofed it will be unusable.

If you are using the stainless-steel bowl method to bake the bread (see page 64), about 30 minutes before you are ready to bake, move one oven rack to the lowest rung and remove the other. Place a large baking stone on the rack and preheat the oven to 450°F. (For all other baking methods, follow the directions on page 64.)

To determine whether the dough is ready to be baked, uncover and gently make a small indentation in the center of the dough with your fingertip. If the indentation slowly and evenly disappears, the bread is ready to bake. If not, follow the instructions on page 63 for additional fermentation.

If the 4 rolls won't fit under your stainless-steel bowl, cover 2 of them with plastic wrap and place in the refrigerator, then bake after the first 2 come out of the oven.

7 BAKING

Cover a bread peel with a sheet of parchment paper. Using your hands, gently remove the rolls from the *couche* and transfer them to the bread peel, top side up.

Carefully slide the rolls on the parchment paper onto the center of the stone, taking care not to touch the hot surface and making sure that they don't "kiss" (touch and get stuck together while baking).

Quickly cover the rolls with the stainless-steel mixing bowl and immediately close the oven door. Bake for 10 minutes; then, lift the edge of the bowl with the tip of a small knife and use oven mitts to carefully remove the hot bowl. Continue to bake until the rolls are a pale golden brown with a lightly floured crust, 10 to 15 minutes more. If you are concerned about the rolls' doneness, insert an instant-read thermometer from the bottom into the center. If it reads 185°F to 210°F the rolls are fully baked.

Transfer the rolls to a cooling rack and let cool for at least 1 hour before cutting with a serrated knife or wrapping for storage.

Sun-Dried Tomato and Basil Ciabatta

MAKES 1 LARGE LOAF OR 4 SMALL ROLLS

To me, this recipe has all the flavors of the height of summer, but it can be made year round. The sweet-acidic sun-dried tomatoes fill the house with the most wonderful aromas as the bread bakes. This is a great sandwich bread and also terrific as a bruschetta base or toasted as crostinis. It is beautiful once cut, with a confetti of ingredients throughout.

16 ounces	454 grams	3½ cups unbleached, unbromated white bread flour
0.31 ounce	9 grams	1½ teaspoons fine sea salt
0.12 ounce	3 grams	1 teaspoon instant dry yeast
13.76 ounces	390 grams	1½ cups plus 2 teaspoons water
0.32 ounce	10 grams	1 tablespoon extra-virgin olive oil, plus about 2 tablespoons to coat the bowl
2.8 ounces	80 grams	½ cup julienned sun-dried tomatoes
1 ounce	28 grams	2 tablespoons julienned fresh basil leaves

1 MEASURING

Scale all of the ingredients.

Place the flour in a large bowl. Add the salt and yeast, making sure that they do not touch each other.

Take the temperature of the water (it should be 65°F to 70°F) and record it in your Dough Log.

2 MIXING AND KNEADING

Pour half of the water into the bowl of the mixer; then, add the dry ingredients. Attach the bowl and dough hook to the mixer.

Begin mixing on low speed ("1" on most mixers), and quickly add enough of the remaining water in a slow, steady stream to make a soft, moist dough that slightly sticks to the sides of the bowl. Take care to add the remaining water immediately; if the water is added too late in the mixing process, the dough will become too firm to mix easily. Stop the mixer often and use a rubber spatula to scrape down the hook and sides of the bowl to ensure that all of the ingredients have been well incorporated.

When all of the water has been added, set a timer and mix for 5 minutes. Stop the mixer and touch your dough; it should be soft and pliable. Taste the dough to check whether you have forgotten the salt. If so, add it now and mix for another 2 minutes.

Increase the speed to medium-low ("2" on most mixers) and mix for 4 minutes, gradually adding 1 tablespoon olive oil. Continue to mix until the oil is thoroughly incorporated, about 1 minute. Add the sun-dried tomatoes and basil and mix until incorporated, about 1 more minute. The dough should be soft and smooth, with a moist, tacky surface.

3 FIRST FERMENTATION

Using an instant-read thermometer, take the temperature of the dough. It should be between 72°F and 80°F. If it is higher or lower, make the necessary adjustments (see page 52). Record the temperature of the dough and the time you finished this step in the Dough Log, and note the time the first fermentation should be completed. This dough will be in the first fermentation for 3 hours, with a fold each hour.

Using your fingertips, coat the inside of a large bowl with the remaining 2 tablespoons olive oil.

Using your bench scraper, scrape the dough into the oil-coated bowl. Using your hands, pull one edge of the dough and fold it into the center and press down slightly. Giving the bowl a quarter turn, continue to fold the dough in and press for 4 additional turns. The dough should begin to form a ball. Roll the ball around in the bowl to coat all sides with olive oil, turning it so that the smooth side is up. The dough does not need to be covered, as the oil prevents dryness.

Place the dough in a warm (75°F to 80°F), draft-free place for 3 hours, folding as above after the first hour and again after the second hour.

4–5 DIVIDING AND SHAPING

Generously coat a clean work surface with flour.

Generously flour the top of the dough and, using a bowl scraper, scrape the dough onto the floured work surface. Lightly dust the exterior of the dough with flour and allow the dough to rest for 30 seconds.

If the dough is very sticky, lightly flour your hands and add more flour to the work surface. If the dough sticks to the table, use your bench scraper to lift it up; do not pull and stretch the dough.

If you are making rolls, lightly press down on the dough with a flat hand, forming the dough into a square. Using a bench scraper, cut the dough in half and then in half again to form 4 rectangles of equal size. For one large loaf, lightly press down on the dough with a flat hand to form 1 large rectangle (about 4 inches by 4 inches). Remember, this is a rather free-form bread, so the shape does not have to be perfect. Place the dough in a lightly floured *couche* (or strong linen towel) as directed on page 62. (If making

4 rolls, make a second ridge in the *couche* to separate the first 2 rolls from the second 2 rolls.) Fold the remaining part of the *couche* over the top of the dough.

6 FINAL FERMENTATION

Place the *couche* in a warm (75°F to 80°F), draft-free place. Record the time in your Dough Log, as well as the exact time required for the final fermentation, and set your timer. It should take from 45 minutes to 1 hour for the final proofing; however, you should keep a close eye on the dough, because if it is overproofed it will be unusable.

If you are using the stainless-steel bowl method to bake the bread (see page 64), about 30 minutes before you are ready to bake, move one oven rack to the lowest rung and remove the other. Place a large baking stone on the rack and preheat the oven to 450°F. (For all other baking methods, follow the directions on page 64.)

To determine whether the dough is ready to be baked, uncover and gently make a small indentation in the center of the dough with your fingertip. If the indentation slowly and evenly disappears, the bread is ready to bake. If not, follow the instructions on page 63 for additional fermentation.

If you are making 4 rolls and they won't all fit under your stainless-steel bowl, cover 2 with plastic wrap and place in the refrigerator, then bake after the first 2 come out of the oven.

7 BAKING

Cover a bread peel with a sheet of parchment paper. Using your hands, gently remove the dough from the *couche* and transfer to the peel, top side up.

Carefully slide the loaf or rolls on the parchment paper onto the center of the stone, taking care not to touch the hot surface. If you are baking

Transfer dough gently to peel.

Place on hot stone.

Cover for first ten minutes of baking.

all 4 rolls together, take care that they don't "kiss" (touch and get stuck together while baking).

Quickly cover the dough with the stainless-steel mixing bowl and immediately close the oven door. Bake for 10 minutes; then, lift the edge of the bowl with the tip of a small knife and, use oven mitts to carefully remove the hot bowl. Continue to bake until the bread is a pale golden brown with a lightly floured crust, about 15 minutes more (rolls will take a few minutes less). If you are concerned about the bread's doneness, insert an instant-read thermometer from the bottom of the bread into the center. If it reads 185°F to 210°F the bread is fully baked.

Transfer the loaf or rolls to a cooling rack and let cool for at least 1 hour before cutting with a serrated knife or wrapping for storage.

Ciabatta Vendée Préfou

MAKES 1 LOAF

This is my version of the regional bread (typically filled with chopped garlic and salted butter) that I loved when I visited my grandparents in Vendée, an area in the southwestern part of France.

Vendée Préfou is a bread with a long history. Originally, the baker in charge of the day's baking would pinch off a small piece of dough, flatten it, and pop it into the oven to test the oven heat before placing the day's worth of bread in it. For centuries, in the quiet of the morning, the first baker would rub the warm bread with a clove of garlic, then spread some freshly churned butter on top to make a baker's snack. Today it is enjoyed throughout the region as a late-afternoon apéritif.

0.8 ounce	23 grams	4 teaspoons, or about 4 large cloves minced garlic
2.9 ounces	82 grams	⅓ cup crème fraîche, at room temperature
4 ounces	113 grams	¼ cup unsalted butter, at room temperature
0.375 ounce	10 grams	⅓ cup finely chopped fresh flat-leaf parsley
0.05 ounce	1.5 grams	¼ teaspoon fine sea salt
0.02 ounce	0.5 gram	¼ teaspoon freshly ground black pepper

1 recipe Ciabatta (page 131)

1 MEASURING
Scale all of the ingredients.

2-3 MIXING AND KNEADING AND FIRST FERMENTATION
To make the *préfou* filling, place the garlic on a cutting board and, with the flat side of a chef's knife, use back and forth movements to mash it until a smooth paste forms. Transfer the garlic to a small mixing bowl and, using a wooden spoon, blend in the crème fraîche and the butter. When blended, mix in the parsley, salt, and pepper. Set aside.

Make the dough according to the directions for Ciabatta through the first fermentation stage.

4 DIVIDING
Since you are making just 1 loaf, skip to Step 5!

5 SHAPING
Generously coat a clean work surface with flour.

Generously flour the top of the dough and, using a bowl scraper, scrape the dough onto the floured work surface. Lightly dust the exterior of the dough with flour and allow the dough to rest for 30 seconds.

If the dough is very sticky, lightly flour your hands and add more flour to the work surface. If the dough sticks to the table, use your bench scraper to lift it up; do not pull and stretch the dough.

Lightly press down on the dough with a flat hand, forming the dough into 1 large rectangle shape, about a foot long.

Place the dough in a lightly floured *couche* (or a strong linen towel) as directed on page 62. Fold the remaining part of the *couche* over the top of the dough.

6 FINAL FERMENTATION
Place the *couche* in a warm (75°F to 80°F), draft-free place for 1 hour. Record the time in your Dough Log, as well as the exact time required for the final fermentation, and set your timer. It should take about 1 hour for the final proofing; however, you should keep a close eye on the dough, because if it is overproofed it will be unusable.

If you are using the stainless-steel bowl method to bake the bread (see page 64), about 30 minutes before you are ready to bake, move one oven rack to the lowest rung and remove the other. Place a large baking stone on the rack and preheat the oven to 450°F. (For all other baking methods, follow the directions on page 64.)

To determine whether the dough is ready to be baked, uncover and gently make a small indentation in the center of the dough with your fingertip. If the indentation slowly and evenly disappears, the bread is ready to bake. If not, follow the instructions on page 63 for additional fermentation.

7 BAKING

Cover a bread peel with a sheet of parchment paper. Using your hands, gently remove the loaf from the *couche* and transfer it to the peel, top side up.

Carefully slide the loaf on the parchment paper onto the center of the stone, taking care not to touch the hot surface.

Quickly cover the loaf with the stainless-steel mixing bowl and immediately close the oven door. Bake for 10 minutes; then, lift the edge of the bowl with the tip of a small knife and use oven mitts to carefully remove the hot bowl. Continue to bake for 10 more minutes; the loaf will go back in the oven after it is coated with the *préfou* filling.

Line a baking sheet with parchment paper. Using the peel, remove the bread from the oven but do not turn off the oven. Wear oven mitts to protect your hands, and use a serrated knife to cut the bread in half horizontally. Separate the halves and, using a sandwich spreader, coat the bottom half with the *préfou* filling. Cover with the top half of the bread and place on the parchment-lined baking sheet.

Carefully slide the filled loaf on the parchment paper onto the center of the stone and bake until the bread is pale golden brown and the filling is very hot and slightly runny, another 5 to 10 minutes. If you are concerned about the bread's doneness, insert an instant-read thermometer from the bottom of the bread into the center. If it reads 185°F to 210°F the bread is fully baked.

Transfer the loaf to a cooling rack and let it cool for at least 1 hour before cutting with a serrated knife or wrapping for storage. Because this is a stuffed bread, some people may prefer to eat it warm.

Note: If you want to reheat the loaf later, wrap it in foil and place in a 350°F oven for about 10 minutes.

Soup Bowls

MAKES 6 TO 8 BOWLS

At La Farm Bakery, I use ciabatta dough to make sturdy, edible bowls to hold our soups. The presentation always draws an "ooh" or even an "ooh la la," and it is great fun to watch diners nibble away at the bowl as they sip their soup. You will need oven-proof crocks that are approximately 4 inches in diameter and about 2½ inches deep to form the bowls. The oil in the dough makes it very elastic and easy to stretch around any solid form.

Bread bowls also make terrific containers for dips to be served with crudités.

1 recipe Ciabatta (page 131)

1–3 MEASURING, MIXING AND KNEADING, AND FIRST FERMENTATION

Make the dough according to the directions for Ciabatta through the first fermentation stage.

4 DIVIDING

Generously coat a clean work surface with flour.

Generously flour the top of the dough and, using a bowl scraper, scrape the dough onto the floured work surface. Lightly dust the exterior of the dough with flour and allow the dough to rest for 30 seconds.

If the dough is very sticky, lightly flour your hands and add more flour to the work surface. If the dough sticks to the table, use your bench scraper to lift it up; do not pull and stretch the dough.

Lightly press down on the dough with a flat hand, forming the dough into a large square. Using a bench scraper, cut the dough in half to form 2 rectangles. Then, again using the bench scraper, cut each piece into 3 or 4 equal-sized rectangles. (The number will depend upon the size of your oven-proof crocks.)

5 SHAPING

Line a baking sheet with parchment paper or a silicone liner. Turn the oven-proof crocks upside-down and spray the exteriors with nonstick vegetable oil spray. Transfer the sprayed crocks to the prepared baking sheet.

Working with one piece of the dough at a time, stretch the dough out

Stretch the dough.

Place dough over greased bowl.

Press excess dough to form a rim.

Continue stretching dough as needed.

and over to completely and evenly cover an inverted, sprayed crock. Don't hesitate to work the dough until it completely covers the crock; any excess can be pressed out to form the rim on the finished bread bowl. Cover the dough-covered crocks with a clean linen towel followed by plastic wrap.

6 FINAL FERMENTATION

Place the baking sheet in a warm (75°F to 80°F), draft-free place for 1 hour. Record the time in your Dough Log, as well as the exact time required for the final fermentation, and set your timer. It should take 45 minutes to 1 hour for the final proofing; however, you should keep a close eye on the dough, because if it is overproofed it will be unusable.

About 30 minutes before you are ready to bake, move the oven rack to one rung below the center. Preheat the oven to 450°F.

To determine whether the dough is ready to be baked, uncover and gently make a small indentation in the center of the dough with your fingertip. If the indentation slowly and evenly disappears, the bread is ready to bake. If not, follow the instructions on page 63 for additional fermentation.

Bake on parchment-lined baking sheet.

Remove bread from bowl.

7 BAKING

Uncover the dough and place the baking sheet in the preheated oven. Bake, rotating the baking sheet after 10 minutes, until the bread bowls are evenly browned and baked through, about 25 minutes. If necessary, rotate the individual bowls occasionally to make sure that they brown evenly.

Remove from the oven and place on cooling racks to cool slightly.

While still slightly warm, carefully tip the baked bread bowls from the crocks and place, still upside-down, on cooling racks to cool completely.

Serve, filled with your favorite soup.

Focaccia

MAKES 1 LOAF

Although its very different name would suggest that focaccia has nothing to do with ciabatta, it is really the same dough shaped and used in other ways. When I consult with bakeries, I always show them how to place ciabatta dough into half-sheet pans (see page 31) and season with sea salt and fresh herbs to serve as a great dipping bread or to use for sandwiches. I also encourage them to add toppings so the bread can be sold by the slice as a light snack or quick lunch. This is focaccia.

In Italy, focaccia is a hearth-baked flat bread topped with herbs and, often, sea salt as well as cheeses, tomatoes, cured meats, onions, or garlic. Although quite like pizza in many ways, focaccia is rarely served as a main course. It is usually considered a snack or used as a sandwich bread. This recipe is for the basic focaccia that we serve every day in the La Farm Bakery Café.

1 recipe Ciabatta (page 131)

3 additional tablespoons extra-virgin olive oil for oiling the pan and seasoning the dough

1–3 MEASURING, MIXING AND KNEADING, AND FIRST FERMENTATION

Make the dough according to the directions for Ciabatta through the first fermentation stage.

4 DIVIDING

Since you are making just 1 loaf, skip to Step 5!

5 SHAPING

Lightly coat a 9-by-13-inch baking pan with 2 tablespoons of the additional olive oil. Set aside.

Generously coat a clean work surface with flour.

Generously flour the top of the dough and, using a bowl scraper, scrape the dough onto the floured work surface. Lightly dust the exterior of the dough with flour and allow the dough to rest for 30 seconds. Sprinkle with additional flour to lightly cover all of the dough.

If the dough is very sticky, lightly flour your hands and add more flour to the work surface. If the dough sticks to the table, use your bench scraper to lift it up; do not pull and stretch the dough.

Lightly press dough into rectangle.

Fold bottom third to center.

Fold top third to center.

Gently transfer to oiled baking pan.

Gently fold dough up to edge of pan.

Gently fold out bottom.

Lightly press down on the dough with a flat hand, forming the dough into a large rectangle. Keeping your hands absolutely flat, continue to gently press the dough into a larger rectangle, approximately the same size and shape as the oiled baking pan. The dough should be an even ½ inch thick. Working from the edge nearest to you, loosely fold the dough into thirds, brushing away any excess flour with a soft pastry brush.

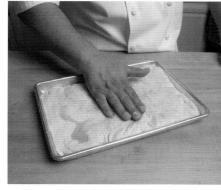

Lightly coat top of dough with oil.

Gently lift the dough onto the oiled baking pan and unfold the dough, using flat hands to carefully fit the dough into the pan so that the pan is evenly covered.

Using a pastry brush (or your hands), lightly coat the top of the dough with the remaining 1 tablespoon olive oil.

6 FINAL FERMENTATION

Place the baking pan in a warm (75°F to 80°F), draft-free place for 1 hour. Record the time in your Dough Log, as well as the exact time required for the final fermentation, and set your timer. It should take 45 minutes to 1 hour for the final proofing; however, you should keep a close eye on the dough, because if it is overproofed it will be unusable.

About 30 minutes before you are ready to bake, move the oven rack to one rung below the center. Preheat the oven to 450°F.

To determine whether the dough is ready to be baked, uncover and gently make a small indentation in the center of the dough with your fingertip. If the indentation slowly and evenly disappears, the bread is ready to bake. If not, follow the instructions on page 63 for additional fermentation.

7 BAKING

Uncover the dough and transfer the baking sheet to the preheated oven. Bake until the dough rises and the crust is golden brown, 20 to 25 minutes.

Remove from the oven and carefully lift the focaccia from the pan. Immediately place on a cooling rack to cool, as the bread will quickly become soggy if left in the pan.

Let cool slightly and then cut into pieces and serve. Cool for at least 1 hour before wrapping for storage.

Focaccia with Herbs, Salt, and Olive Oil

MAKES 1 LOAF

This recipe takes a plain focaccia dough and adds a light but very savory topping. In Italy, focaccia is frequently "dimpled" or poked with the baker's fingertips before baking to create little indentations to absorb extra-virgin olive oil and herbs. This is the La Farm Bakery version. It is an excellent dipping bread and also makes a great accompaniment to soups and salads. Filled with vine-ripened tomatoes, slices of hand-rolled mozzarella, fresh basil, and an aged balsamic reduction, it makes the perfect summer sandwich.

1 recipe Ciabatta (page 131)

3 additional tablespoons extra-virgin olive oil for oiling the pan and seasoning the dough

0.02 ounce	0.5 gram	½ teaspoon chopped fresh rosemary
0.16 ounce	4.5 grams	1 teaspoon coarse sea salt or kosher salt

1–3 MEASURING, MIXING AND KNEADING, AND FIRST FERMENTATION

Make the dough according to the directions for Ciabatta through the first fermentation stage.

4 DIVIDING

Since you are making just 1 loaf, skip to Step 5!

5 SHAPING

Lightly coat a 9-by-13-inch baking pan with 2 tablespoons of the additional olive oil. Set aside.

Generously coat a clean work surface with flour.

Generously flour the top of the dough and, using a bowl scraper, scrape the dough onto the floured work surface. Lightly dust the exterior of the dough with flour and allow the dough to rest for 30 seconds. Sprinkle with additional flour to lightly cover all of the dough.

If the dough is very sticky, lightly flour your hands and add more flour to the work surface. If the dough sticks to the table, use your bench scraper to lift it up; do not pull and stretch the dough.

Lightly press down on the dough with a flat hand, forming the dough into a large rectangle. Keeping your hands absolutely flat, continue to gently press the dough into a larger rectangle, approximately the same size and shape as the oiled baking pan. The dough should be an even ½ inch thick. Working from the edge nearest to you, loosely fold the dough into thirds, brushing away any excess flour with a soft pastry brush.

Gently lift the dough onto the oiled baking pan and unfold the dough, using flat hands to carefully fit the dough into the pan so that the pan is evenly covered.

Using a pastry brush (or your hands), lightly coat the top of the dough with the remaining 1 tablespoon olive oil.

6 FINAL FERMENTATION

Place the baking pan in a warm (75°F to 80°F), draft-free place. Record the time in your Dough Log, as well as the exact time required for the final fermentation, and set your timer. It should take 45 minutes to 1 hour for the final proofing; however, you should keep a close eye on the dough, because if it is overproofed it will be unusable.

About 30 minutes before you are ready to bake, move the oven rack to one rung below the center. Preheat the oven to 450°F.

To determine whether the dough is ready to be baked, uncover and gently make a small indentation in the center of the dough with your fingertip. If the indentation slowly and evenly disappears, the bread is ready to bake. If not, follow the instructions on page 63 for additional fermentation.

7 BAKING

Using your fingertips, randomly poke the dough to create "dimples" all over the top. Evenly sprinkle the rosemary and then the salt all over the top.

Transfer the baking sheet to the preheated oven and bake until the dough rises and the crust is golden brown, 20 to 25 minutes.

Remove from the oven and carefully lift the focaccia from the pan. Immediately place on a cooling rack to cool, as the bread will quickly become soggy if left in the pan.

Let cool slightly and then cut into pieces and serve. Cool for at least 1 hour before wrapping for storage.

Potato and Crème Fraîche Focaccia

MAKES 1 LOAF

This is an especially rich and delicious focaccia I developed after thinking about a favorite recipe from my youth—*pâté aux pommes de terre*, a wonderful peasant dinner, which is simply sliced potatoes layered with onions and herbs and covered with pie pastry. Once baked, a large circle of pastry is cut out of the top and crème fraîche is added to the hot filling. The pastry circle is returned to the top, and when the crème has melted into the filling, it is cut into wedges and served hot and *délicieux*.

You need either a food processor with a thin slicing blade, a mandoline, or a V-slicer to cut the potatoes into paper-thin slices. It is almost impossible to cut slices thin enough by hand, even for a skilled chef, and the thinness is essential; otherwise, the potatoes will not be cooked by the time the bread is done.

FOR THE DOUGH:

1 recipe Ciabatta (page 131)

3 additional tablespoons extra-virgin olive oil for oiling the pan and seasoning the dough

FOR THE TOPPING:

1.25 pounds	570 grams	about 3 medium Yukon gold potatoes, well washed and dried, unpeeled
0.32 ounce	10 grams	1 tablespoon extra-virgin olive oil
0.04 ounce	1 gram	1 teaspoon finely minced fresh rosemary
4.4 ounces	125 grams	½ cup crème fraîche, at room temperature
0.05 ounce	1.5 grams	¼ teaspoon fine sea salt
0.02 ounce	0.5 gram	¼ teaspoon freshly ground black pepper
4 ounces	113 grams	1½ cups shredded Comté or Gruyère cheese (see Note, page 123), at room temperature

1–3 MEASURING, MIXING AND KNEADING, AND FIRST FERMENTATION

Make the dough according to the directions for Ciabatta through the first fermentation stage.

While the dough is in the final period of the first fermentation, prepare the topping. Using a food processor fitted with the thin slicing blade, a mandoline, or a V-slicer, cut the potatoes into very thin slices. Place the sliced potatoes in a mixing bowl. Add the olive oil and rosemary and toss to coat. Very tightly cover the bowl with plastic wrap (to keep the potatoes from oxidizing) and set aside.

4 DIVIDING

Since you are making just 1 loaf, skip to Step 5!

5 SHAPING

Lightly coat a 9-by-13-inch baking pan with 2 tablespoons of the additional olive oil. Set aside.

Generously coat a clean work surface with flour.

Generously flour the top of the dough and, using a bowl scraper, scrape the dough onto the floured work surface. Lightly dust the exterior of the dough with flour and allow the dough to rest for 30 seconds.

If the dough is very sticky, lightly flour your hands and add more flour to the work surface. If the dough sticks to the table, use your bench scraper to lift it up; do not pull and stretch the dough.

Lightly press down on the dough with a flat hand, forming the dough into a large rectangle. Keeping your hands absolutely flat, continue to gently press the dough into a larger rectangle, approximately the same size and shape as the oiled baking pan. The dough should be an even ½ inch thick. Working from the edge nearest to you, loosely fold the dough into thirds, brushing away any excess flour with a soft pastry brush.

Gently lift the dough onto the oiled baking pan and unfold the dough, using flat hands to carefully fit the dough into the pan so that the pan is evenly covered.

Using a pastry brush (or your hands), lightly coat the top of the dough with the remaining 1 tablespoon olive oil.

Place the potatoes in slightly overlapping layers over the entire top of the dough. The potatoes should be placed as close to the edge of the dough as possible and there should be no gaps on the top or the dough will rise up and push the potatoes out of place. Season with salt and pepper. Scatter the shredded cheese over the top of the potatoes to coat completely.

Spread shredded cheese evenly.

6 FINAL FERMENTATION

Place the baking pan in a warm (75°F to 80°F), draft-free place. Record the time in your Dough Log, as well as the exact time required for the final fermentation, and set your timer. It should take 45 minutes to 1 hour for the final proofing; however, you should keep a close eye on the dough, because if it is overproofed it will be unusable.

About 30 minutes before you are ready to bake, move the oven rack to one rung below the center. Preheat the oven to 450°F.

To determine whether the dough is ready to be baked, uncover and gently make a small indentation in the center of the dough with your fingertip. If the indentation slowly and evenly disappears, the bread is ready to bake. If not, follow the instructions on page 63 for additional fermentation.

7 BAKING

Using an offset spatula, coat the top of the dough with the crème fraîche.

Transfer the baking pan to the preheated oven and bake for 30 minutes. Remove from the oven and test a piece of potato for doneness. If the potatoes are not thoroughly cooked, return the pan to the oven until the edges of the focaccia are golden brown, the potatoes are colored around the edges and cooked through, and the cheese has melted and colored slightly, another 5 to 10 minutes.

Remove from the oven and carefully lift the focaccia from the pan. Immediately place on a cooling rack to cool, as the bread will quickly become soggy if left in the pan.

Sautéed Onion Focaccia

MAKES 1 LOAF

When I was consulting for Baker Street Bread, an excellent bakery in Philadelphia, the bakers were making something similar to this focaccia, and it was a favorite of their customers. This is my tribute to the fine bakers there.

This is another tasty accompaniment to soup or salad and is equally good cut into small squares and served with an apéritif. The sweet-savory onion topping for this focaccia can easily be made a couple of days in advance of use and stored, covered, in the refrigerator. It should be brought to room temperature before using.

FOR THE DOUGH:

1 recipe Ciabatta (page 131)

3 additional tablespoons extra-virgin olive oil for oiling the pan and seasoning the dough

FOR THE TOPPING:

0.96 ounce	27 grams	3 tablespoons extra-virgin olive oil
2.5 pounds	1100 grams	about 5 medium yellow onions, thinly sliced crosswise
0.05 ounce	1.5 grams	¼ teaspoon fine sea salt
0.02 ounce	0.5 gram	¼ teaspoon freshly ground black pepper
5.3 ounces	150 grams	1½ cups shredded Comté or Gruyère cheese (see Note, page 123, at room temperature

1–3 MEASURING, MIXING AND KNEADING, AND FIRST FERMENTATION

Make the dough according to the directions for Ciabatta through the first fermentation stage.

While the dough is in the first fermentation, prepare the topping. Heat the olive oil in a large sauté pan over medium heat. Add the sliced onions and sauté, stirring frequently, until well caramelized and aromatic, about 15 minutes. Season with salt and pepper. You may need to lower the heat to keep the onions from burning. Remove from the heat and set aside to cool thoroughly.

4 DIVIDING

Since you are making just 1 loaf, skip to Step 5!

5 SHAPING

Lightly coat a 9-by-13-inch baking pan with 2 tablespoons of the additional olive oil. Set aside.

Generously coat a clean work surface with flour.

Generously flour the top of the dough and, using a bowl scraper, scrape the dough onto the floured work surface. Lightly dust the exterior of the dough with flour and allow the dough to rest for 30 seconds. Sprinkle with additional flour to lightly cover all of the dough.

If the dough is very sticky, lightly flour your hands and add more flour to the work surface. If the dough sticks to the table, use your bench scraper to lift it up; do not pull and stretch the dough.

Lightly press down on the dough with a flat hand, forming the dough into a large rectangle. Keeping your hands absolutely flat, continue to gently press the dough into a larger rectangle, approximately the same size and shape as the oiled baking pan. The dough should be an even ½ inch thick. Working from the edge nearest to you, loosely fold the dough into thirds, brushing away any excess flour with a soft pastry brush.

Spread shredded cheese evenly.

Gently lift the dough onto the oiled baking pan and unfold the dough, using flat hands to carefully fit the dough into the pan so that the pan is evenly covered.

Using a pastry brush (or your hands), lightly coat the top of the dough with the remaining 1 tablespoon olive oil.

Spread the cooled onions over the top of the dough, taking care to coat all of the dough from the edges in. Scatter the shredded cheese over the top of the onions to coat completely.

 6 FINAL FERMENTATION

Place the baking pan in a warm (75°F to 80°F), draft-free place. Record the time in your Dough Log, as well as the exact time required for the final fermentation, and set your timer. It should take 45 minutes to 1 hour for the final proofing; however, you should keep a close eye on the dough, because if it is overproofed it will be unusable.

About 30 minutes before you are ready to bake, move the oven rack to one rung below the center. Preheat the oven to 450°F.

To determine whether the dough is ready to be baked, uncover and gently make a small indentation in the center of the dough with your fingertip. If the indentation slowly and evenly disappears, the bread is ready to bake. If not, follow the instructions on page 63 for additional fermentation.

7 BAKING

Transfer the baking pan to the preheated oven and bake until the cheese has melted and colored slightly and the edges of the bread are golden brown and crisp, about 30 minutes.

Remove from the oven and carefully lift the focaccia from the pan. Immediately place on a cooling rack to cool, as the bread will quickly become soggy if left in the pan.

Let cool slightly and then cut into pieces and serve. Cool for at least 1 hour before wrapping for storage.

Walnut and Gruyère Focaccia

MAKES 1 LOAF

My dear friend Raoul Lucco, a top pastry chef in France, lives on a walnut farm in the Périgord region near Sarlat. I created this recipe in his honor. If you are traveling to France, make a stop at Les Gourmandises de Lucco, Raoul's pastry shop located on his farm, and try his famous walnut cake.

FOR THE DOUGH:

1 recipe Ciabatta (page 131)

3 additional tablespoons extra-virgin olive oil for oiling the pan and seasoning the dough

FOR THE TOPPING:

| 3.15 ounces | 90 grams | ¾ cup coarsely chopped walnuts |
| 5.3 ounces | 150 grams | 1½ cups shredded Comté or Gruyère cheese (see Note, page 123), at room temperature |

1–3 MEASURING, MIXING AND KNEADING, AND FIRST FERMENTATION

Make the dough according to the directions for Ciabatta through the first fermentation stage.

4 DIVIDING

Since you are making just 1 loaf, skip to Step 5!

5 SHAPING

Lightly coat a 9-by-13-inch baking pan with 2 tablespoons of the additional olive oil. Set aside.

Generously coat a clean work surface with flour.

Generously flour the top of the dough and, using a bowl scraper, scrape the dough onto the floured work surface. Lightly dust the exterior of the dough with flour and allow the dough to rest for 30 seconds. Sprinkle with additional flour to lightly cover all of the dough.

If the dough is very sticky, lightly flour your hands and add more flour to the work surface. If the dough sticks to the table, use your bench scraper to lift it up; do not pull and stretch the dough.

Lightly press down on the dough with a flat hand, forming the dough into a large rectangle. Keeping your hands absolutely flat, continue to gently press the dough into a larger rectangle, approximately the same size and shape as the oiled baking pan. The dough should be an even ½ inch thick. Working from the edge nearest to you, loosely fold the dough into thirds, brushing away any excess flour with a soft pastry brush.

Gently lift the dough onto the oiled baking pan and unfold the dough, using flat hands to carefully fit the dough into the pan so that the pan is evenly covered.

Using a pastry brush (or your hands), lightly coat the top of the dough with the remaining 1 tablespoon olive oil.

Using your fingertips, randomly poke the dough to create "dimples" all over the top. Evenly sprinkle the walnuts over the top. Scatter the shredded cheese over the top of the nuts to coat completely.

Spread shredded cheese evenly.

6 FINAL FERMENTATION

Place the baking pan in a warm (75°F to 80°F), draft-free place. Record the time in your Dough Log, as well as the exact time required for the final fermentation, and set your timer. It should take 45 minutes to 1 hour for the final proofing; however, you should keep a close eye on the dough, because if it is overproofed it will be unusable.

About 30 minutes before you are ready to bake, move the oven rack to one rung below the center. Preheat the oven to 450°F.

To determine whether the dough is ready to be baked, uncover and gently make a small indentation in the center of the dough with your fingertip. If the indentation slowly and evenly disappears, the bread is ready to bake. If not, follow the instructions on page 63 for additional fermentation.

BAKING

Transfer the baking pan to the preheated oven and bake until the dough rises slightly, the cheese has melted and colored slightly, and the edges of the bread are golden brown and crisp, about 30 minutes.

Remove from the oven and carefully lift the focaccia from the pan. Immediately place on a cooling rack to cool, as the bread will quickly become soggy if left in the pan.

Let cool slightly and then cut into pieces and serve. Cool for at least 1 hour before wrapping for storage.

Tomato-Basil Focaccia

MAKES 1 LOAF

I developed this focaccia because the tomato-mozzarella combination is one of the most popular flavors among our customers. We started by offering small triangles of this focaccia as a catering option during the holidays, and it was so popular that we now offer it year-round.

FOR THE DOUGH:

1 recipe Ciabatta (page 131)

2 additional tablespoons extra-virgin olive oil for oiling the pan and seasoning the dough

FOR THE TOPPING:

2.5 ounces	70 grams	½ cup Pesto (page 169), at room temperature
12 ounces	340 grams	4 medium Roma tomatoes, cut crosswise into ⅛-inch slices
4.7 ounces	133 grams	⅔ cup shredded mozzarella cheese, at room temperature

1–3 MEASURING, MIXING AND KNEADING, AND FIRST FERMENTATION

Make the dough according to the directions for Ciabatta through the first fermentation stage.

4 DIVIDING

Since you are making just 1 loaf, skip to Step 5!

5 SHAPING

Lightly coat a 9-by-13-inch baking pan with the 2 additional tablespoons olive oil. Set aside.

Generously coat a clean work surface with flour.

Generously flour the top of the dough and, using a bowl scraper, scrape the dough onto the floured work surface. Lightly dust the exterior of the dough with flour and allow the dough to rest for 30 seconds. Sprinkle with additional flour to lightly cover all of the dough.

If the dough is very sticky, lightly flour your hands and add more flour to the work surface. If the dough sticks to the table, use your bench scraper to lift it up; do not pull and stretch the dough.

Lightly press down on the dough with a flat hand, forming the dough into a large rectangle.

Keeping your hands absolutely flat, continue to gently press the dough into a larger rectangle, approximately the same size and shape as the oiled baking pan. The dough should be an even $\frac{1}{2}$ inch thick. Working from the edge nearest to you, loosely fold the dough into thirds, brushing away any excess flour with a soft pastry brush.

Gently lift the dough onto the oiled baking pan and unfold the dough, using flat hands to carefully fit the dough into the pan so that the pan is evenly covered.

Using an offset spatula, coat the top of the dough with the pesto.

Coat dough with pesto.

Layer tomatoes closely and tightly.

Place the tomatoes, slightly overlapping, over the entire surface of the dough. The tomatoes should be placed as close to the edge of the dough as possible, leaving no gaps, or the dough will rise up and push the tomatoes out of place. Scatter the shredded cheese over the tomatoes to coat completely.

6 FINAL FERMENTATION

Place the baking pan in a warm (75°F to 80°F), draft-free place for 1 hour. Record the time in your Dough Log, as well as the exact time required for the final fermentation, and set your timer. It should take about 1 hour for the final proofing; however, you should keep a close eye on the dough, because if it is overproofed it will be unusable.

About 30 minutes before you are ready to bake, move the oven rack to one rung below the center.

Preheat the oven to 450°F.

To determine whether the dough is ready to be baked, uncover and gently make a small indentation in the center of the dough with your fingertip. If the indentation slowly and evenly disappears, the bread is ready to bake. If not, follow the instructions on page 63 for additional fermentation.

7 BAKING

Transfer the baking pan to the preheated oven and bake until the dough rises slightly, the cheese has melted and colored slightly, and the edges of the bread are golden brown and crisp, about 30 minutes.

Remove from the oven and carefully lift the focaccia from the pan. Immediately place on a cooling rack to cool, as the bread will quickly become soggy if left in the pan.

Let cool slightly and then cut into pieces and serve. Cool for at least 1 hour before wrapping for storage.

Pesto

MAKES ABOUT 1 CUP

1 cup packed fresh basil leaves, well washed and dried

¼ cup walnuts or pine nuts

1 large garlic clove, minced

¼ cup fine-quality olive oil

¼ cup finely grated Pecorino Romano or Parmesan cheese

⅛ teaspoon fine sea salt

Freshly ground black pepper

Combine the basil, nuts, and garlic in the bowl of a food processor fitted with the metal blade. Process for 30 seconds to blend.

With the motor running, slowly add the oil through the feed tube. When blended, add the cheese and process for 15 seconds to blend completely.

Scrape the mixture from the processor bowl into a small, nonreactive container. Season to taste with salt and pepper. Use immediately, or cover and refrigerate for up to 2 days.

Fresh Bing Cherry and Pine Nut Focaccia

MAKES 1 LOAF

One morning I spied a farmer at our local farmers' market with a large display of fresh-from-the-tree, deep-red Bing cherries. I bought a large bucket, went right back to the bakery, and created this sweet cherry focaccia to capture the short window of time that local cherries are available. Thank goodness that the season is short, because we all know how much I love pitting (see page 207).

FOR THE DOUGH:

1 recipe Ciabatta (page 131)

3 additional tablespoons extra-virgin olive oil for oiling the pan and seasoning the dough

FOR THE TOPPING:

| 3.2 ounces | 90 grams | ⅓ cup toasted pine nuts |
| 8.6 ounces | 244 grams | 1½ cups pitted fresh Bing cherries |

Sifted confectioners' sugar for dusting

 MEASURING, MIXING AND KNEADING, AND FIRST FERMENTATION

Make the dough according to the directions for Ciabatta through the kneading stage and the addition of the olive oil. Add the toasted pine nuts and mix on low ("1" on most mixers) just until the nuts are incorporated into the dough, but not mashed, about 1 minute. Continue to follow the directions for Ciabatta through the first fermentation stage.

4 DIVIDING

Since you are making just 1 loaf, skip to Step 5!

5 SHAPING

Generously coat a clean work surface with flour.

Generously flour the top of the dough and, using a bowl scraper, scrape the dough onto the floured work surface. Lightly dust the exterior of the dough with flour and allow the dough to rest for 30 seconds.

Lightly press down on the dough with a flat hand, forming the dough into a large rectangle.

Keeping your hands absolutely flat, continue to gently press the dough into a larger rectangle, approximately the same size and shape as the oiled baking pan. The dough should be an even ½ inch thick. Working from the edge nearest to you, loosely fold the dough into thirds, brushing away any excess flour with a soft pastry brush.

Gently lift the dough onto the oiled baking pan and unfold the dough, using flat hands to carefully fit the dough into the pan so that the pan is evenly covered.

Using a pastry brush (or your hands), lightly coat the top of the dough with the remaining 1 tablespoon olive oil.

6 FINAL FERMENTATION

Place the baking pan in a warm (75°F to 80°F), draft-free place for 1 hour. Record the time in your Dough Log, as well as the exact time required for the final fermentation, and set your timer. It should take about 1 hour for the final proofing.

About 30 minutes before you are ready to bake, move the oven rack to one rung below the center.

Preheat the oven to 450°F.

To determine whether the dough is ready to be baked, uncover and gently make a small indentation in the center of the dough with your fingertip. If the indentation slowly and evenly disappears, the bread is ready to bake.

7 BAKING

Randomly place the cherries over the top of the dough, pushing them down until they almost hit the pan. The top should be evenly dotted with cherries.

Transfer the baking pan to the preheated oven and bake until the dough rises slightly and is beginning to brown, about 25 minutes.

Remove from the oven and carefully lift the focaccia from the pan. Immediately place on a cooling rack to cool, as the bread will quickly become soggy if left in the pan.

Let cool slightly and then sift a light dusting of confectioners' sugar over the top. Cut into pieces and serve.

Press cherries evenly into dough.

After cooling, lightly dust with confectioners' sugar.

DOUGH LOG
(Ciabatta)

beginning water temp:
hand mix   82°–84°
(ciabatta dough too wet for stand mixer)

final dough temp:
72°–80°

Dough Type	Measure Water Temp	Mixing Dough Temp	Mixing Finish Mix Time	Rest Time	Bulk Fermentation (1st Proof) 1st Fold	Rest Time	2nd Fold	Rest Time	Divide	Rest Time	Shape	Shape Time	Final Proof Proof Time	Scoring	Baking 450° Baking
Example: Ciabatta Rolls	67°	76°	10:00 am	1 hr		1 hr		1 hr	1:00 pm 4 pieces				45 min–1 hr		1:45 pm
Ciabatta				1 hr		1 hr		1 hr	2 pieces (opt)	1 hr			45 min–1 hr		
Sun-dried Tomato Basil Ciabatta				1 hr		1 hr		1 hr	4 pieces (opt)	1 hr			45 min–1 hr		
Ciabatta Rolls				1 hr		1 hr		1 hr	4 pieces	1 hr			45 min–1 hr		
Vendée Préfou				1 hr		1 hr		1 hr		1 hr			45 min–1 hr		
Soup Bowls				1 hr		1 hr		1 hr	6–8 pieces	1 hr			45 min–1 hr		
Focaccia				1 hr		1 hr		1 hr		1 hr			45 min–1 hr		

Notes: _____

SOURDOUGH BREADS

In recent years, we have come to associate sourdough with the San Francisco sourdough bread; however, not all sourdoughs are highly acidic. At La Farm, we produce sourdough breads that are rounder in flavor and less acidic in taste. The flavor is determined by the baker, and is dependent upon the amount of starter used and the temperature at which the dough is fermented.

Breads made from a natural starter or a liquid *levain* have been made for centuries. All natural starters produce breads that have a chewy interior, a crackling crust, and a long shelf life due to increased moisture and acidity. When using a natural starter, you have time flexibility during final fermentation; you can leave the shaped dough to rise for $2\frac{1}{2}$ to 3 hours, or rest the dough at room temperature for 1 hour then refrigerate loosely covered for 12–16 hours. (Note: the dough will not increase significantly in volume during the first fermentation and will also require additional folding to support the strength of the yeast.)

With understanding of the basics, sourdough breads can easily be turned into a personal statement, with the introduction of your favorite flavors and imaginative shapes.

La Farm Bread
Asiago-Parmesan Bread
Cinnamon Raisin Pecan Bread
Jalapeño-Cheddar Bread
Sesame Semolina Bread
Kalamata Olive Bread
Walnut-Sage Sourdough Bread

LA FARM BREAD QUICK REFERENCE

Once you have learned to make the basic La Farm bread, you can follow this Quick Reference guide for a reminder of the steps involved. It will also work for other breads created from the same basic dough.

- Scale all ingredients.
- Measure the temperature of the water (82°F to 84°F for hand mixing and 65°F to 70°F for using a stand mixer) and note it in your Dough Log (see page 215).
- Mix by hand for 5 to 15 minutes, or with a heavy-duty electric stand mixer for 5 minutes on low speed ("1" on most mixers) and 2 minutes on medium-low speed ("2" on most mixers).
- Measure the dough temperature (72°F to 80°F) and record it in your Dough Log.
- Set aside for the first fermentation for 3 hours, folding the dough each hour.
- Divide and shape.
- Proof for 2½ to 3 hours in a warm (75°F to 80°F), draft-free place or for 12 to 16 hours in the refrigerator.
- Bake at 450°F on a baking stone using the stainless-steel bowl method for 40 minutes.
- Cool and eat, or store at room temperature for up to 3 days.

La Farm Bread

This bread is my "baby." I earned my Master Baker title at the end of my training period at Les Compagnons du Devoir (see page 3) with this classic light country bread, made into a 5-pound loaf. It is a terrific all-purpose bread—toast, sandwiches, on the cheese board, with cold meats—it is the workhorse of all La Farm breads.

Due to the limitations in size of almost all home ovens, I felt that a smaller loaf would be more practical. However, if you look back to page 7 you will find the correct ingredient amounts for the 5-pound loaf, should you have a large enough oven to make it. Because this is our most frequently requested recipe, I will give the instructions for both hand mixing and the stand mixer, so that you might experience making it both ways, even though I strongly recommend that you mix by hand to form your own personal "dough memory."

21.2 ounces	600 grams	4½ cups unbleached, unbromated white bread flour
3.5 ounces	100 grams	¾ cup unbromated whole-wheat bread flour
0.62 ounce	18 grams	1 tablespoon fine sea salt
18.6 ounces	527 grams	2¼ cups plus 1 tablespoon water
6 ounces	170 grams	1 cup plus 2 teaspoons liquid *levain* (see page 20)

1 MEASURING

Scale all of the ingredients.

Take the temperature of the water (it should be 82° to 84°F for hand mixing or 75° to 80°F for a stand mixer) and record it in your Dough Log.

2 MIXING AND KNEADING

To mix by hand:

Place the white and whole-wheat flours in a medium mixing bowl. Add the salt and, using your hands, bring the dry ingredients together. Once blended, quickly form a well in the center of the mix.

Pour half of the water into a mixing bowl, and then pour the *levain* into the water. Gently mix them together. This keeps the *levain* from sticking to the sides of the measuring vessel so that you don't lose any of the yeast, "the spirit of the bakery."

Lionel adding water by hand

Pour levain *into water.*

Add remaining water.

Mix while rotating bowl.

Scrape bowl and fingers often.

Scrape dough onto work surface.

Gradually pour all of the *levain*-water mixture and the remaining water into the well in the center of the flour mixture, rotating the bowl with one hand while simultaneously mixing the wet ingredients into the dry with your hands. Stop often as you work and use the bowl scraper to clean the sides of the bowl and your fingers, making sure that all of the ingredients have been gathered into the dough mass. The bowl should be quite clean and the dough should be soft, slightly wet, and extremely sticky.

Pinch off a bit of dough and taste to see whether you have forgotten the salt. If so, add it now and mix for another minute or so to fully incorporate it into the dough. The dough should just be beginning to come together.

When the dough begins to come together, use your bowl scraper to scrape the dough out onto a lightly floured work surface, making sure not to leave any dough behind. The dough will still be very, very sticky. Do not give in to your temptation to add more flour, since this will alter the flour ratio of the dough. Stick with it; you can do it. The end result will prove it.

Hold your hands, palms facing up, at opposite sides of the dough mass. Slide your fingers under the dough and lift the dough an inch or so from the work surface. Squeeze your thumbs and index fingers together to form

Form "OK" sign and pinch dough.

Pinch through dough.

Continue pinching.

Turn dough and repeat.

Use scraper to incorporate.

a tight "OK" sign through the dough. While holding the "OK" sign, continue to curl your thumbs and index fingers tightly together to pinch off a portion of dough. Working as quickly and smoothly as you can, continue lifting and pinching the dough mass using the same technique, moving up the dough mass in approximately 1-inch to 1½-inch increments until you have gone through the entire mass. You should begin to feel the dough coming together. Remember, your hands are your memory—pay attention to the feel of the dough as it comes together.

Turn the dough a quarter turn and continue lifting, pinching, and turning the dough until it begins to take on an identifiable shape and is less and less sticky. This can take anywhere from 5 to 15 minutes. Remember, do not add any flour to speed the process. Use your scraper to

Lift dough from front.

Quickly fold over.

Repeat 4 to 5 times.

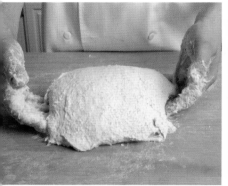

Ball shape forms.

Touch to confirm that it's not sticky.

Take dough temperature.

keep incorporating all of the dough into the mass. The dough is sufficiently kneaded when it can be formed into a ball. You do not want a stiff, dry dough; you want a soft, pliable mass that still holds its shape.

To form the dough into a ball, using both hands, lift it up from the front and fold it over and onto itself in one swift motion, quickly dropping it down on the work surface. Repeat this process 4 to 5 times until a ball forms. At all times, use the scraper to ensure that you are gathering all of the dough.

Touch the dough with the back of your hand to make sure that it is no longer sticky. If it is, use the OK-sign pinching method to knead up and down the dough once or twice more, quickly folding the dough over itself 4 to 5 times. Touch the top of the dough again to be sure that it is no longer sticky. If it is, repeat the folding process until it is no longer sticky.

To mix using a stand mixer:

Place the white and whole-wheat flours and salt in a medium mixing bowl, stirring to blend well.

Using an instant-read thermometer, take the temperature of the water. It should read 65°F to 70°F. Note the temperature in your Dough Log.

Pour levain-water mixture into bowl.

Add dry ingredients.

Mix until incorporated.

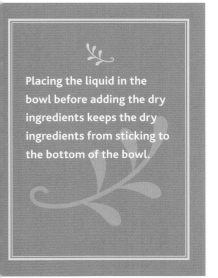

Placing the liquid in the bowl before adding the dry ingredients keeps the dry ingredients from sticking to the bottom of the bowl.

In a small mixing bowl, combine half of the water, and then add the liquid *levain*, stirring to blend well.

Pour the *levain*-water mixture into the bowl of the electric stand mixer. Add the flour-salt mixture. Then, attach the dough hook to the mixer. Begin mixing on low speed ("1" on most mixers) and gradually add the remaining water. Continue to mix until the dough becomes soft and moist, about 5 minutes, frequently stopping the mixer and scraping down the sides and the bottom of the bowl with a bowl scraper or rubber spatula to make sure that all of the ingredients are incorporated into the dough.

Pinch off a bit of dough and taste to see whether you have forgotten the salt. If so, add it now and mix for another minute or so to fully incorporate it into the dough. The dough should just be beginning to come together.

Stop the mixer and move the dough hook out of the way. Using your bowl scraper, scrape down the sides to make sure that all of the ingredients are combined in the dough.

Return the dough hook to its original position. Increase the speed to medium-low ("2" on most mixers) and mix until the dough is soft and smooth with a moist, tacky surface, about 2 minutes.

3   FIRST FERMENTATION

Using an instant-read thermometer, take the temperature of the dough. It should be between 72°F and 80°F. If it is not, immediately make the necessary adjustments (see page 52). Record the temperature of the dough and the time you finished this step in your Dough Log, and note the time the first fermentation should be complete. This dough will be in the first fermentation for 3 hours, with a fold each hour.

Lightly dust a large glass or metal bowl with flour. Transfer the dough to the floured bowl, throw a light film of flour over the top to keep the plastic from sticking, tightly cover with plastic wrap, and place in a warm (75°F to 80°F), draft-free place for 1 hour.

182

Take dough temperature.

Cover with plastic wrap.

Lightly flour top of dough.

Place dough on lightly floured surface.

Pat dough into thick square.

Lift and fold past center.

Lightly pat down seams.

Repeat lifting and folding past center.

Place dough seam side down and cover.

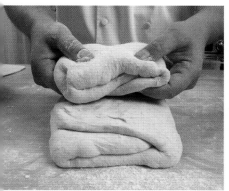

Lift bottom and fold past center.

Lift top and fold past center.

Roll dough over.

Lightly dust a clean work surface with flour.

Because this is a wetter dough, it is "overfolded" to give the dough extra strength (see page 54). Using cupped hands, pat the dough into a thick square. Lift the right corners and fold them *past* the center of the square, lightly patting the seam down. Lift the left corners and fold them *past* the center of the square, overlapping the seams. Again, lightly pat down the seams. Repeat this process with the top two corners and then the bottom two corners.

Lightly flour the bowl and return the dough to it, seam side down. Cover with plastic wrap and return to the warm (75°F to 80°F), draft-free place for another hour.

Repeat the above process and again place the dough in a warm (75°F to 80°F), draft-free place to rise for a third and final hour. At this point the dough should have increased in body and be less sticky.

4–5 DIVIDING AND SHAPING

Lightly dust a clean work surface with flour.

Uncover the dough and use a bowl scraper to scrape the dough onto the floured work surface. If the dough is very sticky, lightly flour your hands, but do not add more flour to the dough. If the dough sticks to the table, use your bench scraper to lift it up; do not pull and stretch the dough.

For one large loaf, lightly press down on the dough with a flat hand, forming the dough into a large rectangle. If you are making two small loaves, lightly press down on the dough with a flat hand, forming the dough into a square. Using a bench scraper, cut the dough in half to form two rectangles.

Lift the dough to make sure that it is not sticking to the work surface. If it is sticking, use the dough scraper to lift it. If it continues to stick, again lightly dust the work surface with flour. Then, carefully shape the dough into 1 large or 2 small *boule*s (see page 56).

Place the dough in a lightly floured *couche* (or strong linen towel) as directed on page 62. (If making 2 small loaves, make a second ridge in the

Place dough on lightly floured couche.

Pull couche *up to hold dough.*

couche to separate them.) Fold the remaining part of the *couche* over the top of the dough.

6 FINAL FERMENTATION

Place the *couche* in a warm (75°F to 80°F), draft-free place for 2½ to 3 hours or, alternatively, proof for 1 hour and then place in the refrigerator for 12 to 16 hours. You should keep a close eye on the dough, because if it is overproofed it will be unusable. If the dough has been refrigerated, let it come to room temperature for 1 hour before baking.

If you are using the stainless-steel bowl method to bake the bread (see page 64), about 30 minutes before you are ready to bake, move one oven rack to the lowest rung and remove the other. Place a large baking stone on the rack and preheat the oven to 450°F. (For all other baking methods, follow the directions given on page 64.)

To determine whether the dough is ready to be baked, uncover it and gently make a small indentation in the center of the dough with your fingertip. If the indentation slowly and evenly disappears, the bread is ready to bake. If not, follow the instructions on page 63 for additional fermentation.

If you are making two loaves and both won't fit under your stainless-steel bowl, cover one with plastic wrap and place in the refrigerator, then bake after the first loaf comes out of the oven.

7 BAKING

Cover a bread peel with a sheet of parchment paper. Using your hands, gently remove the loaf from the *couche* and transfer it, top side up, onto the peel.

Throw a light dusting of flour over the top of the loaf. Working quickly and using a lamé or single-edged razor blade, score the top of the loaf (see page 65). Cut in quick, decisive slashes, marking into the dough by no more than ⅛ inch.

Lightly flour top of loaf.

Score loaf.

Place on hot stone.

Cover for first 10 minutes of baking.

Carefully slide the loaf on the parchment paper onto the center of the stone, taking care not to touch the hot surface. If you are baking two loaves together, take care that they don't "kiss" (touch and get stuck together while baking).

Quickly cover the loaf with the stainless-steel mixing bowl. Immediately close the oven door. Bake for 10 minutes; then lift the edge of the bowl with the tip of a small knife and use oven mitts to carefully remove the hot bowl. Continue to bake until the bread is a deep golden brown, about 30 minutes more. (It is a good idea to check after the bread has been baking for about 20 minutes to make sure it is browning evenly. If not, rotate the bread.) If you are concerned about the bread's doneness, insert an instant-read thermometer from the bottom of the bread into the center. If it reads 185°F to 210°F the bread is fully baked.

Transfer the loaf to a cooling rack and let it cool for at least 1 hour before cutting with a serrated knife or wrapping for storage.

Finished baking

Asiago-Parmesan Bread

MAKES 1 *BOULE*

In my travels as a consultant, I worked with Missy's company (before she was my wife) in Virginia. They wanted a new twist on a hot sandwich made with artisanal bread that would really set them apart from others. Missy's boss, Dick Ripp, had a great saying—"Think Ben and Jerry's"—and thought that bigger chunks of savory, salty hard cheeses baked in a sourdough bread would do the trick for his bread. I chose the sharpness of Parmesan and the creaminess of Asiago, both cheeses that wouldn't melt away as the bread baked, and developed this very popular bread. It has since been recognized by a number of national publications, including *Saveur* magazine, as one of the best breads in the country. I hope that your version becomes a family favorite.

16 ounces	454 grams	3½ cups unbleached, unbromated white bread flour
0.21 ounce	6 grams	1 teaspoon fine sea salt
10 ounces	285 grams	1 cup plus 3 tablespoons plus 1 teaspoon water
3.5 ounces	100 grams	½ cup liquid *levain* (see page 20)
2.3 ounces	65 grams	about ½ cup ¼-by-½-inch pieces Asiago cheese, at room temperature
2.3 ounces	65 grams	about ½ cup ¼-by-½-inch pieces Parmesan cheese, at room temperature

1 MEASURING

Scale all of the ingredients.

Using an instant-read thermometer, take the temperature of the water. It should read between 65°F and 70°F. Record it in your Dough Log.

2 MIXING AND KNEADING

(These instructions are for using a stand mixer; see page 177 for instructions for mixing by hand.)

Place the flour and salt in a medium mixing bowl, stirring to blend well.

Pour half of the water into a mixing bowl, and then add the liquid *levain*, stirring to blend.

Pour the *levain*-water mixture into the bowl of the electric stand mixer. Add the flour-salt mixture. Then, attach the dough hook to the mixer. Begin mixing on low speed ("1" on most mixers) and gradually add the remaining water. Continue to mix until the dough becomes soft and moist, about 5 minutes, frequently stopping the mixer and scraping down the sides of the bowl with a bowl scraper or rubber spatula to make sure that all of the ingredients are incorporated into the dough.

Taste the dough to see whether you have forgotten the salt. If so, add it now and mix for another minute. The dough should just be beginning to come together.

Stop the mixer and move the dough hook out of the way. Using your bowl scraper, scrape down the sides to make sure that all of the ingredients are combined in the dough.

Return the dough hook to its original position. Increase the speed to medium-low ("2" on most mixers) and mix until the dough is soft and smooth, with a moist, tacky surface, about 2 minutes.

Stop the mixer and move the dough hook out of the way. Using your bowl scraper, scrape down the sides of the bowl to make sure that all of the ingredients are combined in the dough.

Return the dough hook to its original position. Add the Asiago and Parmesan cheeses, reduce the speed to low, and continue to mix until the cheeses are completely incorporated into the dough.

3 FIRST FERMENTATION

Using an instant-read thermometer, take the temperature of the dough. It should be between 72°F and 80°F. If it is not, immediately make the necessary adjustments (see page 52). Record the temperature of the dough and the time you finished this step in the Dough Log, and note the time the first fermentation should be completed. This dough will be in the first fermentation for 3 hours, with a fold each hour.

Lightly dust a large glass or metal bowl with flour. Transfer the dough to the floured bowl, throw a light film of flour over the top to keep the plastic from sticking, tightly cover the bowl with plastic wrap, and place in a warm (75°F to 80°F), draft-free place for 1 hour.

Lightly dust a clean work surface with flour.

Uncover the dough and place it on the floured work surface. If the dough is very sticky, lightly flour your hands, but do not add more flour to the dough. If the dough sticks to the table, use your bench scraper to lift it up; do not pull and stretch the dough. Let the dough rest for 30 seconds. Using cupped hands, pat the dough into a thick square. Lift the right corners and fold them into the center of the square, lightly patting the seam down. Lift the left corners and fold them into the center of the square, again lightly patting the seam down. Repeat this process with the top two corners and then the bottom two corners, meeting in the middle of the square and lightly patting down the seams.

Lightly flour the bowl and return the dough to it, seam side down. Cover with plastic wrap and return to a warm (75°F to 80°F), draft-free place for another hour.

Repeat the above process and again place the dough in a warm (75°F to 80°F), draft-free place to rise for a third and final hour. At this point the dough should have increased in body and be less sticky.

4 DIVIDING

Since you are making just 1 loaf, skip to Step 5!

5 SHAPING

Lightly dust a clean work surface with flour.

Uncover the dough and use a bowl scraper to scrape the dough onto the floured work surface. If the dough is very sticky, lightly flour your hands, but do not add more flour to the dough. If the dough sticks to the table, use your bench scraper to lift it up; do not pull and stretch the dough.

Using a flat hand, lightly press the dough into a thick rectangle. Lift the dough to make sure that it is not sticking to the work surface. If it is sticking, use the dough scraper to lift it. If it continues to stick, again lightly dust the work surface with flour. Then, carefully shape the dough into a *boule* (see page 56).

Lightly dust a *banneton* with flour. Place the dough in the *banneton*, seam side up. Throw a light film of flour over the top to keep the plastic from sticking, and cover tightly with plastic wrap.

6 FINAL FERMENTATION

Place the *banneton* in a warm (75°F to 80°F), draft-free place for 2½ to 3 hours or, alternatively, proof for 1 hour and then place in the refrigerator for 12 to 16 hours. If the dough has been refrigerated, let it come to room temperature for 1 hour before baking.

If you are using the stainless-steel bowl method to bake the bread (see

Lightly flour banneton.

Place dough seam side up.

page 64), about 30 minutes before you are ready to bake, move one oven rack to the lowest rung and remove the other. Place a large baking stone on the rack and preheat the oven to 450°F. (For all other baking methods, follow the directions on page 64.)

To determine whether the dough is ready to be baked, uncover and gently make a small indentation in the center of the dough with your fingertip. If the indentation slowly and evenly disappears, the bread is ready to bake. If not, follow the instructions on page 63 for additional fermentation.

7 BAKING

Place a piece of parchment paper on a bread peel. Then, turn the dough onto the peel, bottom side up.

Working quickly and using a lamé or single-edged razor blade, score the top of the loaf (see page 65). Cut in quick, decisive slashes, marking into the dough by no more than ⅛ inch.

Slide the loaf on the parchment paper onto the center of the stone, taking care not to touch the hot surface. Quickly cover with the stainless-steel mixing bowl. Immediately close the oven door. Bake for 10 minutes; then, lift the edge of the bowl with the tip of a small knife and use oven

Turn dough on parchment.

Bottom-side up

Start at top to score.

Then score again around loaf.

mitts to carefully remove the hot bowl. Continue to bake until the bread is a deep golden brown, about 30 minutes more. (It is a good idea to check after the bread has been baking for about 20 minutes to make sure it is browning evenly. If not, rotate the bread.) If you are concerned about the bread's doneness, insert an instant-read thermometer from the bottom of the bread into the center. If it reads 185°F to 210°F, the bread is fully baked.

Cover for first 10 minutes of baking.

Transfer the loaf to a cooling rack and let it cool for at least 1 hour before cutting with a serrated knife or wrapping for storage.

Note: I leave the dough on parchment paper when baking breads with oily ingredients, such as cheese, on a baking stone to prevent the oils from soaking into the stone.

Finished baking

Cinnamon Raisin Pecan Bread

MAKES 2 SMALL BÂTARDS

I first learned about using cinnamon in bread doughs when working with Nancy Silverton, one of America's premier bakers. In France, cinnamon is not used very often, and it took Nancy to convince me of its importance to baking in this country

The addition of pecans to this slightly sweet loaf makes it a wonderful bread for breakfast, toasted or not, or toasted to serve with a cheese platter.

11.03 ounces	315 grams	2½ cups unbleached, unbromated white bread flour
2.28 ounces	65 grams	½ cup unbromated whole-wheat bread flour
0.31 ounce	9 grams	1½ teaspoons fine sea salt
10 ounces	285 grams	1 cup plus 3 tablespoons plus 1 teaspoon water
3.5 ounces	100 grams	½ cup liquid *levain* (see page 20)
2.75 ounces	80 grams	about ½ cup organic raisins
2 ounces	56 grams	about ½ cup chopped toasted pecans (see Note, page 196)
0.08 ounce	2 grams	1 teaspoon ground cinnamon

1 MEASURING

Scale all of the ingredients.

Using an instant-read thermometer, take the temperature of the water. It should read between 65˚F and 70˚F. Record it in your Dough Log.

2 MIXING AND KNEADING

(These instructions are for using a stand mixer; see page 177 for instructions for mixing by hand.)

Place the white and whole-wheat flours and salt in a mixing bowl, stirring to blend well.

Pour half of the water into a mixing bowl, and then add the liquid *levain*, stirring to blend.

Pour the *levain*-water mixture into the bowl of the electric stand mixer. Add the flour-salt mixture. Then, attach the dough hook to the mixer. Begin mixing on low speed ("1" on most mixers) and gradually add the remaining water. Continue to mix until the dough becomes soft and moist, about 5 minutes, frequently stopping the mixer and scraping down the sides and bottom of the bowl with a bowl scraper (or rubber spatula) to make sure that all of the ingredients are incorporated into the dough.

Taste the dough to see whether you have forgotten the salt. If so, add it now and mix for another minute. The dough should just be beginning to come together.

Stop the mixer and move the dough hook out of the way. Using your bowl scraper, scrape down the sides to make sure that all of the ingredients are combined in the dough.

Return the dough hook to its original position. Increase the speed to medium-low ("2" on most mixers) and mix until the dough is soft and smooth, with a moist, tacky surface, about 2 minutes.

Stop the mixer and move the dough hook out of the way. Using your bowl scraper, scrape down the sides of the bowl to make sure that all of the ingredients are combined in the dough.

Return the dough hook to its original position. Add the raisins, pecans, and cinnamon, reduce the speed to low, and continue to mix until everything is completely incorporated into the dough.

3 FIRST FERMENTATION

Using an instant-read thermometer, take the temperature of the dough. It should be between 72°F and 80°F. If it is not, immediately make the necessary adjustments (see page 52). Record the temperature of the dough and the time you finished this step in the Dough Log, and note the time the first fermentation should be completed. This dough will be in the first fermentation for 3 hours, with a fold each hour.

Lightly dust a large glass or metal bowl with flour. Transfer the dough to the floured bowl, throw a light film of flour over the top to keep the plastic from sticking, tightly cover the bowl with plastic wrap, and place in a warm (75°F to 80°F), draft-free place for 1 hour.

Lightly dust a clean work surface with flour.

Uncover the dough and place it on the floured work surface. If the dough is very sticky, lightly flour your hands, but do not add more flour to the dough. If the dough sticks to the table, use your bench scraper to lift it up; do not pull and stretch the dough. Let the dough rest for 30 seconds. Using cupped hands, pat the dough into a thick square. Lift the right corners and fold them into the center of the square, lightly patting the seam down. Lift the left corners and fold them into the center of the square, again lightly patting the seam down. Repeat this process with the top two corners and then the bottom two corners, meeting in the middle of the square and lightly patting down the seams.

Lightly flour the bowl and return the dough to it, seam side down. Cover with plastic wrap and return to the warm (75°F to 80°F), draft-free place for another hour.

Repeat the above process and again place the dough in a warm (75°F to

80˚F), draft-free place to rise for a third and final hour. At this point the dough should have increased in body and be less sticky.

4–5 DIVIDING AND SHAPING

Lightly dust a clean work surface with flour.

Transfer the dough to the floured surface and, using a flat hand, lightly press the dough into a thick rectangle. Lift the dough to make sure that it is not sticking to the work surface. If it is sticking, use the dough scraper to lift it. If it continues to stick, again lightly dust the work surface with flour.

Divide the dough into 2 equal pieces. Shape each piece into a *bâtard* (see page 60).

Place the first baguette in a lightly floured *couche* (or a strong linen towel) as directed on page 62. It does not matter whether you have the smooth side up or down for the final proofing as long as you bake it smooth side up. Make a second ridge next to the first loaf and place the second loaf against it. Fold the remaining *couche* over the top.

6 FINAL FERMENTATION

Place the *couche* in a warm (about 75˚F to 80˚F), draft-free place for 2½ to 3 hours or, alternatively, proof for 1 hour and then place in the refrigerator for 12 to 16 hours. You should keep a close eye on the dough, because if it is overproofed it will be unusable. If the dough has been refrigerated, let it come to room temperature for 1 hour before baking.

If you are using the stainless-steel bowl method to bake the bread (see page 64), about 30 minutes before you are ready to bake, move one oven rack to the lowest rung and remove the other. Place a large baking stone on the rack and preheat the oven to 450˚F. (For all other baking methods, follow the directions on page 64.)

To determine whether the dough is ready to be baked, uncover and gently make a small indentation in the center of the dough with your fingertip. If the indentation slowly and evenly disappears, the bread is ready to bake. If not, follow the instructions on page 63 for additional fermentation.

7 BAKING

Lightly dust a bread peel with flour and carefully transfer the loaves to it, top side up.

Throw a light dusting of flour over the top of the loaf. Working quickly and using a lamé or single-edged razor blade, score the top of each loaf (see page 65). Cut in quick, decisive slashes, marking into the dough by no more than ⅛ inch.

Carefully transfer loaves.

Lightly floured bread peel

Lightly dust top of loaves.

Score top of each loaf.

Remove cover after first 10 minutes of baking.

Finished baking

Slide the loaves onto the center of the stone, taking care not to touch the hot surface and making sure that the loaves are not touching. Quickly cover with the stainless-steel mixing bowl. Immediately close the oven door. Bake for 10 minutes; then, lift the edge of the bowl with the tip of a small knife and use oven mitts to carefully remove the hot bowl. Continue to bake until the bread is a deep golden brown, about 30 minutes more. (It is a good idea to check after the bread has been baking for about 20 minutes to make sure it is browning evenly. If not, rotate the bread.) If you are concerned about the bread's doneness, insert an instant-read thermometer from the bottom of the bread into the center. If it reads 185°F to 210°F the bread is fully baked.

Transfer the loaf to a cooling rack and let it cool for at least 1 hour before cutting with a serrated knife or wrapping for storage.

Note: Toasted nuts have a richer flavor and keep their shape better when mixed into dough. All nuts will generally toast to an aromatic golden brown in about 5 minutes in a 350°F oven. Check frequently as the oils they contain can cause them to burn quickly.

Jalapeño-Cheddar Bread

MAKES 1 BÂTARD

Since my Asiago-Parmesan Bread is so popular at La Farm, I took the same basic idea and added some spice to it in honor of my many Hispanic friends. In the bakery, we always feature it for Cinco de Mayo. It is a terrific summer bread and is the base for our Monte Cristo Chicken *Tartine*. And, believe it or not, sliced very thin and toasted, it also makes a great replacement for chips as a dipper for guacamole and salsas.

16 ounces	454 grams	3½ cups unbleached, unbromated white bread flour
0.21 ounce	6 grams	1 teaspoon fine sea salt
10 ounces	285 grams	1 cup plus 3 tablespoons plus 1 teaspoon water
3.5 ounces	100 grams	½ cup liquid *levain* (see page 20)
4 ounces	112 grams	about 1 cup shredded sharp cheddar cheese, at room temperature, plus an additional 2 ounces / 56 grams (½ cup) for topping
0.5 ounce	15 grams	2 tablespoons minced jalapeño

1 MEASURING

Scale all of the ingredients.

Using an instant-read thermometer, take the temperature of the water. It should read between 65°F and 70°F. Record it in your Dough Log.

2 MIXING AND KNEADING

(These instructions are for using a stand mixer; see page 177 for instructions for mixing by hand.)

Place the flour and salt in a medium mixing bowl, stirring to blend well.

Pour half of the water into a mixing bowl, and then add the liquid *levain*, stirring to blend.

Pour the *levain*-water mixture into the bowl of the electric stand mixer. Add the flour-salt mixture. Then, attach the dough hook to the mixer. Begin mixing on low speed ("1" on most mixers) and gradually add the remaining water. Continue to mix until the dough becomes soft and moist, about 5 minutes, frequently stopping the mixer and scraping down the sides and bottom of the bowl with a bowl scraper or rubber spatula to ensure that all of the ingredients are incorporated into the dough.

Taste the dough to see whether you have forgotten the salt. If so, add it now and mix for another minute. The dough should just be beginning to come together.

Stop the mixer and move the dough hook out of the way. Using your bowl scraper, scrape down the sides to make sure that all of the ingredients are combined in the dough.

Return the dough hook to its original position. Increase the speed to medium-low ("2" on most mixers) and mix until the dough is soft and smooth, with a moist, tacky surface, about 2 minutes.

Add the 4 ounces/112 grams cheddar along with the jalapeño, reduce the speed to low, and continue to mix until the cheese is completely incorporated into the dough.

3 FIRST FERMENTATION

Using an instant-read thermometer, take the temperature of the dough. It should be between 72°F and 80°F. If it is not, immediately make the necessary adjustments (see page 52). Record the temperature of the dough and the time you finished this step in the Dough Log, and note the time the first fermentation should be completed. This dough will be in the first fermentation for 3 hours, with a fold after each hour.

Lightly dust a large glass or metal bowl with flour. Transfer the dough to the floured bowl, throw a light film of flour over the top to keep the plastic from sticking, tightly cover the bowl with plastic wrap, and place in a warm (75°F to 80°F), draft-free place for 1 hour.

Mise en place

Lightly dust a clean work surface with flour.

Uncover the dough and place it on the floured work surface. If the dough is very sticky, lightly flour your hands, but do not add more flour to the dough. If the dough sticks to the table, use your bench scraper to lift it up; do not pull and stretch the dough. Let the dough rest for 30 seconds. Using cupped hands, pat the dough into a thick square. Lift the right corners and fold them into the center of the square, lightly patting the seam down. Lift the left corners and fold them into the center of the square, again lightly patting the seam down. Repeat this process with each of the top two corners and then the bottom two corners, meeting in the middle of the square and lightly patting down the seams.

Lightly flour the bowl and return the dough to it, seam side down. Cover with plastic wrap and return to the warm (75°F to 80°F), draft-free place for another hour.

Repeat the above process and again place the dough in a warm (75°F to 80°F), draft-free place to rise for a third and final hour. At this point the dough should have increased in body and be less sticky.

4 DIVIDING
Since you are making just 1 loaf, skip to Step 5!

5 SHAPING
Lightly dust a clean work surface with flour.

Transfer the dough to the floured surface and, using a flat hand, lightly press the dough into a thick rectangle. Lift the dough to make sure that it is not sticking to the work surface. If it is sticking, use the dough scraper to lift it. If it continues to stick, again lightly dust the work surface with flour. Then, carefully shape the dough into a *bâtard* (see page 60).

6 FINAL FERMENTATION
Place the dough in a lightly floured *couche* (or a strong linen towel) as directed on page 62. Fold the remaining part of the *couche* over the top of the dough.

Place the *couche* in a warm (75°F to 80°F), draft-free place for 2½ to 3 hours or, alternatively, proof for 1 hour and then place in the refrigerator for 12 to 16 hours. You should keep a close eye on the dough, because if it is overproofed it will be unusable. If the dough has been refrigerated, let it come to room temperature for 1 hour before baking.

If you are using the stainless-steel bowl method to bake the bread (see page 64), about 30 minutes before you are ready to bake, move one oven rack to the lowest rung and remove the other. Place a large baking stone on the rack and preheat the oven to 450°F. (For all other baking methods, follow the directions on page 64.)

To determine whether the dough is ready to be baked, uncover and gently make a small indentation in the center of the dough with your fingertip. If the indentation slowly and evenly disappears, the bread is ready to bake. If not, follow the instructions on page 63 for additional fermentation.

7 **BAKING**

Place a piece of parchment paper on a bread peel. Then, turn the dough onto the peel, top side up.

Working quickly and using a lamé or single-edged razor blade, score the top of the loaf (see page 65). Cut in quick, decisive slashes, marking into the dough by no more than ⅛ inch. Quickly sprinkle the remaining 2 ounces/56 grams cheddar over the top of the dough.

Sprinkle cheese over top.

Slide the loaf on the parchment paper onto the center of the stone, taking care not to touch the hot surface. Quickly cover with the stainless-steel mixing bowl. Immediately close the oven door. Bake for 10 minutes; then, lift the edge of the bowl with the tip of a small knife and use oven mitts to carefully remove the hot bowl. Continue to bake until the bread is a deep golden brown, about 30 minutes more. (It is a good idea to check after the bread has been baking for about 20 minutes to make sure it is browning evenly. If not, rotate the bread.) If you are concerned about the bread's doneness, insert an instant-read thermometer from the bottom of the bread into the center. If it reads 185°F to 210°F the bread is fully baked.

Transfer the loaf to a cooling rack and let it cool for at least 1 hour before cutting with a serrated knife or wrapping for storage.

Note: Don't hesitate to experiment with the amount or variety of chile you add to this bread; it really is a matter of taste. But whatever type you use, remember that the heat is in the seeds and ribs, and you should always wash your hands carefully after working with chiles as you can burn your skin or your eyes should you rub them.

Sesame Semolina Bread

MAKES 1 S-SHAPED BAGUETTE

My first exposure to semolina flour was in Italian bakeries in New York and New Jersey, where I watched bakers smoothly slide their loaves into the oven after coating the bottom of the dough with semolina. I found the bread somewhat bland, so I added sesame seeds to the dough for added texture and nuttiness and as a topping to give an extra crunch to the crust. This is a great sandwich bread, particularly toasted for BLTs, and is perfect served alongside a big bowl of pasta.

11.03 ounces	315 grams	2½ cups unbleached, unbromated white bread flour
1.5 ounces	43 grams	¼ cup semolina flour
0.31 ounce	9 grams	1½ teaspoons fine sea salt
1 ounce	28 grams	2 tablespoons unsalted butter, at room temperature
7.35 ounces	210 grams	¾ cup plus 1 tablespoon plus 2 teaspoons water
3.5 ounces	100 grams	½ cup liquid *levain* (see page 20)
1.5 ounces	45 grams	about ⅓ cup sesame seeds, plus 0.5 ounce/14 grams (2 tablespoons) for the topping

1 MEASURING

Scale all of the ingredients.

Using an instant-read thermometer, take the temperature of the water. It should read between 65°F and 70°F. Record it in your Dough Log.

2 MIXING AND KNEADING

(These instructions are for using a stand mixer; see page 177 for instructions for mixing by hand.)

Place the white and semolina flours and salt in a mixing bowl, stirring to blend well. Add the butter and incorporate into the dough.

Pour half of the water into a mixing bowl, and then add the liquid *levain*, stirring to blend.

Pour the *levain*-water mixture into the bowl of the electric stand mixer. Add the flour-butter mixture. Attach the dough hook to the mixer. Begin mixing on low speed ("1" on most mixers) and continue to mix until the dough becomes soft and moist, about 5 minutes, frequently stopping the mixer and scraping down the sides and bottom of the bowl with a bowl scraper or rubber spatula to be sure that all of the ingredients are incorporated into the dough.

Taste the dough to see whether you have forgotten the salt. If so, add it now and mix for another minute. The dough should just be beginning to come together.

Stop the mixer and move the dough hook out of the way. Using your bowl scraper, scrape down the sides to make sure that all of the ingredients are combined in the dough.

Return the dough hook to its original position. Increase the speed to medium-low ("2" on most mixers) and mix until the dough is soft and smooth, with a moist, tacky surface, about 2 minutes.

Add the 1.5 ounces/45 grams sesame seeds, reduce the speed to low, and continue to mix until they are completely incorporated into the dough.

3 FIRST FERMENTATION

Using an instant-read thermometer, take the temperature of the dough. It should be between 72°F and 80°F. If it is not, immediately make the necessary adjustments (see page 52). Record the temperature of the dough and the time you finished this step in the Dough Log, and note the time the first fermentation should be completed. This dough will be in the first fermentation for 3 hours, with a fold each hour.

Lightly dust a large glass (or metal) bowl with flour. Transfer the dough to the floured bowl, throw a light film of flour over the top to keep the plastic from sticking, tightly cover with plastic wrap, and place in a warm (75°F to 80°F), draft-free place for 1 hour.

Lightly dust a clean work surface with flour.

Uncover the dough and, using a bowl scraper, scrape the dough onto the floured work surface. If the dough is very sticky, lightly flour your hands, but do not add more flour to the dough. If the dough sticks to the table, use your bench scraper to lift it up; do not pull and stretch the dough. Let the dough rest for 30 seconds. Using cupped hands, pat the dough into a thick square. Lift the right corners and fold them into the center of the square, lightly patting the seam down. Lift the left corners and fold them into the center of the square, again lightly patting the seam down. Repeat this process with the top two corners and then the bottom two corners, meeting in the middle of the square and lightly patting down the seams.

Lightly flour the bowl and return the dough to it, seam side down. Cover with plastic wrap and return to the warm (75°F to 80°F), draft-free place for another hour.

Repeat the above process and again place the dough in a warm (75°F to 80°F), draft-free place to rise for a third and final hour. At this point the dough should have increased in body and be less sticky.

4 DIVIDING

Since you are making just 1 loaf, skip to Step 5!

5 SHAPING

Line a baking sheet with a silicone liner or parchment paper. Set aside.

Lightly dust a clean work surface with flour.

Transfer the dough to the floured surface and, using a flat hand, lightly press the dough into a thick rectangle. Lift the dough to make sure that it is not sticking to the work surface. If it is sticking, use the dough scraper to lift it. If it continues to stick, again lightly dust the work surface with flour. Then, carefully shape the dough into a baguette (see page 58).

Place the remaining 0.5 ounce/14 grams sesame seeds on a baking pan and carefully roll the dough in them to generously cover.

Carefully roll dough in seeds.

Elongate dough and curl tips.

Continue in opposite directions.   *Make an "S" shape.*

Gently curl each end of the loaf in opposite directions to make an "S" shape. Turn the shaped dough onto the lined baking sheet, seam side down. Cover lightly with a linen cloth.

6 FINAL FERMENTATION

Place the baking sheet in a warm (75°F to 80°F), draft-free place for 2½ to 3 hours or, alternatively, proof for 1 hour and then place in the refrigerator for 12 to 16 hours. If the dough has been refrigerated, let it come to room temperature for 1 hour before baking.

If you are using the stainless-steel bowl method to bake the bread (see page 64), about 30 minutes before you are ready to bake, move one oven rack to the lowest rung and remove the other. Place a large baking stone on the rack and preheat the oven to 450°F. (For all other baking methods, follow the directions on page 64.)

To determine whether the dough is ready to be baked, uncover and gently make a small indentation in the center of the dough with your fingertip. If the indentation slowly and evenly disappears, the bread is ready to bake. If not, follow the instructions on page 63 for additional fermentation.

Placed on lined baking sheet.   *Cover for first 10 minutes of baking.*

BAKING

Lightly dust a bread peel with flour and carefully transfer the loaf to it, top side up. Slide the loaf onto the center of the stone, taking care not to touch the hot surface.

Quickly cover with the stainless-steel mixing bowl. Immediately close the oven door. Bake for 10 minutes; then, lift the edge of the bowl with the tip of a small knife and use oven mitts to carefully remove the hot bowl. Continue to bake until the bread is a deep golden brown, about 30 minutes more. (It is a good idea to check after the bread has been baking for about 20 minutes to make sure it is browning evenly. If not, rotate the bread.) If you are concerned about the bread's doneness, insert an instant-read thermometer from the bottom of the bread into the center. If it reads 185°F to 210°F the bread is fully baked.

Transfer the loaf to a cooling rack and let it cool for at least 1 hour before cutting with a serrated knife or wrapping for storage.

Kalamata Olive Bread

MAKES 1 BOULE

One of the stops on my Guild Tour de France was Nîmes, where a *fougasse* (a French take on focaccia) with olives is the bread of choice. When I began baking in the United States, I added olives to my sourdough bread. It was instantly popular, which did not make me happy because the only olives available still had their pits. I spent more time pitting olives than making bread—not a fun job! Thankfully, pitted kalamata olives are now readily available in the United States. Try this bread to make a tuna Niçoise sandwich—a very French lunch.

3.23 ounces	92 grams	about ¾ cup pitted kalamata olives, well drained and patted dry (see Note, page 210)
2.28 ounces	65 grams	½ cup unbromated whole-wheat bread flour, plus .35 ounce/10 grams (2 teaspoons) for the olives
11.03 ounces	315 grams	2½ cups unbleached, unbromated white bread flour
0.21 ounce	6 grams	1 teaspoon fine sea salt
9.5 ounces	270 grams	1 cup plus 3 tablespoons plus 1 teaspoon water
3.5 ounces	100 grams	½ cup liquid *levain* (see page 20)

Cornmeal for dusting

1 MEASURING

Scale all of the ingredients.

Using a chef's knife, cut each olive into 6 pieces and place them in a small bowl. Add the .35 ounce/10 grams whole-wheat flour and stir to lightly coat each piece of olive, allowing the flour to absorb any remaining moisture. Set aside.

Using an instant-read thermometer, take the temperature of the water. It should read between 65°F and 70°F. Record it in your Dough Log.

Lightly flour olives.

2 MIXING AND KNEADING

(These instructions are for using a stand mixer; see page 177 for instructions for mixing by hand.)

Place the 11.03 ounces/315 grams whole-wheat flour, the white flour, and the salt in a medium mixing bowl, stirring to blend well.

Pour half of the water into a mixing bowl, and then add the liquid *levain*, stirring to blend.

Pour the *levain*-water mixture into the bowl of the electric stand mixer. Add the flour-salt mixture. Then, attach the dough hook to the mixer. Begin mixing on low speed ("1" on most mixers) and continue to mix until the dough becomes soft and moist, about 5 minutes, frequently stopping the mixer and scraping down the sides of the bowl with a bowl scraper or rubber spatula to make sure that all of the ingredients are incorporated into the dough.

Taste the dough to see whether you have forgotten the salt. If so, add it now and mix for another minute. The dough should just be beginning to come together.

Stop the mixer and move the dough hook out of the way. Using your bowl scraper, scrape down the sides to make sure that all of the ingredients are combined in the dough.

Return the dough hook to its original position. Increase the speed to medium-low ("2" on most mixers) and mix until the dough is soft and smooth, with a moist, tacky surface, about 2 minutes.

Add the floured olives, reduce the speed to low, and continue to mix until the olives are completely incorporated into the dough.

3 FIRST FERMENTATION

Using an instant-read thermometer, take the temperature of the dough. It should be between 72°F and 80°F. If it is not, immediately make the necessary adjustments (see page 52). Record the temperature of the dough and the time you finished this step in the Dough Log, and note the time the first fermentation should be completed. This dough will be in the first fermentation for 3 hours, with a fold each hour.

Lightly dust a large glass or metal bowl with flour. Transfer the dough to the floured bowl, throw a light film of flour over the top to keep the plastic from sticking, tightly cover the bowl with plastic wrap, and place in a warm (75°F to 80°F), draft-free place for 1 hour.

Lightly dust a clean work surface with flour.

Uncover the dough and place it on the floured work surface. If the dough is very sticky, lightly flour your hands, but do not add more flour to the dough. If the dough sticks to the table, use your bench scraper to lift it up; do not pull and stretch the dough. Let the dough rest for 30 seconds. Using cupped hands, pat the dough into a thick square. Lift the right corners and fold them into the center of the square, lightly patting the seam down. Lift the left corners and fold them into the center of the square, again lightly patting the seam down. Repeat this process with the top two corners and then the bottom two corners, meeting in the middle of the square and lightly patting down the seams.

Lightly flour the bowl and return the dough to it, seam side down. Cover with plastic wrap and return to the warm (75°F to 80°F), draft-free place for another hour.

Repeat the above process and again place the dough in a warm (75°F to 80°F), draft-free place to rise for a third and final hour. At this point the dough should have increased in body and be less sticky.

4 DIVIDING
Since you are making just 1 loaf, skip to Step 5!

5 SHAPING
Lightly dust a clean work surface with flour.

Transfer the dough to the floured surface and, using a flat hand, lightly press the dough into a thick rectangle. Lift the dough to make sure that it is not sticking to the work surface. If it is sticking, use the dough scraper to lift it. If it continues to stick, again lightly dust the work surface with flour. Then, carefully shape the dough into a *boule* (see page 56).

Lightly dust a *banneton* with flour. Place the dough in the *banneton*, seam side up. Throw a light film of flour over the top to keep the plastic from sticking, and cover tightly with plastic wrap.

6 FINAL FERMENTATION
Place the *banneton* in a warm (75°F to 80°F), draft-free place for 2½ to 3 hours or, alternatively, proof for 1 hour and then place in the refrigerator for 12 to 16 hours. If the dough has been refrigerated, let it come to room temperature for 1 hour before baking.

If you are using the stainless-steel bowl method to bake the bread (see page 64), about 30 minutes before you are ready to bake, move one oven rack to the lowest rung and remove the other. Place a large baking stone on the rack and preheat the oven to 450°F. (For all other baking methods, follow the directions on page 64.)

To determine whether the dough is ready to be baked, uncover and gently make a small indentation in the center of the dough with your fingertip. If the indentation slowly and evenly disappears, the bread is ready to bake. If not, follow the instructions on page 63 for additional fermentation.

Working quickly, score top.

Score all around top.

7 BAKING

Lightly dust a bread peel with cornmeal and carefully transfer the loaf to it, top side up.

Working quickly and using a lamé or single-edged razor blade, score the top of the loaf (see page 65). Cut in quick, decisive slashes, marking into the dough by no more than 1/8 inch.

Slide the loaf onto the center of the stone, taking care not to touch the hot surface. Quickly cover with the stainless-steel mixing bowl. Immediately close the oven door. Bake for 10 minutes; then, lift the edge of the bowl with the tip of a small knife and use oven mitts to carefully remove the hot bowl. Continue to bake until the bread is a deep golden brown, about 30 minutes more. (It is a good idea to check after the bread has been baking for about 20 minutes to make sure it is browning evenly. If not, rotate the bread.) If you are concerned about the bread's doneness, insert an instant-read thermometer from the bottom of the bread into the center. If it reads 185°F to 210°F the bread is fully baked.

Transfer the loaf to a cooling rack and let it cool for at least 1 hour before cutting with a serrated knife or wrapping for storage.

Note: Kalamata olives are deep black Greek olives that are packed in either oil or vinegar. I use those packed in vinegar, but the oil-packed would work also. Just make sure that you pat them as dry as possible. And, buy pitted if you can!

Walnut-Sage Sourdough Bread

MAKES 1 BOULE

Walnut bread was the first style of bread that I wanted to bring home to my parents during my guild training in France, particularly because it is often an accompaniment to the cheeses they enjoy at the end of their meal. Years later, when I was demonstrating a walnut bread for a bakery in Brooklyn, the bakers had the great idea to add some fresh herbs to the mix. We threw in some sage and it turned out to be one of my favorite combinations. We offer the bread at La Farm Bakery during the holidays to serve with stews and other heartier foods and on cheese platters. I always use sage, but you can use any fresh herb you like.

11.03 ounces	315 grams	2½ cups unbleached, unbromated white bread flour
2.28 ounces	65 grams	½ cup unbromated whole-wheat bread flour
0.31 ounce	9 grams	1½ teaspoons fine sea salt
9.88 ounces	280 grams	1¼ cups water
3.5 ounces	100 grams	½ cup liquid *levain* (see page 20)
4 ounces	112 grams	1 cup toasted walnut pieces (see Note, page 196)
0.16 ounce	4 grams	2 tablespoons chopped fresh sage leaves

Cornmeal for dusting

1 MEASURING

Scale all of the ingredients.

Using an instant-read thermometer, take the temperature of the water. It should read between 65°F and 70°F. Record it in your Dough Log.

2 MIXING AND KNEADING

(These instructions are for using a stand mixer; see page 177 for instructions for mixing by hand.)

Place the white and whole-wheat flours and salt in a mixing bowl, stirring to blend well.

Pour half of the water into a mixing bowl, and then add the liquid *levain*, stirring to blend.

Mise en place

Pour the *levain*-water mixture into the bowl of the electric stand mixer. Add the flour-salt mixture. Then, attach the dough hook to the mixer. Begin mixing on low speed ("1" on most mixers) and continue to mix until the dough becomes soft and moist, about 5 minutes, frequently stopping the mixer and scraping down the sides of the bowl with a bowl scraper or rubber spatula to make sure that all of the ingredients are incorporated into the dough.

Taste the dough to see whether you have forgotten the salt. If so, add it now and mix for another minute. The dough should just be beginning to come together.

Stop the mixer and move the dough hook out of the way. Using your bowl scraper, scrape down the sides to make sure that all of the ingredients are combined in the dough.

Increase the speed to medium-low ("2" on most mixers) and mix until the dough is soft and smooth, with a moist, tacky surface, about 2 minutes.

Add the walnuts and sage, reduce the speed to low, and continue to mix until the nuts and sage are completely incorporated into the dough.

3 FIRST FERMENTATION

Using an instant-read thermometer, take the temperature of the dough. It should be between 72°F and 80°F. If it is not, immediately make the necessary adjustments (see page 52). Record the temperature of the dough and the time you finished this step in the Dough Log, and note the time the first fermentation should be completed. This dough will be in the first fermentation for 3 hours, with a fold each hour.

Lightly dust a large glass or metal bowl with flour. Transfer the dough to the floured bowl, throw a light film of flour over the top to keep the plastic from sticking, tightly cover the bowl with plastic wrap, and place in a warm (75°F to 80°F), draft-free place for 1 hour.

Lightly dust a clean work surface with flour.

Uncover the dough and place it on the floured work surface. If the dough is very sticky, lightly flour your hands, but do not add more flour to the dough. If the dough sticks to the table, use your bench scraper to lift it up; do not pull and stretch the dough. Let the dough rest for 30 seconds. Using cupped hands, pat the dough into a thick square. Lift the right corners and fold them into the center of the square, lightly patting the seam down. Lift the left corners and fold them into the center of the square, again lightly patting the seam down. Repeat this process with the top two corners and then the bottom two corners, meeting in the middle of the square and lightly patting down the seams.

Lightly flour the bowl and return the dough to it, seam side down. Cover with plastic wrap and return to the warm (75°F to 80°F), draft-free place for another hour.

Repeat the above process and again place the dough in a warm (75°F to 80°F), draft-free place to rise for a third and final hour. At this point the dough should have increased in body and be less sticky.

DIVIDING
Since you are making just 1 loaf, skip to Step 5!

SHAPING
Lightly dust a clean work surface with flour.

Transfer the dough to the floured surface and, using a flat hand, lightly press the dough into a thick rectangle. Lift the dough to make sure that it is not sticking to the work surface. If it is sticking, use the dough scraper to lift it. If it continues to stick, again lightly dust the work surface with flour. Then, carefully shape the dough into a *boule* (see page 56).

Lightly dust a *banneton* with flour. Place the dough in the *banneton*, seam side up. Throw a light film of flour over the top to keep the plastic from sticking, and cover tightly with plastic wrap.

FINAL FERMENTATION
Place the *banneton* in a warm (75°F to 80°F), draft-free place for 2½ to 3 hours or, alternatively, proof for 1 hour and then place in the refrigerator for 12 to 16 hours. You should keep a close eye on the dough, because if it is overproofed it will be unusable.

If the dough has been refrigerated, let it come to room temperature for 1 hour before baking.

If you are using the stainless-steel bowl method to bake the bread (see page 64), about 30 minutes before you are ready to bake, move one oven rack

Carefully transfer loaf to bread peel. *Place loaf onto center of hot stone.*

to the lowest rung and remove the other. Place a large baking stone on the rack and preheat the oven to 450°F. (For all other baking methods, follow the directions on page 64.)

To determine whether the dough is ready to be baked, uncover and gently make a small indentation in the center of the dough with your fingertip. If the indentation slowly and evenly disappears, the bread is ready to bake. If not, follow the instructions on page 63 for additional fermentation.

 BAKING

Lightly dust a bread peel with cornmeal and carefully transfer the loaf to it, top side up.

Working quickly and using a lamé or single-edged razor blade, score the top of the loaf (see page 65). Cut in quick, decisive slashes, marking into the dough by no more than ⅛ inch.

Slide the loaf onto the center of the stone, taking care not to touch the hot surface. Quickly cover with the stainless-steel mixing bowl. Immediately close the oven door. Bake for 10 minutes; then, lift the edge of the bowl with the tip of a small knife and use oven mitts to carefully remove the hot bowl. Continue to bake until the bread is a deep golden brown, about 30 minutes more. (It is a good idea to check after the bread has been baking for about 20 minutes to make sure it is browning evenly. If not, rotate the bread). If you are concerned about the bread's doneness, insert an instant-read thermometer from the bottom of the bread into the center. If it reads 185°F to 210°F the bread is fully baked.

Transfer the loaf to a cooling rack and let it cool for at least 1 hour before cutting with a serrated knife or wrapping for storage.

DOUGH LOG
(Sourdough)

| Dough Type | Measure | Mixing | | Bulk Fermentation (1st Proof) | | | | | | Divide | | | Shape | | | Final Proof | | Scoring | Baking |
	Water Temp	Dough Temp	Finish Mix Time	Rest Time	1st Fold	Rest Time	2nd Fold	Rest Time		Divide	Rest Time		Shape	Shape Time		Proof Time		Scoring	Baking 450°
Example: La Farm Bread (hand mix)	83°	77°	2:00 pm	1 hr	3:00 pm	1 hr	4:00 pm	1 hr		5:00 pm 2 pieces (opt)	10–15 min		round	5:15 pm		3 hr min 12–16 hr in fridge			9:00 am
La Farm Bread				1 hr		1 hr		1 hr		2 pieces (opt)	10–15 min		round			3 hr min 12–16 hr in fridge			
Asiago Parmesan				1 hr		1 hr		1 hr			10–15 min		round			3 hr min 12–16 hr in fridge			
Cinnamon Raisin				1 hr		1 hr		1 hr		2 pieces	10–15 min		batard			3 hr min 12–16 hr in fridge			
Jalapeño Cheddar				1 hr		1 hr		1 hr		2 pieces (opt)	10–15 min		batard			3 hr min 12–16 hr in fridge			
Kalamata Olive				1 hr		1 hr		1 hr			10–15 min		round			3 hr min 12–16 hr in fridge			
Sesame Semolina				1 hr		1 hr		1 hr			10–15 min		S-shaped			3 hr min 12–16 hr in fridge			
Walnut Sage				1 hr		1 hr		1 hr			10–15 min		round			3 hr min 12–16 hr in fridge			

Notes: _____

WHOLE-GRAIN BREADS

Whole-grain breads, whether yeasted or made with a natural starter, are generally more deeply flavored than are breads made with unbleached, unbromated white flour. And those enriched with seeds and other whole grains in addition to whole-grain flours are even more intensely flavored. However, beyond the flavor, artisanal breads made with whole-grain flours carry terrific nutritional values. In fact, some scientific research shows that the nutrients in whole grains—antioxidants, lignans, phenolic acids, and phytochemicals—may help reduce the risk of cancer, heart disease, and diabetes. This is because whole grains still contain their bran and germ and offer more fiber, folic acid, and vitamins, all of which are recommended for a healthy diet.

In this section, I offer two types of whole-grain breads: those made with yeast and those made with a liquid *levain*. Each has its own distinct flavor profile, so I suggest that you try them all to find your favorite.

Yeasted Grain Breads
100% Whole-Wheat Bread
Honey Whole-Wheat Bread
Spelt Bread
A Frenchman's Cornbread

Liquid *Levain* Breads
Multigrain Sourdough Bread
Rye Bread
Raisin Rye Bread
Seeded Rye Bread

MILLED
JAN 2 2 2013

100% Whole-Wheat Bread

MAKES 1 BOULE OR 2 SMALL LOAVES

When developing this recipe, I wanted to create a bread that was different from most whole-wheat breads. I was aiming for a lighter texture and an airy crumb without a lot of competing flavors. I did not want to hide the earthy flavor of the whole wheat, which happens with many commercial whole-wheat breads because so many softening ingredients, such as milk, are added to them. We are fortunate to have an excellent new organic local flour in North Carolina—Carolina Ground Flour—and I encourage you to seek out your local whole-wheat flour for this bread. But any will work well. Our daughters love it when Missy makes a classic grilled cheese with this bread and sharp cheddar, and offers it with a side of fresh fruit, and we have the satisfaction of knowing this is a delicious and nutrient-rich lunch.

16 ounces	454 grams	3½ cups unbromated whole-wheat bread flour
0.31 ounce	9 grams	1½ teaspoons fine sea salt
0.1 ounce	3 grams	¾ teaspoon instant dry yeast
12 ounces	340 grams	1½ cups water

Cornmeal for dusting

1 MEASURING

Scale all of the ingredients.

Place the flour in a medium mixing bowl. Add the salt and yeast, making sure that they do not touch each other.

Place the water in a small bowl. Using an instant-read thermometer take the temperature of the water (it should read between 65°F and 70°F) and record it in your dough log.

2 MIXING AND KNEADING

Pour half of the water into the bowl of the electric stand mixer. Add the flour mixture. Then, attach the dough hook to the mixer. Begin mixing on low speed ("1" on most mixers) and then immediately start to add the remaining water in a slow, steady stream. Continue to mix on low speed for 5 minutes.

Taste the dough to see whether you have forgotten the salt. If so, add it now and mix for another minute.

Stop the mixer and move the dough hook out of the way. Using your bowl scraper, scrape down the sides and into the bottom of the bowl to insure that all of the ingredients are combined in the dough.

Add water and mix on low speed.

Check dough for consistency.

Scrape down sides and bottom of bowl.

Return the dough hook to its original position. Increase the speed to medium-low ("2" on most mixers) and mix until the dough is soft and smooth, with a moist, tacky surface, about 2 minutes.

3   FIRST FERMENTATION

Using an instant-read thermometer, take the temperature of the dough. It should be between 72°F and 80°F. If it is not, immediately make the necessary adjustments (see page 52). Record the temperature of the dough and the time you finished this step in the Dough Log, and note the time the first fermentation should be completed. This dough will be in the first fermentation for 90 minutes, with a fold halfway through.

Lightly dust a large bowl (preferably glass to allow observation of the process) with flour. The bowl should be large enough to allow the dough to rise without coming in contact with the plastic wrap that will cover it. Transfer the dough to the bowl, smooth side up, and cover the bowl with plastic wrap. Place in a warm (75°F to 80°F), draft-free place for 45 minutes.

Place dough in lightly floured bowl.

Lightly dust a clean work surface with flour.

Uncover the dough and, using cupped hands, lift the dough from the bowl and place it on the floured work surface. Using flat hands, pat the dough into a thick square. Lift the right corners and fold them into the center of the square, lightly patting the seam down. Lift the left corners and fold them into the center of the square, again lightly patting the seam down. Repeat this process with the top two corners and then the bottom two corners, meeting in the middle of the square and lightly patting down the seams.

Lightly flour the bowl and return the dough to it, seam side down. Cover with plastic wrap and place in a warm (75°F to 80°F), draft-free place for another 45 minutes.

DIVIDING AND SHAPING

Lightly dust a clean work surface with flour.

Uncover the dough and, using a bowl scraper, scrape the dough onto the floured work surface. If the dough is very sticky, lightly flour your hands, but do not add more flour to the dough. If the dough sticks to the table, use your bench scraper to lift it; do not pull and stretch the dough.

For one large loaf, lightly press down on the dough with a flat hand, forming the dough into a large rectangle. If you are making two small loaves, lightly press down on the dough with a flat hand, forming the dough into a square. Using a bench scraper, cut the dough in half to form two rectangles.

Lift the dough to make sure that it is not sticking to the work surface. If it is sticking, use the dough scraper to lift it. If it continues to stick, again lightly dust the work surface with flour. Then, carefully shape the dough into 1 large or 2 small *boules* (see page 56).

Place the *boule* in a lightly floured *couche* (or a strong linen towel) as directed on page 62. (If making 2 small loaves, make a second ridge in the *couche* to separate them.) Fold the remaining part of the *couche* over the top of the dough.

FINAL FERMENTATION

Place the *couche* in a warm (75°F to 80°F), draft-free place for 1 hour; however, you should keep a close eye on the dough, because if it is overproofed it will be unusable.

If you are using the stainless-steel bowl method to bake the bread (see page 64), about 30 minutes before you are ready to bake, move one oven rack to the lowest rung and remove the other. Place a large baking stone on the rack and preheat the oven to 450°F. (For all other baking methods, follow the directions on page 64.)

To determine whether the dough is ready to be baked, uncover and gently make a small indentation in the center of the dough with your fingertip. If the indentation slowly and evenly disappears, the bread is ready to bake. If not, follow the instructions on page 63 for additional fermentation.

If you are making two loaves and both won't fit under your stainless-steel bowl, cover one with plastic wrap and place in the refrigerator, then bake after the first loaf comes out of the oven.

7 BAKING

Lightly dust a bread peel with cornmeal and place the dough on it, seam side down.

Working quickly and using a lamé or single-edged razor blade, score the top of the loaf (see page 65). Cut in quick, decisive slashes, marking into the dough by no more than ⅛ inch.

Slide the loaf, seam side down, onto the center of the stone, taking care not to touch the hot surface. If you are baking two loaves together, take care that they don't "kiss" (touch and get stuck together while baking).

Quickly cover with the stainless-steel mixing bowl. Immediately close the oven door. Bake for 10 minutes; then, lift the edge of the bowl with the tip of a small knife and use oven mitts to carefully remove the hot bowl. Continue to bake until the bread is a chestnut-brown and sounds hollow when tapped on the bottom, about 30 minutes more. (It is a good idea to check after the bread has been baking for about 20 minutes to make sure it is browning evenly. If not, rotate the bread.) If you are concerned about the bread's doneness, insert an instant-read thermometer from the bottom of the bread into the center. If it reads 185°F to 210°F the bread is fully baked.

Transfer the loaf to a cooling rack and let it cool for at least 1 hour before cutting with a serrated knife or wrapping for storage.

Honey Whole-Wheat Bread

MAKES 1 BÂTARD

Here, I use a balance of white and whole-wheat flours for a lighter bread; the added touch of honey brings out the sweetness of the wheat. While I'm not a peanut butter fan, a number of our customers say that this bread is their children's favorite for peanut butter and jelly sandwiches. Made with an electric stand mixer and baked in a loaf pan, it is a great sandwich bread; however, you can shape it, proof it in a *couche*, and bake it directly on the hot baking stone if you like.

I encourage you to use a local honey; try locating a beekeeper at a farmers' market, which is how I found my local beekeeper. Don't hesitate to throw in some sunflower seeds or other seeds or grains to add a nice crunch.

12.5 ounces	354 grams	2¾ cups unbleached, unbromated white bread flour
3.5 ounces	100 grams	²/₃ cup unbromated whole-wheat bread flour
0.31 ounce	9 grams	1½ teaspoons fine sea salt
0.01 ounce	3 grams	¾ teaspoon instant dry yeast
11.26 ounces	320 grams	1¼ cups plus 2 tablespoons water
1.1 ounces	30 grams	1½ tablespoons honey

1 MEASURING

Scale all of the ingredients.

Using an instant-read thermometer, take the temperature of the water. It should read between 65°F and 70°F. Record it in your Dough Log.

2 MIXING AND KNEADING

(These instructions are for using a stand mixer; see page 45 for instructions for mixing by hand.)

Place the white and whole-wheat flours in a medium mixing bowl. Add the salt and yeast, making sure that they do not touch each other.

Add the honey to the water, stirring to blend well. This ensures that rather than sticking to the bowl, all of the honey will be incorporated into the water.

Pour half of the water-honey mixture into the bowl of the electric stand mixer. Add the flour mixture. Then, attach the dough hook to the mixer. Begin mixing on low speed ("1" on most mixers) and then immediately start to add the remaining water-honey mixture in a slow, steady stream. Continue to mix on low speed for 5 minutes.

Taste the dough to see whether you have forgotten the salt. If so, add it now and mix for another minute.

Stop the mixer and move the dough hook out of the way. Using your bowl scraper, scrape down the sides of the bowl to make sure that all of the ingredients are combined in the dough.

Return the dough hook to its original position. Increase the speed to medium-low ("2" on most mixers) and mix until the dough is soft and smooth, with a moist, tacky surface, about 2 minutes.

Salt and yeast should not touch.

3 FIRST FERMENTATION

Using an instant-read thermometer, take the temperature of the dough. It should be between 72°F and 80°F. If it is not, immediately make the necessary adjustments (see page 52). Record the temperature of the dough and the time you finished this step in the Dough Log, and note the time the first fermentation should be completed. This dough will be in the first fermentation for 90 minutes, with a fold halfway through.

Lightly dust a large bowl (preferably glass to allow observation of the process) with flour. The bowl should be large enough to allow the dough to rise without coming in contact with the plastic wrap that will cover it. Transfer the dough to the bowl, smooth side up, and cover the bowl with plastic wrap. Place in a warm (75°F to 80°F), draft-free place for 45 minutes.

Lightly dust a clean work surface with flour.

Uncover the dough and, using cupped hands, pat the dough into a thick square. Lift the right corners and fold them into the center of the square, lightly patting the seam down. Lift the left corners and fold them into the center of the square, again lightly patting the seam down. Repeat this process with the top two corners and then the bottom two corners, meeting in the middle of the square and lightly patting down the seams.

Lightly flour the bowl and return the dough to it, seam side down. Cover with plastic wrap and return to a warm (75°F to 80°F), draft-free place for an additional 45 minutes.

DIVIDING
Since you are making just 1 loaf, skip to Step 5!

SHAPING
Lightly butter the interior of a 10-by-4-by-3-inch loaf pan. Add just enough flour to coat, holding the pan upside down and tapping on the bottom to eliminate any excess flour. Set aside.

Lightly dust a clean work surface with flour.

Uncover the dough and place it on the lightly floured surface. If the dough is very sticky, lightly flour your hands, but do not add more flour to the dough. If the dough adheres to the table, use your bench scraper to lift it; do not pull and stretch the dough.

Using a flat hand, lightly press down on the dough, forming a large rectangle. Then, using your hands, gently pick up the dough to make sure that it is not sticking to the work surface. If it is, lightly flour the work surface. Then, carefully shape the dough into a *bâtard* (see page 60).

Transfer the loaf to the prepared pan, seam side down. Cover with a linen towel followed by plastic wrap.

FINAL FERMENTATION
Place the pan in a warm (75°F to 80°F), draft-free place for 1 hour.

If you are using the stainless-steel bowl method to bake the bread (see page 64), about 30 minutes before you are ready to bake, move one oven rack to the lowest rung and remove the other. Place a large baking stone on the rack and preheat the oven to 450°F. (For all other baking methods, follow the directions on page 64.)

To determine whether the dough is ready to be baked, uncover and gently make a small indentation in the center of the dough with your fingertip. If the indentation slowly and evenly disappears, the bread is ready to bake. If not, follow the instructions on page 63 for additional fermentation.

BAKING
For this particular bread, I dust the top with flour, as I prefer the color contrast that occurs when the bread is baked; however, this is totally

Remove plastic wrap.

Lightly dust top with flour.

Score top of loaf.

optional. Working quickly and using a lamé or single-edged razor blade, score the top of the loaf (see page 65). Cut in quick, decisive slashes, marking into the dough by no more than ⅛ inch.

Transfer the pan onto the center of the stone, taking care not to touch the hot surface.

Quickly cover with the stainless-steel mixing bowl. Immediately close the oven door. Bake for 10 minutes; then, lift the edge of the bowl with the tip of a small knife and use oven mitts to carefully remove the hot bowl. Continue to bake until the bread is a chestnut-brown and sounds hollow when popped out of the pan and tapped on the bottom, about 30 minutes more. (It is a good idea to check after the bread has been baking for about 20 minutes to make sure it is browning evenly. If not, rotate the bread.) If you are concerned about the bread's doneness, insert an instant-read thermometer from the bottom of the bread into the center. If it reads 185°F to 210°F the bread is fully baked.

Transfer the loaf to a cooling rack and let it cool for at least 1 hour before removing from the pan and cutting with a serrated knife or wrapping for storage.

Finished baking

Spelt Bread

MAKES 4 MINI-LOAVES

Spelt is one of the oldest grains known; breads were made from it in ancient Egypt. I had tried a number of spelt breads but found them to be too dense and dry for my taste. I wanted to make a lighter, moister bread for customers who could not tolerate regular wheat flour, and I think this recipe does the trick.

16 ounces	454 grams	3½ cups spelt flour
0.31 ounce	9 grams	1½ teaspoons fine sea salt
0.1 ounce	3 grams	¾ teaspoon instant dry yeast
12 ounces	340 grams	1½ cups water

1 MEASURING

Scale all of the ingredients.

Using an instant-read thermometer, take the temperature of the water. It should read between 65°F and 70°F. Record it in your dough log.

2 MIXING AND KNEADING

(These instructions are for using a stand mixer; see page 45 for instructions for mixing by hand.)

Place the spelt flour in a medium mixing bowl. Add the salt and yeast, making sure that they do not touch each other.

Pour half of the water into the bowl of the electric stand mixer. Add the flour mixture to the bowl. Then, attach the dough hook to the mixer. Begin mixing on low speed ("1" on most mixers) and then immediately start to add the remaining water in a slow, steady stream. Continue to mix on low speed for 5 minutes.

Taste the dough to see whether you have forgotten the salt. If so, add it now and mix for another minute.

Stop the mixer and move the dough hook out of the way. Using your bowl scraper, scrape down the sides to make sure that all of the ingredients are combined in the dough.

Return the dough hook to its original position. Turn on the mixer, increase the speed to medium-low ("2" on most mixers) and mix until the dough is soft and smooth, with a moist, tacky surface, about 2 minutes.

3 FIRST FERMENTATION

Using an instant-read thermometer, take the temperature of the dough. It should be between 72°F and 80°F. If it is not, immediately make the necessary adjustments (see page 52). Record the temperature of the dough and the time you finished this step in the Dough Log, and note the time the first fermentation should be completed. This dough will be in the first fermentation for 90 minutes, with a fold halfway through.

Lightly dust a large glass or metal bowl with flour. Transfer the dough to the floured bowl, throw a light film of flour over the top to keep the plastic from sticking, tightly cover with plastic wrap, and place in a warm (75°F to 80°F), draft-free place for 45 minutes.

Lightly dust a clean work surface with flour.

Uncover the dough and, using cupped hands, pat the dough into a thick square. Lift the right corners and fold them into the center of the square, lightly patting the seam down. Lift the left corners and fold them into the center of the square, again lightly patting the seam down. Repeat this process with the top two corners and then the bottom two corners, meeting in the middle of the square and lightly patting down the seams.

Lightly flour the bowl and return the dough to it, seam side down. Cover with plastic wrap and return to a warm (75°F to 80°F), draft-free place for another 45 minutes.

DIVIDING AND SHAPING

Lightly butter the interiors of four mini-loaf (5½-by-3-by-2-inch) pans. Add just enough flour to coat, holding the pans upside down and tapping on the bottoms to eliminate any excess flour. Set aside.

Lightly dust a clean work surface with flour.

Using a flat hand, lightly press the dough into a thick rectangle. Lift the dough to make sure that it is not sticking to the work surface. If it is sticking, use the dough scraper to lift it. If it continues to stick, again lightly dust the work surface with flour.

Using a bench scraper, divide the dough into 4 equal pieces. Then, carefully shape each piece into a *bâtard* (see page 60). Place a loaf into each of the prepared pans. When all of the loaves have been shaped and placed in a pan, throw a thin film of flour over the tops to keep the plastic from sticking, and cover with plastic wrap.

Place loaf into prepared pan.

FINAL FERMENTATION

Place the pans in a warm (75°F to 80°F), draft-free place for 1 hour.

Preheat the oven to 450°F.

If you are using the stainless-steel bowl method to bake the bread (see page 64), about 30 minutes before you are ready to bake, move one oven rack to the lowest rung and remove the other. Place a large baking stone on the rack and preheat the oven to 450°F. (For all other baking methods, follow the directions on page 64.)

To determine whether the dough is ready to be baked, uncover and gently make a small indentation in the center of the dough with your fingertip. If the indentation slowly and evenly disappears, the bread is ready to bake. If not, follow the instructions on page 63 for additional fermentation.

If all four loaves won't fit under your stainless-steel bowl, cover two with plastic wrap and place in the refrigerator, then bake after the first loaves comes out of the oven.

BAKING

If you like, lightly dust the top of each loaf with flour. Then, working quickly and using a lamé or single-edged razor blade, score the top of each

Lightly dust top of loaf.

Score with "S" shape.

loaf (see page 65) in an "S" shape (for spelt). Cut in a quick, decisive slash, marking into the dough by no more than ⅛ inch.

Transfer the pans onto the center of the stone, taking care not to touch the hot surface.

Quickly cover with the stainless-steel mixing bowl. Immediately close the oven door. Bake for 10 minutes; then, lift the edge of the bowl with the tip of a small knife and use oven mitts to carefully remove the hot bowl. Continue to bake until the bread is a chestnut-brown and sounds hollow when popped out of the pan and tapped on the bottom, about 30 minutes more. (It is a good idea to check after the bread has been baking for about 20 minutes to make sure it is browning evenly. If not, rotate the loaf pans.) If you are concerned about the bread's doneness, insert an instant-read thermometer from the bottom of the bread into the center. If it reads 185°F to 210°F the bread is fully baked.

Transfer the loaves to a cooling rack and let them cool for at least 1 hour before removing from the pans and cutting with a serrated knife or wrapping for storage.

Finished baking

A Frenchman's Cornbread

MAKES 1 LOAF

Yates Mill

We are lucky to have a renovated mill not far from La Farm Bakery that makes stone-ground cornmeal. A group of dedicated millers start up this old mill and grind North Carolina corn into old-fashioned cornmeal. I wanted to do something with this great cornmeal, so I called upon my friends at Terra Bread in Vancouver, since they make a wonderful and unusual corn soufflé-bread that I love. I took the same flavor profile and created a hearth-baked cornbread more typical of the South.

12.5 ounces	354 grams	2¾ cups unbleached, unbromated white bread flour
3.5 ounces	100 grams	⅔ cup stone-ground cornmeal, plus more for dusting
0.31 ounce	9 grams	1½ teaspoons fine sea salt
0.1 ounce	3 grams	¾ teaspoon instant dry yeast
10 ounces	290 grams	1 cup plus 3 tablespoons buttermilk, at room temperature
1.76 ounces	50 grams	¼ cup water
0.7 ounce	20 grams	1 tablespoon honey
1.1 ounces	32 grams	3 tablespoons finely diced chives
1.1 ounces	32 grams	3 tablespoons finely diced red onion
1.1 ounces	32 grams	½ cup finely sliced scallions

Mise en place

1 MEASURING

Scale all of the ingredients.

Using an instant-read thermometer, take the temperature of the water. It should read between 65°F and 70°F. Record it in your Dough Log. The temperature of the buttermilk should also read between 65°F and 70°F.

2 MIXING AND KNEADING

(These instructions are for using a stand mixer; see page 45 for instructions for mixing by hand.)

Place the flour and cornmeal in a mixing bowl, stirring to blend well. Add the salt and yeast, making sure that they do not touch each other.

Combine the buttermilk with the water and honey, stirring to blend.

Pour half of the buttermilk mixture into the bowl of a heavy-duty electric stand mixer. Add the flour mixture. Then, attach the dough hook to the mixer. Begin mixing on low speed ("1" on most mixers), immediately add the remaining buttermilk mixture, and continue to mix for 5 minutes.

Taste the dough to see whether you have forgotten the salt. If so, add it now and mix for another minute.

Stop the mixer and move the dough hook out of the way. Using your bowl scraper, scrape down the sides to make sure that all of the ingredients are combined in the dough.

Return the dough hook to its original position. Increase the speed to medium-low ("2" on most mixers), and mix until the dough is soft and smooth, with a moist, tacky surface, about 2 minutes. Add the chives, red onion, and scallions and mix to just incorporate.

3 FIRST FERMENTATION

Using an instant-read thermometer, take the temperature of the dough. It should be between 72°F and 80°F. If it is not, immediately make the necessary adjustments (see page 52). Record the temperature of the dough and the time you finished this step in the Dough Log, and note the time the first fermentation should be completed. This dough will be in the first fermentation for 90 minutes, with a fold halfway through.

Lightly dust a large bowl (preferably glass to allow observation of the process) with flour. The bowl should be large enough to allow the dough to rise without coming in contact with the plastic wrap that will cover it. Transfer the dough to the bowl and cover the bowl with plastic wrap. Place in a warm (75°F to 80°F), draft-free place for 45 minutes.

Lightly dust a clean work surface with flour.

Uncover the dough and, using cupped hands, lift the dough from the bowl and place it on the floured work surface. Using flat hands, pat the dough into a thick square. Lift the right corners and fold them into the center of the square, lightly patting the seam down. Lift the left corners and fold them into the center of the square, again lightly patting the seam down. Repeat this process with the top two corners and then the bottom two corners, meeting in the middle of the square and lightly patting down the seams.

Lightly flour the bowl and return the dough to it, seam side down. Cover with plastic wrap and return to a warm (75°F to 80°F), draft-free place for 45 minutes.

4 DIVIDING

Since you are making just 1 loaf, skip to Step 5!

5 SHAPING

Lightly coat a baking sheet with cornmeal. Set aside.

Lightly dust a clean work surface with flour.

Uncover the dough and, using a bowl scraper, scrape the dough onto the floured work surface. If the dough is very sticky, lightly flour your hands, but do not add more flour to the dough. If the dough sticks to the table, use your bench scraper to lift it; do not pull and stretch the dough.

Using a flat hand, lightly press the dough into a thick rectangle. Lift the dough to make sure that it is not sticking to the work surface. If it is sticking, use the dough scraper to lift it. If it continues to stick, again lightly dust the work surface with flour. Then, carefully shape the dough into a *boule* (see page 56).

Gently coat in cornmeal.

Place elbow in center.

Using thumbs, open indentation.

Lift dough gently.

Stretch hole to 3 inches.

Place dough on couche.

Transfer the dough to the prepared baking sheet and gently turn it to coat all sides in cornmeal. Let rest for 5 minutes.

Now shape the dough into a crown. Put your bare elbow (nice and clean, of course) into the center of the dough and push it down into the dough until you reach the work surface. Using your thumbs, open up the indentation you have created with your elbow to make an opening rather like a hole in a bagel. Lift the dough from the baking sheet and gently stretch the hole out to a roughly 3-inch opening by gently rotating the dough.

Place the dough in a lightly floured *couche* (or a strong linen towel) as directed on page 62. Fold the remaining part of the *couche* over the top of the dough.

6 FINAL FERMENTATION

Place the *couche* in a warm (75°F to 80°F), draft-free place for 1 hour.

If you are using the stainless-steel bowl method to bake the bread (see page 64), about 30 minutes before you are ready to bake, move one oven rack to the lowest rung and remove the other. Place a large baking stone on the rack and preheat the oven to 450°F. (For all other baking methods, follow the directions on page 64.)

To determine whether the dough is ready to be baked, uncover and gently make a small indentation in the center of the dough with your fingertip. If the indentation slowly and evenly disappears, the bread is ready to bake. If not, follow the instructions on page 63 for additional fermentation.

7 BAKING

Lightly dust a bread peel with cornmeal and transfer the crown to it. Working quickly and using a lamé or single-edged razor blade, score the top of the loaf (see page 65). Cut in quick, decisive slashes, marking into the dough by no more than ⅛ inch.

Slide the loaf, top side up, onto the center of the stone, taking care not to touch the hot surface.

Quickly cover with the stainless-steel mixing bowl. Immediately close the oven door. Bake for 10 minutes; then, lift the edge of the bowl with the tip of a small knife and use oven mitts to carefully remove the hot bowl. Continue to

Score top of loaf.

bake until the bread is golden-brown and sounds hollow when tapped on the bottom, about 30 minutes more. (It is a good idea to check after the bread has been baking for about 20 minutes to make sure it is browning evenly. If not, rotate the bread.) If you are concerned about the bread's doneness, insert an instant-read thermometer from the bottom of the bread into the center. If it reads 185°F to 210°F the bread is fully baked.

Transfer the loaf to a cooling rack and let it cool for at least 1 hour before cutting with a serrated knife or wrapping for storage.

Multigrain Sourdough Bread

MAKES 1 LOAF

This is a very healthy, grainy bread that makes great toast in the morning. It has about all the fiber and nutrients you need to start the day with a bang. You have to plan ahead to make this bread, as the grains need to be soaked overnight to soften before being added to the dough. You can use any mixture of seeds and grains you have on hand. The mixture here is very similar to the one I use at La Farm Bakery.

I also add just a hint of a great local honey. Its sweetness balances the earthiness of the grains, plus it is good for your immune system. Being French, I always try to think of health benefits when I create a recipe.

FOR THE DOUGH:

10.05 ounces	285 grams	1 cup plus 3 tablespoons plus 1 teaspoon water
0.7 ounce	20 grams	2 tablespoons steel-cut oats
0.67 ounce	19 grams	2 tablespoons whole flaxseeds
0.67 ounce	19 grams	2 tablespoons sunflower seeds
0.67 ounce	19 grams	2 tablespoons millet
0.31 ounce	9 grams	1 tablespoon #2 cracked bulgur wheat
0.28 ounce	8 grams	1 tablespoon pearl barley
4 ounces	113 grams	½ cup cold water
8.5 ounces	240 grams	2 cups unbleached, unbromated white bread flour
2.5 ounces	72 grams	½ cup unbromated whole-wheat bread flour
2.25 ounces	65 grams	½ cup medium rye flour
0.31 ounce	9 grams	1½ teaspoons fine sea salt
3.5 ounces	100 grams	½ cup liquid *levain* (see page 20)
0.75 ounce	21 grams	1 tablespoon honey

FOR THE TOPPING:
2 tablespoons old-fashioned rolled oats

1 MEASURING
Scale all of the ingredients.

Using an instant-read thermometer, take the temperature of the 10.05 ounces/285 grams water. It should read between 65°F and 70°F. Record it in your Dough Log.

Combine the steel-cut oats, flaxseeds, sunflower seeds, millet, bulgur, and barley in a small bowl. Add the 4 ounces/113 grams cold water, cover with plastic wrap, and set aside to soak for at least 8 hours or overnight.

2 MIXING AND KNEADING

(These instructions are for using a stand mixer; see page 45 for instructions for mixing by hand.)

Place the white, whole-wheat, and rye flours and salt in a mixing bowl, stirring to blend well.

Pour half of the water into a mixing bowl, and then add the *levain*, stirring to blend. In another small bowl, stir the honey into the remaining water to blend.

Pour the *levain*-water mixture into the bowl of a heavy-duty electric stand mixer. Add the flour-salt mixture. Then, attach the dough hook to the mixer. Begin mixing on low speed ("1" on most mixers) and then immediately add the water-honey mixture in a slow, steady stream. Continue to mix on low speed for 5 minutes.

Taste the dough to see whether you have forgotten the salt. If so, add it now and mix for another minute.

Stop the mixer and move the dough hook out of the way. Using your bowl scraper, scrape down the sides and bottom of the bowl to make sure that all of the ingredients are combined in the dough.

Return the dough hook to its original position. Increase the speed to medium-low ("2" on most mixers) and mix until the dough is soft and smooth, with a moist, tacky surface, about 2 minutes.

Add the soaked grains, reduce the speed to low, and continue to mix until the grains are completely incorporated into the dough, about 1 minute.

3 FIRST FERMENTATION

Using an instant-read thermometer, take the temperature of the dough. It should be between 75°F and 80°F. If it is not, immediately make the necessary adjustments (see page 52). Record the temperature of the dough and the time you finished this step in the Dough Log, and note the time the first fermentation should be completed. This dough will have a first fermentation of 3 hours, with a fold each hour.

Lightly dust a large bowl (preferably glass to allow observation of the process) with flour. Transfer the dough to the bowl, throw a light film of flour over the top to keep the plastic from sticking, tightly cover the bowl with plastic wrap, and place in a warm (75°F to 80°F), draft-free place for 1 hour.

Lightly dust a clean work surface with flour.

Uncover the dough and, using cupped hands, pat the dough into a thick square. Lift the right corners and fold them into the center of the square, lightly patting the seam down. Lift the left corners and fold them into the center of the square, again lightly patting the seam down. Repeat this process with the top two corners and then the bottom two corners, meeting in the middle of the square and lightly patting down the seams.

Lightly flour the bowl and return the dough to it, seam side down. Cover with plastic wrap and return to a warm (75°F to 80°F), draft-free place for another hour. Record the time in your Dough Log.

Repeat the folding process and again place the dough in a warm (75°F to 80°F), draft-free place to rise for a third and final hour.

4 DIVIDING
Since you are making just 1 loaf, skip to Step 5!

5 SHAPING
Lightly butter the interior of a 9-by-5-by-3-inch loaf pan. Add just enough flour to coat, holding the pan upside-down and tapping on the bottom to eliminate any excess flour. Set aside.

Lightly dust a clean work surface with flour.

Uncover the dough and, using a bowl scraper, scrape the dough onto the floured work surface. If the dough is very sticky, lightly flour your hands, but do not add more flour to the dough. If the dough sticks to the table, use your bench scraper to lift it up. Do not pull and stretch the dough.

Using a flat hand, lightly press the dough into a thick rectangle. Lift the dough to make sure that it is not sticking to the work surface. Using a flat hand, lightly press down on the dough. Then, shape the dough into a *bâtard* (see page 60).

Place the old-fashioned oats in a shallow pan and roll the top of the dough in the oats to cover generously.

Cover generously in oats.

Place in prepared loaf pan.

Transfer the dough to the prepared loaf pan, seam side down. Throw a light film of flour over the top to keep the plastic from sticking and tightly cover with plastic wrap.

6 FINAL FERMENTATION

Place the pan in a warm (75°F to 80°F), draft-free place for 2½ to 3 hours or, alternatively, proof for 1 hour and then place in the refrigerator for 12 to 16 hours. If you have refrigerated the dough, let it come to room temperature for 1 hour before baking.

If you are using the stainless-steel bowl method to bake the bread (see page 64), about 30 minutes before you are ready to bake, move one oven rack to the lowest rung and remove the other. Place a large baking stone on the rack and preheat the oven to 450°F. (For all other baking methods, follow the directions on page 64.)

To determine whether the dough is ready to be baked, uncover and gently make a small indentation in the center of the dough with your fingertip. If the indentation slowly and evenly disappears, the bread is ready to bake. If not, follow the instructions on page 63 for additional fermentation.

7 BAKING

Working quickly and using the back side of a lamé or a cake tester, score the loaf (see page 65) by poking 3 times evenly across the top—or create your own score mark.

Transfer the pan to the center of the hot baking stone, taking care not to touch the hot surface. Immediately cover with the stainless-steel mixing bowl. Quickly close the oven door. Bake for 10 minutes; then, lift the edge of the bowl with the tip of a small knife and use oven mitts to carefully remove the hot bowl. Continue to bake until the bread is a deep golden brown and sounds hollow when popped out of the pan and tapped on the

Score by evenly poking 3 times.

Place on hot stone.

Cover for first 10 minutes of baking.

bottom, about 30 minutes more. (It is a good idea to check after the bread has been baking for about 20 minutes to make sure it is browning evenly. If not, rotate the bread.) If you are concerned about the bread's doneness, insert an instant-read thermometer from the bottom of the bread into the center. If it reads 185°F to 210°F the bread is fully baked.

Transfer the loaf to a cooling rack and let it cool for at least 1 hour before cutting with a serrated knife or wrapping for storage.

Note: Multigrain Sourdough Bread can also be baked in a 10-by-4-by-3-inch loaf pan as for Honey Whole-Wheat Bread (see page 223).

Finished baking

Rye Bread

MAKES 1 BÂTARD

Rye bread stirs up memories of my childhood holidays, especially Christmas, when we always had rye bread with fresh oysters. We would squeeze lemon juice on the plump oysters and then eat them with a bite of rye bread slathered with fresh creamery butter and a sprinkle of sea salt. The oysters came from La Tranche-sur-Mer, just slightly north of my parents' home in La Rochelle. Today, I celebrate in the same way with my girls and Missy's family, racking oysters in Southport, off the coast of North Carolina, where Missy's parents live. A feast of oysters and rye bread—the tradition continues!

8.8 ounces	250 grams	1⅓ cups plus 1 tablespoon plus 2 teaspoons unbleached, unbromated white bread flour
4.6 ounces	130 grams	1 cup plus 1 tablespoon medium rye flour
0.31 ounce	9 grams	1½ teaspoons fine sea salt
8.5 ounces	240 grams	1 cup plus 1 teaspoon water
3.5 ounces	100 grams	½ cup liquid *levain* (see page 20)

1

MEASURING

Scale all of the ingredients.

Using an instant-read thermometer, take the temperature of the water. It should read between 65°F and 70°F. Record it in your Dough Log.

2

MIXING AND KNEADING

(These instructions are for using a stand mixer; see page 45 for instructions for mixing by hand.)

Place the wheat and rye flours and the salt in a mixing bowl, stirring to blend well.

Pour half of the water into a mixing bowl, and then add the *levain*, stirring to blend.

Pour the *levain*-water mixture into the bowl of a heavy-duty electric stand mixer. Add the flour-salt mixture. Then, attach the dough hook to the mixer. Begin mixing on low speed ("1" on most mixers) and then immediately start to add the remaining water in a slow, steady stream. Continue to mix on low speed for 5 minutes.

Taste the dough to see whether you have forgotten the salt. If so, add it now and mix for another minute.

Stop the mixer and move the dough hook out of the way. Using your bowl scraper, scrape down the sides and bottom of the bowl to make sure that all of the ingredients are combined in the dough.

Return the dough hook to its original position. Increase the speed to medium-low ("2" on most mixers) and mix until the dough is soft and smooth, with a moist, tacky surface, about 2 minutes.

3

FIRST FERMENTATION

Using an instant-read thermometer, take the temperature of the dough. It should be between 72°F and 80°F. If it is not, immediately make the necessary adjustments (see page 52). Record the temperature of the dough and the time you finished this step in the Dough Log, and note the time the first fermentation should be completed. This dough will have a first fermentation of 3 hours, with a fold each hour.

Lightly dust a large bowl (preferably glass to allow observation of the process) with flour. Transfer the dough to the bowl, throw a light film of flour over the top to keep the plastic from sticking, tightly cover the bowl with plastic wrap, and place in a warm (75°F to 80°F), draft-free place for 1 hour.

Lightly dust a clean work surface with flour.

Uncover the dough and, using cupped hands, pat the dough into a thick square. Lift the right corners and fold them into the center of the square, lightly patting the seam down. Lift the left corners and fold them into the center of the square, again lightly patting the seam down. Repeat this process with the top two corners and then the bottom two corners, meeting in the middle of the square and lightly patting down the seams.

Lightly flour the bowl and return the dough to it, seam side down. Cover with plastic wrap and return to a warm (75°F to 80°F), draft-free place for another hour. Record the time in your Dough Log.

Repeat the above process and again place the dough in a warm (75°F to 80°F), draft-free place to rise for a third and final hour. At this point the dough should have increased in body and be less sticky.

4 DIVIDING

Since you are making just 1 loaf, skip to Step 5!

5 SHAPING

Lightly dust a clean work surface with flour.

Using a flat hand, lightly press the dough into a thick rectangle. Lift the dough to make sure that it is not sticking to the work surface. If it is sticking, use the dough scraper to lift it. If it continues to stick, again lightly dust the work surface with flour.

Carefully lift the dough, turning the short side to face you. Using a flat hand, press down on the dough. Then, shape the dough into a *bâtard* (see page 60).

Place the dough in a lightly floured *couche* (or a strong linen towel) as directed on page 62. Fold the remaining part of the *couche* over the top of the dough.

6 FINAL FERMENTATION

Place the *couche* in a warm (75°F to 80°F), draft-free place for 2½ to 3 hours or, alternatively, proof for 1 hour and then place in the refrigerator for 12 to 16 hours. If the dough has been refrigerated, let it come to room temperature for 1 hour before baking.

If you are using the stainless-steel bowl method to bake the bread (see page 64), about 30 minutes before you are ready to bake, move one oven rack to the lowest rung and remove the other. Place a large baking stone on the rack and preheat the oven to 450°F. (For all other baking methods, follow the directions on page 64.)

To determine whether the dough is ready to be baked, uncover and gently make a small indentation in the center of the dough with your fingertip. If the indentation slowly and evenly disappears, the bread is ready to bake. If not, follow the instructions on page 63 for additional fermentation.

Place dough on couche.

Light dusting of flour.　　　　　*Score top of loaf.*

7 BAKING

Throw a light dusting of flour over the dough and transfer to a bread peel or the back of a sheet pan. Working quickly and using a lamé or single-edged razor blade, score the top of the loaf (see page 65). Cut in quick, decisive slashes, marking into the dough by no more than ⅛ inch.

Slide the loaf, top side up, onto the center of the stone, taking care not to touch the hot surface. Quickly cover with the stainless-steel mixing bowl. Immediately close the oven door. Bake for 10 minutes; then, lift the edge of the bowl with the tip of a small knife and use oven mitts to carefully remove the hot bowl. Continue to bake until the bread is a deep golden brown and sounds hollow when tapped on the bottom, about 30 minutes more. (It is a good idea to check after the bread has been baking for about 20 minutes to make sure it is browning evenly. If not, rotate the bread.) If you are concerned about the bread's doneness, insert an instant-read thermometer from the bottom of the bread into the center. If it reads 185°F to 210°F the bread is fully baked.

Transfer the loaf to a cooling rack and let it cool for at least 1 hour before cutting with a serrated knife or wrapping for storage.

Finished baking

Raisin Rye Bread

MAKES 1 BOULE

You can incorporate many different flavors into rye flour. I've used dried apricots, dried cherries, and dried cranberries, as well as raisins and currants. I always plump dried fruit in water the night before I'm going to bake to add moistness. Of course, I drain the fruit well before adding to my dough. This raisin version makes a great breakfast toast.

3.5 ounces	100 grams	¾ cup organic raisins
8.5 ounces	240 grams	1 cup plus 1 teaspoon water, plus 1.75 ounces/50 grams (3½ tablespoons) for plumping the raisins
8.8 ounces	250 grams	1⅓ cups plus 1 tablespoon plus 2 teaspoons unbleached, unbromated white bread flour
4.6 ounces	130 grams	1 cup plus 1 tablespoon medium rye flour
0.31 ounce	9 grams	1½ teaspoons fine sea salt
3.5 ounces	100 grams	½ cup liquid *levain* (see page 20)

1 MEASURING

Scale all of the ingredients.

Using an instant-read thermometer, take the temperature of the 8.5 ounces/240 grams water. It should read between 65°F and 70°F. Record it in your Dough Log.

Place the raisins in a small bowl. Add the 1.75 ounces/50 grams water, cover, and set aside at room temperature to rehydrate for at least 4 hours or overnight.

Rehydrate raisins.

2 MIXING AND KNEADING

(These instructions are for using a stand mixer; see page 45 for instructions for mixing by hand.)

Place the wheat and rye flours and salt in a mixing bowl, stirring to blend well.

Pour half of the water into a mixing bowl, and then add the *levain*, stirring to blend.

Pour the *levain*-water mixture into the bowl of a heavy-duty electric stand mixer. Add the flour-salt mixture. Then, attach the dough hook to the mixer. Begin mixing on low speed ("1" on most mixers) and then immediately start to add the remaining water in a slow, steady stream. Continue to mix on low speed for 5 minutes.

Taste the dough to see whether you have forgotten the salt. If so, add it now and mix for another minute.

Stop the mixer and move the dough hook out of the way. Using your bowl scraper, scrape down the sides of the bowl to insure that all of the ingredients are combined in the dough.

Return the dough hook to its original position. Increase the speed to medium-low ("2" on most mixers) and mix until the dough is soft and smooth, with a moist, tacky surface, about 2 minutes.

Drain the raisins well and add them to the dough. Mix on low speed for 2 minutes to incorporate.

3 FIRST FERMENTATION

Using an instant-read thermometer, take the temperature of the dough. It should be between 72°F and 80°F. If it is not, immediately make the necessary adjustments (see page 52). Record the temperature of the dough and the time you finished this step in the Dough Log, and note the time the first fermentation should be completed. This dough will have a first fermentation of 3 hours, with a fold each hour.

Lightly dust a large bowl (preferably glass to allow observation of the process) with flour. Transfer the dough to the bowl, throw a light film of flour over the top to keep the plastic from sticking, tightly cover the bowl with plastic wrap, and place in a warm (75°F to 80°F), draft-free place for 1 hour.

Lightly dust a clean work surface with flour.

Uncover the dough and place it on the floured work surface. Using cupped hands, pat the dough into a thick square. Lift the right corners and fold them into the center of the square, lightly patting the seam down. Lift the left corners and fold them into the center of the square, again lightly patting the seam down. Repeat this process with the top two corners and then the bottom two corners, meeting in the middle of the square and lightly patting down the seams.

Lightly flour the bowl and return the dough to it, seam side down. Cover with plastic wrap and return to a warm (75°F to 80°F), draft-free place for another hour. Record the time in your Dough Log.

Repeat the above process and again place the dough in a warm (75°F to 80°F), draft-free place to rise for a third and final hour. At this point the dough should have increased in body and be less sticky.

4 DIVIDING

Since you are making just 1 loaf, skip to Step 5!

5 SHAPING

Lightly dust a clean work surface with flour.

Using a flat hand, lightly press the dough into a thick rectangle. Lift the dough to make sure that it is not sticking to the work surface. If it is sticking, use the dough scraper to lift it. If it continues to stick, again lightly dust the work surface with flour.

Shape the dough into a *boule* (see page 56).

Place the dough in a lightly floured *banneton*, seam side up. Throw a

Lightly dust banneton *with flour.*

Place dough in banneton *seam side up.*

light film of flour over the top to keep the plastic from sticking, and tightly cover with plastic wrap.

6 FINAL FERMENTATION

Place the *banneton* in a warm (75°F to 80°F), draft-free place for 2½ to 3 hours or, alternatively, proof for 1 hour and then place in the refrigerator for 12 to 16 hours. If the dough has been refrigerated, let it come to room temperature for 1 hour before baking.

If you are using the stainless-steel bowl method to bake the bread (see page 64), about 30 minutes before you are ready to bake, move one oven rack to the lowest rung and remove the other. Place a large baking stone on the rack and preheat the oven to 450°F. (For all other baking methods, follow the directions on page 64.)

To determine whether the dough is ready to be baked, uncover and gently make a small indentation in the center of the dough with your fingertip. If the indentation slowly and evenly disappears, the bread is ready to bake. If not, follow the instructions on page 63 for additional fermentation.

7 BAKING

Throw a light dusting of flour over the dough and transfer to a bread peel or the back of a sheet pan. Working quickly and using a lamé or single-edged razor blade, score the top of the loaf (see page 65). Cut in quick, decisive slashes, marking into the dough by no more than ⅛ inch.

Slide the loaf, top side up, onto the center of the stone, taking care not to touch the hot surface. Quickly cover with the stainless-steel mixing bowl. Immediately close the oven door. Bake for 10 minutes; then, lift the edge of the bowl with the tip of a small knife and use oven mitts to carefully remove the hot bowl. Continue to bake until the bread is a deep golden brown and sounds hollow when tapped on the bottom, about 30 minutes more. (It is a good idea to check after the bread has been baking for about 20 minutes to make sure it is browning evenly. If not, rotate the bread.) If you are concerned about the bread's doneness, insert an instant-read thermometer from the bottom of the bread into the center. If it reads 185°F to 210°F the bread is fully baked.

Transfer the loaf to a cooling rack and let it cool for at least 1 hour before cutting with a serrated knife or wrapping for storage.

Seeded Rye Bread

MAKES 1 BÂTARD

This rye bread uses caraway seed, a very popular flavor with our customers. In France, the seed is known as cumin and it doesn't seem as strong as the seeds we have here. I don't use a lot, but if you really like the flavor to be assertive, add as much as you like. This style of rye bread is frequently referred to as Jewish rye.

8.8 ounces	250 grams	1⅓ cups plus 1 tablespoon plus 2 teaspoons unbleached, unbromated white bread flour
4.6 ounces	130 grams	1 cup plus 1 tablespoon medium rye flour
0.31 ounce	9 grams	1½ teaspoons fine sea salt
8.5 ounces	240 grams	1 cup plus 1 teaspoon water
3.5 ounces	100 grams	½ cup liquid *levain* (see page 20)
0.12 ounce	4 grams	3 teaspoons caraway seeds

1 MEASURING

Scale all of the ingredients.

Using an instant-read thermometer take the temperature of the water. It should read between 65°F and 70°F. Record it in your Dough Log.

Mise en place

MIXING AND KNEADING

(These instructions are for using a stand mixer; see page 45 for instructions for mixing by hand.)

Place the wheat and rye flours and the salt in a mixing bowl, stirring to blend well.

Pour half of the water into a mixing bowl, and then add the *levain*, stirring to blend.

Pour the *levain*-water mixture into the bowl of a heavy-duty electric stand mixer. Add the flour-salt mixture. Then, attach the dough hook to the mixer. Begin mixing on low speed ("1" on most mixers) and then immediately start to add the remaining water in a slow, steady stream. Continue to mix on low speed for 5 minutes.

Taste the dough to see whether you have forgotten the salt. If so, add it now and mix for another minute.

Stop the mixer and move the dough hook out of the way. Using your bowl scraper, scrape down the sides and bottom of the bowl to make sure that all of the ingredients are combined in the dough.

Return the dough hook to its original position. Increase the speed to medium-low ("2" on most mixers) and mix until the dough is soft and smooth, with a moist, tacky surface, about 2 minutes.

Add the caraway seeds, reduce the speed to low, and continue to mix until they are completely incorporated into the dough, about 1 minute.

FIRST FERMENTATION

Using an instant-read thermometer, take the temperature of the dough. It should be between 72°F and 80°F. If it is not, immediately make the necessary adjustments (see page 52). Record the temperature of the dough and the time you finished this step in the Dough Log, and note the time the first fermentation should be completed. This dough will have a first fermentation of 3 hours, with a fold each hour.

Lightly dust a large bowl (preferably glass to allow observation of the process) with flour. Transfer the dough to the bowl, throw a light film of flour over the top to keep the plastic from sticking, tightly cover the bowl with plastic wrap, and place in a warm (75°F to 80°F), draft-free place for 1 hour.

Lightly dust a clean work surface with flour.

Uncover the dough and place it on the floured work surface. Using cupped hands, pat the dough into a thick square. Lift the right corners and fold them into the center of the square, lightly patting the seam down. Lift the left corners and fold them into the center of the square, again lightly patting the seam down. Repeat this process with the top two corners and then the bottom two corners, meeting in the middle of the square and lightly patting down the seams.

Lightly flour the bowl and return the dough to it, seam side down. Cover with plastic wrap and return to a warm (75°F to 80°F), draft-free place for another hour. Record the time in your Dough Log.

Repeat the above process and again place the dough in a warm (75°F to 80°F), draft-free place to rise for a third and final hour. At this point the dough should have increased in body and be less sticky.

4　DIVIDING

Since you are making just 1 loaf, skip to Step 5!

5　SHAPING

Lightly dust a clean work surface with flour.

Using your bowl scraper, transfer the dough to the work surface. Carefully lift the dough, turning the short side to face you. Using a flat hand, press down on the dough and then shape the dough into a *bâtard* (see page 60).

Place the dough in a lightly floured *banneton*, seam side up. Throw a light film of flour over the top to keep the plastic from sticking, and tightly cover with plastic wrap.

6　FINAL FERMENTATION

Place the *banneton* in a warm (75°F to 80°F), draft-free place for 2½ to 3 hours or, alternatively, proof for 1 hour and then place in the refrigerator for 12 to 16 hours. If the dough has been refrigerated, let it come to room temperature for 1 hour before baking.

If you are using the stainless-steel bowl method to bake the bread (see page 64), about 30 minutes before you are ready to bake, move one oven rack to the lowest rung and remove the other. Place a large baking stone on the rack and preheat the oven to 450°F. (For all other baking methods, follow the directions on page 64.)

To determine whether the dough is ready to be baked, uncover and gently make a small indentation in the center in the center of the dough with your fingertip. If the indentation slowly and evenly disappears, the bread is ready to bake. If not, follow the instructions on page 63 for additional fermentation.

7　BAKING

Again, throw a light dusting of flour over the dough and transfer it to a bread peel or the back of a sheet pan.

Working quickly and using a lamé or single-edged razor blade, score the top of the loaf (see page 65). Cut in quick, decisive slashes, marking into the dough by no more than ⅛ inch.

Transfer to bread peel.　　　*Score top of loaf.*　　　*Form into a figure-eight shape.*

Slide the loaf onto the center of the stone, taking care not to touch the hot surface. Quickly cover with the stainless-steel mixing bowl. Immediately close the oven door. Bake for 10 minutes; then, lift the edge of the bowl with the tip of a small knife and use oven mitts to carefully remove the hot bowl. Continue to bake until the bread is a deep golden brown and sounds hollow when tapped on the bottom, about 30 minutes more. (It is a good idea to check after the bread has been baking for about 20 minutes to make sure it is browning evenly. If not, rotate the bread.) If you are concerned about the bread's doneness, insert an instant-read thermometer from the bottom of the bread into the center. If it reads 185°F to 210°F the bread is fully baked.

Transfer the loaf to a cooling rack and let it cool for at least 1 hour before cutting with a serrated knife or wrapping for storage.

DOUGH LOG
(Whole Grain)

beginning water temp:
hand mix 82°–84°
stand mixer 65°–70°

final dough temp:
72°–80°

If dividing (opt) then 10–15 min rest time

Dough Type	Measure Water Temp	Mixing Dough Temp	Mixing Finish Mix Time	Bulk Fermentation (1st Proof) Rest Time	1st Fold	Rest Time	2nd Fold	Rest Time	Divide	Rest Time	Shape	Shape Time	Final Proof Time	Scoring	Baking 450°
Yeasted Breads:															
Example: 100% Whole Wheat (hand mix)	83°	75°	8:00 am	45 min	8:45 am	45 min					boule	9:30 am	1 hr	(crosshatch circle)	10:30 am
100% Whole Wheat				45 min		45 min					boule		1 hr	(crosshatch oval)	
Honey Whole Wheat				45 min		45 min					batard		1 hr	(single line)	
Spelt				45 min		45 min			4 pieces (opt)	10–15 min	mini batards		1 hr	(curved line)	
Corn Bread				45 min		45 min					crown		1–1.5 hr	(concentric circles)	
Natural Levain Starter Breads:															
Example: Multi-Grain (hand mix)	82°	77°	12:00 pm	1 hr	1:00 pm	1 hr	2:00 pm	1 hr	3:00 pm 2 pieces (opt)	10–15 min	(mini) batard	3:15 pm	3 hr min 12–16 hr in fridge	(three dots)	6:15 pm
Multi-Grain				1 hr		1 hr		1 hr			batard		3 hr min 12–16 hr in fridge	(three dots)	
Rye				1 hr		1 hr		1 hr			batard		3 hr min 12–16 hr in fridge	(crosshatch oval)	
Rye with Raisins				1 hr		1 hr		1 hr			boule		3 hr min 12–16 hr in fridge	(crosshatch oval)	
Seeded Rye with Cumin				1 hr		1 hr		1 hr			batard		3 hr min 12–16 hr in fridge	(infinity)	

Notes:

BETWEEN, ON, AND AROUND THE BREAD

When we opened La Farm Bakery, we didn't think beyond making great artisanal bread. However, almost from the beginning, customers asked for more: "Your bakery is so crowded, why don't you expand?" "Too bad you don't have a place to sit." "Your bread is so good, won't you make us some sandwiches?" And since the customer is always right, we expanded with an adjacent café, designed with salvaged bricks and wooden beams, which helped to create the rustic, warm, and inviting interior that remind us of *boulangeries* throughout the French countryside. We developed the café menu based on some of my best food memories, and our mission remained the same—to offer our artisan breads in as many delicious ways as possible.

Early in 2008, on the weekend that our first child, Léa, was born, the La Farm Bakery Café opened to cheers from our customers. We started with limited hours, but within weeks it grew to a full-time business. The menu continues, as it began, to be built by customer demand. We now operate an espresso bar and serve breakfast, lunch, and dinner in our café, as well as a Sunday brunch. And we love every minute of it.

Tomato-Basil Bisque
Pumpkin Soup with Goat Cheese Cream
Soupe à l'Oignon
Avocado-Cucumber Soup
Gazpacho
Croque Madame
Boeuf Champignon
Asparagus and Prosciutto *Tartine*
Oven-Baked Grilled Cheese Sandwich
Quatre Fromages
Cocotte
Walnut-Cranberry Bread Stuffing

Tomato-Basil Bisque

SERVES 6

What could be better than a bowl of homemade tomato soup and a cheese sandwich? This is a favorite combo at the La Farm Bakery Café. Since we use canned San Marzano tomatoes, known for their richness, this soup can be made all year round. A touch of sugar helps the inherent sweetness of ripe tomatoes balance their acidity, and a good dose of fresh basil puts a hint of summer in the bowl. If you plan ahead, this soup is particularly delicious served in a homemade bread Soup Bowls (see page 148).

¼ cup extra-virgin olive oil

6 carrots, peeled and coarsely chopped (about 3 cups)

2 large onions, coarsely chopped (about 3 cups)

One 28-ounce can San Marzano whole tomatoes, undrained

⅓ cup packed chopped fresh basil, plus more for garnish

4 cups homemade chicken stock or low-sodium, nonfat canned chicken broth

1 teaspoon fine sea salt

¼ teaspoon freshly ground black pepper

3 cups heavy cream

1 tablespoon sugar, optional

Garlic Croutons (page 260), optional

Heat the olive oil in a large saucepan over medium heat. When hot, add the carrots and onions and cook, stirring frequently, until the vegetables have begun to soften, about 10 minutes.

Add the tomatoes along with their liquid and 3 tablespoons of the basil. Stir in the stock and season to taste with salt and pepper. Bring to a simmer, lower the heat, and simmer for 20 minutes.

Remove the pan from the heat. Blend the soup to a smooth puree using a handheld immersion blender. Or you can puree the soup, in batches, in a blender or food processor fitted with the metal blade. If using a blender, hold the lid of the blender down with a kitchen towel to keep the heat from forcing the liquid up and out—a messy outcome that you want to avoid!

If pureed in the saucepan, return it to medium-low heat. If processed in a blender or food processor, return the puree to a clean saucepan and place over medium-low heat.

*Pumpkin Soup, Gazpacho,
Tomato-Basil Bisque,
Avocado-Cucumber Soup*

Stir in the cream and the sugar (if using), and bring to a simmer, stirring occasionally. Simmer for 10 minutes. Taste and, if necessary, adjust the seasoning with additional salt, pepper, and sugar.

Remove from the heat and stir in the remaining 2 tablespoons basil.

Ladle into warm soup bowls, garnish with chopped basil, and top with Garlic Croutons, if desired. Serve immediately.

Garlic Croutons

MAKES 4 CUPS

¼ cup unsalted butter, melted

1 medium garlic clove, minced

4 cups ½-inch cubes stale bread

Fine sea salt and freshly ground black pepper

Preheat the oven to 350°F. Line a sheet pan with a silicone liner or parchment paper. Set aside.

Combine the melted butter and garlic in a large mixing bowl. Add the bread cubes, season to taste with salt and pepper, and toss to coat evenly.

Spread the seasoned bread cubes in a single layer on the prepared pan. Transfer to the preheated oven and bake, stirring occasionally, until golden brown and fragrant, 15 to 20 minutes.

Remove from the oven and allow to cool. When cool, store, tightly covered, at room temperature for up to 1 week.

Pumpkin Soup with Goat Cheese Cream

SERVES 4 TO 6

This soup brings back memories of my grandmother, who made it throughout the fall. It always made me laugh because my dad hated pumpkin (*citrouille* in French), and it was fun to see him try to get out of eating it. I loved it then and still do. Pumpkin soup was the soup of French peasants—a thin, watery soup thickened by a bit of tapioca. In America, it is just the opposite—a rich, creamy dish that is part of our fall and winter holiday celebrations. This is now one of our most requested fall soups, served with a large wedge of Multigrain Sourdough Bread (see page 237). It is a wonderful soup for the home cook as it can be made up to 3 days in advance of use and stored, covered and refrigerated, until ready to serve; it also freezes very well.

The Goat Cheese Cream is easy to make and adds a little something extra to the soup. The cream can also be served on toasted La Farm Bread triangles sprinkled with fresh thyme.

¼ cup unsalted butter, at room temperature

1 small celery rib, finely chopped (about ¼ cup)

1 small yellow onion, finely chopped (about ¼ cup)

2 tablespoons all-purpose flour

4 cups warm homemade chicken stock or low-sodium, nonfat canned chicken broth

1 teaspoon pumpkin pie spice

½ teaspoon fine sea salt

¼ teaspoon freshly ground black pepper

One 15-ounce can pumpkin puree

1 cup warm half-and-half

Goat Cheese Cream (recipe follows), for optional garnish

Place the butter in a large saucepan over medium heat. When melted, immediately add the celery and onions. Don't let the butter brown. Cook, stirring constantly, until the onions begin to be translucent, about 3 minutes.

Whisking constantly, stir in the flour. Cook until the flour has been completely incorporated into the butter and vegetable juices, about 2 minutes.

Still whisking constantly, beat in the warm stock. Continue whisking until the soup comes to a boil. The soup will begin to thicken.

Add the pumpkin pie spice and season with salt and pepper. Cook, stirring frequently, and allow to simmer for 2 minutes.

Whisk in the pumpkin puree, raise the heat, and bring to a boil. Immediately reduce the heat, cover, and cook at a bare simmer for 10 minutes.

Remove the soup from the heat and whisk in the half-and-half. Taste and, if necessary, adjust the seasoning with additional salt and pepper.

Ladle into warm soup bowls and serve garnished with a dollop of Goat Cheese Cream on top, if desired.

Goat Cheese Cream

MAKES 1 CUP

4 ounces fresh goat cheese, at room temperature (about ½ cup)

½ cup heavy cream

½ teaspoon minced fresh thyme leaves

¼ teaspoon freshly ground black pepper

Place the cheese in the bowl of a food processor fitted with the metal blade. With the motor running, slowly add the cream through the feed tube. When all of the cream has been incorporated, add the thyme and pepper and process to just blend.

If not using immediately, use a rubber spatula to scrape the mixture into a nonreactive container. Cover and refrigerate up to 1 week.

Here are some ideas for pairing croutons made with a variety of La Farm breads from this book:

❈ Walnut-Sage Sourdough Croutons (see page 211) on salads with blue cheese

❈ Asiago-Parmesan Croutons (see page 187) to make *panzanella* (Italian bread salad)

❈ Multigrain Sourdough Croutons (see page 237) with hearty stews and thick winter soups

❈ Sesame Semolina Croutons (see page 201) on cheese-based soups

❈ Kalamata Olive Croutons (see page 207) on tossed green salads

❈ Focaccia Croutons (see page 151) on Caesar salads

Soupe à l'Oignon

SERVES 6

Classic French onion soup is rich, deeply colored, and deeply satisfying on a cold winter day. My brother, Laurent, is a chef, and he helped La Farm create an authentic French soup. According to Laurent, *Soupe à l'Oignon* was traditionally made in the early morning following a wedding or other celebration to hide the alcohol on the breath of the partiers.

It is not difficult to make, but you do need to let the onions really caramelize to achieve the full-bodied flavor that defines the dish. My trick is to use a mix of sweet yellow and red onions and shallots—yellow for their meatiness, red for sweetness, and shallots for their zest. If you take the time to fully caramelize the mix over low heat, your soup will be perfect. Slices of fresh (or not-so-fresh) bread are toasted to create the required "lid" for the soup.

2 tablespoons unsalted butter

2 tablespoons extra-virgin olive oil

4 medium yellow onions, thinly sliced

2 large red onions, thinly sliced

2 small shallots, thinly sliced

3 tablespoons dry white wine

3 tablespoons dry sherry

8 cups homemade beef stock or low-sodium, nonfat canned beef broth

1 bay leaf

2 tablespoons Worcestershire sauce

2 tablespoons chopped flat-leaf parsley

1 tablespoon freshly ground black pepper

Six ⅛-inch-thick slices La Farm Bread (page 177) or Baguette (page 79), toasted (see Note)

Six ¼-inch-thick slices Gruyère or Comté cheese or ¼ cup shredded Gruyère or Comté cheese (see Note, page 123)

Preheat the broiler to 500°F. Line a baking sheet—small enough to fit under the broiler and large enough to hold six 8-ounce ovenproof crocks—with parchment paper. Place the crocks on the lined baking sheet and set aside.

Combine the butter and oil in a large (6- to 8-quart) heavy-bottomed saucepan over medium-low heat. When melted, add both the yellow and red

onions along with the shallots. Cook, stirring frequently, until the onions are caramelized (golden brown and almost sugary), about 1 hour.

Add the white wine and sherry to the saucepan, stirring to scrape up the brown bits on the bottom of the pan. Cook, stirring, until the wine has begun to evaporate, 4 to 5 minutes. Add the stock, along with the bay leaf, Worcestershire sauce, parsley, and pepper, and bring to a boil. Immediately lower the heat and simmer for 15 minutes.

Remove from the heat and discard the bay leaf. Ladle an equal portion of the onion soup into each crock, filling each about three-quarters full. Top each one with a piece of toast followed by either a slice of cheese or an equal amount of shredded cheese.

Transfer the baking sheet to the preheated oven and broil until the cheese is melted and golden brown, about 5 minutes. Serve immediately.

Note: The bread should be cut in a shape that will exactly fit the top of the soup crocks. If you use dry, stale bread, there will be no need to toast it.

Avocado-Cucumber Soup

SERVES 4

This is a refreshing and easy-to-make cold soup. Our customers love it—thick and icy-cold—all through our hot and humid North Carolina summers. We turn it into a complete meal when served with a *tartine* made with Jalapeño-Cheddar Bread (see page 197) topped with grilled chicken, aged cheddar or Monterey Jack cheese, grilled onions, and roasted peppers.

3 scallions (green parts only), sliced

3 ripe avocados, halved, pitted, and scooped out, reserve 1 avocado for garnish

3 cucumbers, peeled, seeded, and coarsely chopped, reserve 1 cucumber for garnish

2½ cups buttermilk

2 tablespoons freshly squeezed lemon juice

2 tablespoons seeded and finely diced jalapeño peppers

2 tablespoons chopped fresh cilantro

1 medium garlic clove, minced

½ teaspoon Tabasco or other hot pepper sauce

2 teaspoons fine sea salt

½ teaspoon ground cumin

¼ teaspoon ground white pepper

¼ cup plain, nonfat Greek-style yogurt, for optional garnish

Combine the scallions, scooped-out avocados, cucumbers, buttermilk, and lemon juice in a large nonreactive bowl. Using a handheld immersion blender, begin to process the mixture into a puree. While still chunky, add the jalapeños, cilantro, garlic, and hot sauce and continue to blend. Then, add the salt, cumin, and pepper and process until very smooth. (Alternatively, puree the soup, in batches, in a blender or food processor fitted with the metal blade.) Taste and, if necessary, adjust the seasoning with additional salt, pepper, or hot sauce.

Ladle the soup into shallow soup bowls and garnish the center with a dollop of yogurt, if desired, and then add an equal portion of diced avocado and cucumber. Serve.

Gazpacho

SERVES 6

My brother, Laurent, who is a chef in Switzerland, created this recipe especially for the Café at La Farm Bakery. We use leftover La Farm Bread, our signature light sourdough, to make this smooth version of the classic chilled summertime vegetable soup. However, if you don't have a loaf on hand, any light sourdough bread could be used. As an accompaniment, warm Jalapeño-Cheddar Bread (see page 197) or any fresh warm crusty bread will turn the soup into a complete meal.

Two 28-ounce cans crushed San Marzano tomatoes

3 cups tomato juice, preferably low-sodium organic

1½ cups chopped fresh cilantro

1 medium cucumber, peeled, seeded, and chopped (about 1 cup)

1 large red bell pepper, seeded and chopped (about 1 cup)

1 cup cubed stale La Farm Bread (page 177) or other light sourdough bread

2 tablespoons extra-virgin olive oil

2 tablespoons red wine vinegar

½ teaspoon Tabasco or other hot pepper sauce

1 teaspoon fine sea salt

1 teaspoon freshly ground black pepper

1 small red onion, finely diced (about ½ cup), for garnish

1 medium red bell pepper, seeded and finely diced (about ½ cup), for garnish

1 medium cucumber, peeled, seeded, and finely diced (about ½ cup), for garnish

Combine the crushed tomatoes, tomato juice, cilantro, chopped cucumber, chopped bell pepper, bread cubes, and oil in a deep bowl. Cover and refrigerate until well chilled, at least 2 hours and up to 24 hours.

Use a handheld immersion blender to puree the soup until very smooth. Or you can puree the soup, in batches, in a blender or food processor fitted with the metal blade.

Stir in the vinegar and hot sauce and season with salt and pepper.

Pour an equal portion of the soup into each of six shallow soup bowls. Garnish the center of each bowl with finely diced red onion, bell pepper, and cucumber. Serve immediately.

Croque Madame

SERVES 2

Croque Monsieur or *Croque Madame*? I'll always opt for the feminine of the two, which is, of course, the richer and more inviting. I've often wondered if the two fried eggs on top had more than a little suggestive meaning—and, being French, I think they do.

Croque Madame is a favorite from my childhood. On those days when my mother didn't have a lot of time to prepare dinner, these rich, filling sandwiches were frequently on the menu. Mom used a crusty bread found in bistros and homes throughout France, but I use our signature La Farm Bread. You could also use Country French Bread (see page 75).

Unlike the standard American-style grilled cheese sandwich, a *Croque Madame* is baked with melted cheese inside and out. Since it is extremely rich and filling, it can be served for brunch, lunch, or even dinner. In the morning, accompany the sandwich with a fresh fruit salad; later on, a salad of tender greens lightly tossed with a light vinaigrette is all that is needed to complete the meal.

Four ¾-inch-thick slices La Farm Bread (page 177)

Four ⅛-inch-thick slices Comté or Gruyère cheese (see Note, page 123)

2 thin slices French-style boiled ham or other unsmoked ham

¼ cup Mornay Sauce (page 270)

½ cup shredded mozzarella cheese

4 teaspoons clarified butter

4 large eggs, at room temperature

Fine sea salt and freshly ground black pepper

2 teaspoons chopped fresh chives, optional

Preheat the oven to 450°F.

Line a baking sheet with a silicone liner or parchment paper. Place 2 slices of bread on the lined pan. Place a slice of cheese on each slice of bread; then, place a slice of ham on top of the cheese. Top the ham with the final slice of cheese and cover with the remaining slice of bread.

Spread 2 tablespoons of the Mornay Sauce on top of each sandwich, making sure that the entire top is completely covered with sauce. Sprinkle an equal portion of the mozzarella on top of each sandwich.

Clarified butter is simply butter that has been slowly heated over very low heat until the butterfat and milk solids have separated. The milk-solid proteins are what cause butter to burn when heated so, once separated, the clear butter is poured off and the milk solids discarded. By using clarified butter, higher heat can be used when frying and sautéing. The clarifying process can be done on the stovetop or in a microwave oven. One stick (½ cup / 8 tablespoons) unsalted butter will yield about ⅓ cup clarified butter.

To make clarified butter:

MICROWAVE METHOD:
Place one stick (½ cup/8 tablespoons) unsalted butter, in its wrapper and at room temperature, in a 1-quart glass measuring cup. Place in the microwave and heat on high until completely melted, about 2 minutes. Discard the wrapper. Cool until the butter separates into three distinct layers, 5 minutes. Proceed to the final step (below).

STOVETOP METHOD:
Place one stick (½ cup/8 tablespoons) unsalted butter in a small, heavy-bottomed saucepan over low heat. Cook until completely melted, 2 minutes. Remove from the heat and cool until the butter separates into three distinct layers, 5 minutes. Proceed to the final step.

FINAL STEP: Using a small ladle, skim off and discard the foamy milk-fat solids from the top. Carefully pour the clear, bright yellow butter into a clean container. Discard the milky solids that have settled on the bottom. Set the clarified butter aside to cool. Cover and refrigerate up to one month.

Place in the preheated oven and bake until the sandwiches are golden brown and bubbling, about 10 minutes.

While the sandwiches are baking, heat 2 teaspoons of clarified butter in each of two small frying pans over medium heat.

Carefully break 2 eggs into each of two small ramekins (this is to ensure that no contamination on the shell makes its way into the cooking eggs). Carefully tip the eggs into each pan. Season with salt and pepper to taste and cook for 1 minute. Using a flexible spatula, turn the eggs and cook to the desired degree of doneness. (At La Farm Bakery, we prefer an oozy, runny yolk to mix in with the melted cheese.)

Place each hot, bubbling sandwich on a warm luncheon plate. Transfer 2 eggs to the top of each sandwich, season to taste with salt and pepper, garnish with chopped chives (if using), and serve immediately.

Mornay Sauce

MAKES 1 GENEROUS CUP

¾ cup heavy cream

2 tablespoons unsalted butter, at room temperature

1½ tablespoons all-purpose flour

1 ounce (about ¾ cup) shredded Comté or Gruyère cheese (see Note, page 123)

½ teaspoon fine sea salt

Place the heavy cream in a small saucepan over medium heat and bring to a bare simmer. Remove from the heat and cover to keep warm.

Place the butter in a medium saucepan over medium heat. When melted, stir in the flour and cook, stirring constantly, until the flour has been completely incorporated into the butter, about 2 minutes. Do not allow the mixture to brown.

Immediately whisk in the warm cream and bring to a simmer. Add the cheese and season with salt. Cook, stirring constantly, until the cheese has melted and the sauce is thick and smooth.

Remove from the heat and set aside to cool until firm enough to spread easily, about 30 minutes. The sauce may be made up to 3 days in advance and stored, covered and refrigerated, until ready to use.

Boeuf Champignon

SERVES 2

This sandwich is terrific on a crusty French bread. It captures the classic flavors of my country with a *soupçon*—just a hint—of spiciness. Actually, you can make the *aïoli* as spicy as you like by adjusting the amount of cayenne, but don't use too little as it is necessary to balance the richness of the beef. Be sure to add the *aïoli* just as you're putting the sandwich together; otherwise the heat will cause it to separate.

In the La Farm Bakery Café we strain the onions from our *Soupe à l'Oignon* (see page 263) to make this sandwich. If you are feeling particularly ambitious, make the soup and do the same. They are delicious!

To use for a party, double the recipe and cut the sandwiches, crosswise, into bite-sized pieces or small finger sandwiches.

2 teaspoons extra-virgin olive oil

1 teaspoon unsalted butter, at room temperature

1 small Vidalia or other sweet onion, sliced crosswise into rings

4 ounces button or cremini mushrooms, sliced (about ½ cup)

Fine sea salt and freshly ground black pepper

½ pound medium-rare roast beef, sliced

2 Baguettes (page 79) or other small baguette-style breads, halved lengthwise

2 ounces (¼ cup) Saint Agur or other blue cheese, at room temperature (see Notes, page 273)

¼ cup Cayenne Aïoli (page 273)

Twelve ½-inch-thick strips roasted red bell pepper

Cornichons, optional (see Notes, page 273)

Preheat the oven to 450°F. Line a baking sheet with a silicone liner or parchment paper and set aside.

Combine the oil and butter in a medium frying pan over medium heat. When hot but not smoking, add the onion, stirring to coat. Cook, stirring frequently, until the onion is translucent, about 5 minutes. Add the mushrooms, lightly season with salt and pepper, and continue to cook, stirring

occasionally, until the mushrooms have sweated their liquid, about 5 minutes. Remove from the heat.

Form the roast beef into 2 equal mounds in the same shape as the baguettes and place the mounds on the prepared baking sheet. Place 2 equal portions of the onion/mushroom mixture next to the mounds of beef. Place in the preheated oven and bake for 5 minutes.

Lightly coat the cut side of each baguette top with half of the blue cheese. Place the baguette tops, cheese side up, on the baking sheet next to the beef and onion/mushroom mixture and continue to bake just until heated through, about 3 minutes.

Spread half of the *aïoli* on the cut side of each baguette heel. Place a mound of hot roast beef on top of each cheese-coated baguette piece, followed by a mound of onion/mushroom mixture. Top each with 6 strips of roasted pepper. Cover with the aioli-coated baguette half and press down lightly.

Using a serrated knife, cut each sandwich on the diagonal into two equal pieces. Serve warm with some cornichons on the side, if desired.

Cayenne Aïoli

1 cup fine-quality mayonnaise (see Notes)

2 tablespoons sour cream

1 tablespoon freshly squeezed lemon juice

1 large garlic clove, minced

1 teaspoon Dijon mustard

¼ teaspoon cayenne pepper

¼ teaspoon fine sea salt

Combine all of the ingredients in a small mixing bowl, whisking to blend thoroughly. Taste and add more salt if needed.

Cover and refrigerate for 30 minutes to allow the flavors to balance. The *aïoli* can be stored, covered and refrigerated, for up to 3 days.

Notes: Saint Agur is an aged, double-cream French cheese from the Auvergne region that is intensely flavored. It is very smooth and spreadable, made quite tangy by the green mold veins that marble it. It is not as salty as most other blue cheeses. It was developed in the mid 1980s and its name is a mystery as there is no person or place called Saint Agur!

Cornichons are tiny French sour pickles often served as a garnish for pâtés, cured meats, and cheeses. They are available in specialty food stores and many supermarkets.

At home in France, we always make our own mayonnaise. It is so easy to do and tastes so fresh. To make 1 cup homemade mayonnaise, simply whisk 1 large egg yolk with 1½ teaspoons freshly squeezed lemon juice (strained), 1 teaspoon white wine vinegar, ¾ teaspoon Dijon mustard, and a pinch of sugar; then whisk in about ¾ cup extra-virgin olive oil. When blended, season with fine sea salt and white pepper. *Et, voilà! Mayonnaise, très délicieuse!*

Asparagus and Prosciutto Tartine

SERVES 2

A *tartine* is nothing more than the French version of an open-faced sandwich, with either a simple or an extravagant topping. This *tartine* is the latter, with its mix of asparagus, cheese, artichokes, and prosciutto. It also has two components, Oven-Roasted Tomatoes and Tapenade, that are great to have on hand to jazz up all sorts of other dishes—pastas, salads, grilled fish, or poultry—so don't hesitate to double or even triple the recipes for them.

Growing up, a *tartine* was on the menu daily. One of my father's favorites was the simplest of all: a long slice of baguette, lightly coated with sweet butter, sprinkled with sea salt from the nearby Île de Ré, and topped with a thin bar of his special dark chocolate. My mom would say that you could set your watch by Dad's afternoon break, promptly at 2:00 p.m. daily. The schedule never varied.

Gary Wood, our great friend who has been instrumental in every aspect of the café, helped me develop this recipe in the spring when we opened. It's become a local favorite, and was even featured in *Food & Wine* magazine.

4 pencil-thin asparagus spears, tough ends trimmed

1 tablespoon extra-virgin olive oil

1 medium shallot, finely diced

Two ¾-inch-thick slices Asiago-Parmesan Bread (see page 187)

Two ¼-inch-thick slices fresh mozzarella, each torn into 3 pieces

2 teaspoons Tapenade (page 277)

2 slices Comté or Gruyère cheese (see Note, page 123)

2 ounces fresh goat cheese

4 paper-thin slices prosciutto

2 Oven-Roasted Tomatoes (page 276)

1 marinated artichoke, cut into quarters

Aged balsamic vinegar, for drizzling

Line a baking sheet small enough to fit under the broiler with a silicone liner or parchment paper. Set aside.

Fill a shallow sauté pan with about an inch of cold water and place over medium heat. Bring to a boil. Add the asparagus, lower the heat,

One of my favorite summer *tartines* is an open baguette slathered with slightly soft sweet butter, sprinkled with crunchy sea salt, and topped with really, really ripe strawberries that have been mashed with a bit of sugar. I let it sit for about 15 minutes so that the berry juices can sink into the bread.

and simmer until crisp-tender but still bright green, about 2 minutes. Immediately remove from the heat and drain well. Place the asparagus in a bowl and cover with ice to quickly cool down. When cool, drain well and pat dry. Set aside.

Place the oil in a small frying pan over medium heat. Add the shallot and cook, stirring frequently, until the shallot is soft and translucent, about 4 minutes. Remove from the heat and scrape the shallots onto a small plate to cool to room temperature.

Preheat the broiler.

Place the bread on the prepared baking sheet. Spread half of the cooled shallots on each slice of bread. Top each with 3 pieces of the torn mozzarella and drizzle half of the tapenade over the mozzarella. Then, place 2 asparagus spears on top of each, followed by 1 slice of Comté cheese.

Place the baking sheet under the broiler and broil until the cheese melts and begins to brown, about 2 minutes.

Remove from the broiler and immediately top each *tartine* with equal dollops of goat cheese, followed by 2 slices of prosciutto. Place a roasted tomato in the center of each.

Slice each *tartine* in half on the diagonal. Garnish each half with an artichoke quarter, drizzle with balsamic vinegar, and serve.

Oven-Roasted Tomatoes

MAKES 8

4 whole plum tomatoes, halved lengthwise and seeded

1 tablespoon extra-virgin olive oil

1 teaspoon dried Italian herb blend

½ teaspoon fine sea salt

½ teaspoon freshly ground black pepper

Preheat the oven to 325°F. Line a rimmed baking sheet with a silicone liner or parchment paper. Set aside.

Combine the tomatoes with the olive oil, herb blend, salt, and pepper in a medium mixing bowl, tossing to coat well. Place the tomatoes, cut side up, on the prepared baking sheet.

Bake until the tomatoes are very soft and beginning to dry around the edges, about 1 hour.

Remove from the oven and set aside to cool. Store, coated with a layer of olive oil, in a covered container in the refrigerator for up to 1 week.

Tapenade

MAKES ½ CUP

¾ cup pitted kalamata olives

2 tablespoons capers, drained

2 tablespoons extra-virgin olive oil

½ teaspoon minced fresh flat-leaf parsley

1 small garlic clove, minced

¼ teaspoon diced anchovies packed in oil (see Notes)

¼ teaspoon freshly squeezed lemon juice

Combine all of the ingredients in the bowl of a small food processor and process until the mixture is coarsely chopped, about 15 seconds. Do not overprocess or the tapenade will be too smooth.

If not serving immediately, scrape into a clean container, cover, and refrigerate. Tapenade will keep for about 1 month.

Notes: Tapenade, a classic and quite traditional Provençal spread, is easy to make, but it is also available from specialty food stores and many supermarkets. Tapenade is often served on small squares of toasted baguette as a light snack with an apéritif. It can also be used as a condiment for grilled fish or chicken.

If you don't like (or are allergic to) anchovies, replace them with an equal amount of sun-dried tomatoes packed in oil.

Oven-Baked Grilled Cheese Sandwich

MAKES 2

At La Farm Bakery Café we created a unique twist on the classic grilled cheese sandwich—a blend of three cheeses melted around a vine-ripened tomato. Our deeply flavored La Farm Bread stands up to all of the bold flavors in the sandwich. If you don't have it on hand, use an artisanal sourdough or even a multigrain bread. We use the oven because cooking a grilled cheese sandwich on the stovetop always seems to burn the bread before the cheese is meltingly wonderful.

Four ¾-inch-thick slices La Farm Bread (page 177)

¼ cup Mornay Sauce (page 270)

4 thin slices beefsteak tomato

Two ⅛-inch-thick slices red onion, separated into rings

Two ⅛-inch-thick slices cheddar cheese

½ cup shredded mozzarella cheese

2 teaspoons grated Pecorino Romano cheese

2 teaspoon Chipotle Aïoli (page 280)

2 teaspoons unsalted butter, at room temperature

Preheat the oven to 475°F. Line a baking sheet with a silicone liner or parchment paper.

Lightly coat 2 slices of bread with 2 tablespoons of the Mornay Sauce each. Place them, coated side up, on the prepared baking sheet.

Top each slice of bread with 2 slices of tomato, followed by 2 to 3 onion rings. Cover with a slice of cheddar and half of the mozzarella, and then sprinkle on half of the Pecorino.

Spread the remaining 2 slices of bread with 1 teaspoon of the Chipotle Aïoli each. Place the bread, coated side down, on top of the sandwiches.

Spread the top of each sandwich with 1 teaspoon butter.

Transfer the baking sheet to the preheated oven and bake until golden brown and oozing cheese, about 10 minutes.

Remove from the oven and transfer to a cutting board. Using a serrated knife, cut the sandwiches in half on the diagonal, and serve immediately.

Chipotle Aïoli

MAKES 1 GENEROUS CUP

1 cup homemade or fine-quality mayonnaise (see Notes, page 273)

2 tablespoons chopped canned chipotle peppers in adobo, including sauce (see Note)

2 tablespoons freshly squeezed lemon juice

2 tablespoons cold water

½ teaspoon fine sea salt

Combine the mayonnaise with the chipotles and lemon juice in a small mixing bowl. Add the cold water and whisk to blend thoroughly. Add the salt and whisk to blend.

Cover and refrigerate for at least 30 minutes to allow the flavors to blend. The *aïoli* can be stored, covered and refrigerated, for up to 3 days.

Note: Chipotle peppers in adobo are available from Latin markets, specialty food stores, and many large supermarkets. They are smoked jalapeños that are packed in a seasoned tomato sauce. They are quite hot, with a deep earthy-smoky flavor.

Quatre Fromages

SERVES 8 TO 10

In France, nothing is wasted when it comes to bread; even the crumbs are collected from the cutting board. One way we use stale bread is to make breadcrumbs. This recipe is all about the classic cheese and pasta mix with great breadcrumbs providing the extra crispness that I love. I grew up on *pâtes coquillettes*, a simple dish of elbow macaroni mixed with tomato paste and Gruyère cheese. The first time I ate American mac 'n' cheese, it was made with processed cheese, which didn't hold much appeal to me.

When we opened the Café at La Farm Bakery I wanted to use our breadcrumbs in a way that would highlight the variety of flavors that come together in the combination of all of our breads. Together, our team created this marvelous and complex cheese flavor using four cheeses that thoroughly met with my approval. We ended up with a really cheesy mac 'n' cheese—a bit sharp and very smooth—that satisfies everyone.

2 cups whole milk

1 cup heavy cream

2 tablespoons unsalted butter

2 tablespoons all-purpose flour

12 ounces (about 3 cups) shredded cheddar cheese

4 ounces (about 1 cup) shredded mozzarella cheese

2 ounces (about ½ cup) shredded Comté or Gruyère cheese (see Note, page 123)

2 ounces (about ¼ cup) grated Pecorino Romano cheese

½ teaspoon fine sea salt

¼ teaspoon freshly ground black pepper

1 pound elbow macaroni, cooked and drained according to package directions

2 cups Breadcrumbs (page 283)

Preheat the oven to 350°F. Lightly coat a 9-by-13-by-2-inch ovenproof baking dish with nonstick vegetable spray and set aside.

Combine the milk and cream in a medium saucepan over medium-low heat and cook just until bubbles begin to form around the edges of the pan, about 4 minutes. Immediately remove from the heat and cover to keep warm. (Alternatively, combine the milk and cream in a microwaveable bowl and heat on high for 3 minutes.)

Here are some other great combos for oven-baked cheese sandwiches:

❋ Cinnamon Raisin Pecan Bread (see page 193) with brie and fig jam

❋ White Chocolate Mini-Baguette (see page 111) with ham, turkey, Dijon mustard, and cheddar

❋ Walnut-Sage Sourdough Bread (see page 211) with blue cheese, pears, and honey

❋ Kalamata Olive Bread (see page 207) with feta cheese, Oven-Roasted Tomatoes (see page 276), and red onions

❋ Sesame Semolina Bread (see page 201) with provolone or mozzarella and mortadella, capicola, or salami, plus Oven-Roasted Tomatoes (see page 276) and fresh basil leaves

Place the butter in a large, heavy-bottomed saucepan over low heat. When melted, stir in the flour and cook, stirring constantly, until a roux has formed, about 2 minutes.

Whisking constantly, add the warm milk mixture and cook, continuing to whisk, until the mixture comes to a boil, about 4 minutes. Immediately lower the heat and stir in all of the cheeses. Cook, stirring constantly, until the cheeses have melted and the sauce is very smooth, about 5 minutes. Season with salt and pepper.

Add the cooked macaroni, stirring to blend completely. Taste and, if necessary, season with additional salt and pepper.

Pour the mac 'n' cheese into the prepared dish and smooth the top. Generously sprinkle the breadcrumbs evenly over the top.

Place in the preheated oven and bake until bubbling and golden brown on top, about 20 minutes.

Remove from the oven and serve.

Breadcrumbs

MAKES 2 CUPS

2 cups stale bread cubes

2 tablespoons unsalted butter, melted

Preheat the oven to 350°F. Line a baking sheet with a silicone liner or parchment paper. Set aside.

Place the bread cubes in the bowl of a food processor fitted with the metal blade and process until very fine crumbs have formed.

Transfer the crumbs to a medium mixing bowl. Add the butter and toss to blend well. Spill the buttered crumbs out onto the prepared baking sheet, spreading them out into a thin layer.

Place in the preheated oven and bake until golden and aromatic, about 10 minutes.

Remove from the oven and set aside to cool. When cool, place in a resealable plastic bag and freeze for up to 3 months.

Cocotte

SERVES 10 TO 12

You can use any style of bread or even a mixture of many different varieties to make a *cocotte* (casserole). Ours is a breakfast *cocotte* filled with spicy sausage, smoked ham, sautéed mushrooms, and shallots tossed with bread cubes in a delicious egg custard and then topped with breadcrumbs before baking. It is a good idea to freeze the ends of bread that don't get used for that "rainy day" when a breakfast *cocotte* is just the thing to warm hearts and tummies. A *cocotte* is also terrific for easy entertaining, as it has to be made the night before it is to be served, allowing the host to spend very little time in the kitchen while the brunch gathering is going on. La Farm customers often buy our savory bread pudding and then reheat it to serve for an easy Sunday morning brunch along with sparkling mimosas.

1 loaf La Farm Bread (page 177), slightly stale, cut into 1-inch cubes

1 Baguette (page 79), slightly stale, cut into 1-inch cubes (about 2 pounds total)

1 tablespoon canola oil

1 pound pork breakfast sausage, crumbled

8 ounces button mushrooms, quartered

6 shallots or 1 medium onion, finely chopped

4 garlic cloves, finely chopped

¼ cup dry white wine

½ pound smoked ham, finely diced

2 cups shredded mozzarella cheese

½ cup grated Comté or Gruyère cheese (see Note, page 123)

12 large eggs, at room temperature

3 cups heavy cream

1 tablespoon fine sea salt

1 teaspoon freshly ground black pepper

Lightly coat a 9-by-13-by-2-inch baking dish with nonstick vegetable spray.

Combine the sourdough and baguette cubes in a large mixing bowl, tossing to blend well. Place half of the bread cubes in the prepared baking dish. Set aside.

Heat the oil in a large frying pan over medium heat. Add the sausage and fry, stirring frequently, until nicely browned, about 10 minutes. Using a slotted spoon, transfer the sausage crumbles to a double layer of paper towels to drain, leaving the fat in the pan.

Keeping the pan on medium heat, add the mushrooms and cook, stirring frequently, for 4 minutes. Add the shallots and fry, stirring frequently, for 2 additional minutes. Stir in the garlic and fry for 1 additional minute.

Add the wine and cook, stirring to deglaze the pan, for 1 minute. Remove from the heat and set aside.

Sprinkle half of the ham over the bread cubes in the baking dish, followed by half of the sausage. Spoon half of the mushroom mixture over the sausage and then sprinkle with half of the mozzarella. Cover with the remaining bread cubes and then repeat the layering of ham, sausage, mushrooms, and mozzarella. Cover the top with the Comté cheese. Set aside.

Combine the eggs and cream in a large mixing bowl, whisking to blend well. Season with salt and pepper and then pour over the top of the casserole. Cover the pan with foil.

Transfer to the refrigerator and allow the bread to absorb the flavors and the liquid for at least 4 hours or up to 12 hours.

Remove the *cocotte* from the refrigerator 1 hour before baking and set aside, still covered, to come to room temperature. It's important to bring the casserole to room temperature before baking or the bottom will burn before it is cooked through.

About 30 minutes before baking, preheat the oven to 375°F.

Place the casserole on a baking sheet in the preheated oven. (The sheet will catch any liquid that bubbles over the top.) Bake for 1 hour. Then, uncover and bake until golden brown and bubbling, about 15 minutes more.

Remove from the oven and let rest for 10 to 15 minutes before cutting and serving.

Walnut-Cranberry Bread Stuffing

MAKES 8 CUPS

I have very fond memories of my mom making holiday stuffing from chestnuts that had been roasted on a woodstove. Even today, the smell of roasting chestnuts says Christmas to me. I'm sure this came from lean years, when poor folks made the best with what the land offered and chestnuts could be picked in the wild.

I now use walnuts in my stuffing, although you could replace them with roasted chestnuts if you like. This is a wonderful stuffing not only for poultry and other meats, but for winter squashes, too.

2 teaspoons poultry seasoning

2 teaspoons minced dried onion

½ teaspoon garlic powder

½ teaspoon fine sea salt

½ teaspoon freshly ground black pepper

3 tablespoons water

1 tablespoon canola oil

2 medium yellow onions, chopped

3 large celery ribs, chopped

8 cups ½-inch cubes stale La Farm Bread (page 177) or other artisanal bread

1 large tart apple, peeled, cored, and diced, optional

½ cup fresh cranberries, optional

½ cup chopped walnuts, optional

1¾ cups homemade chicken stock or low-sodium, nonfat canned chicken broth

Preheat the oven to 350°F. Generously butter a 2-quart casserole and set aside.

Combine the poultry seasoning, dried onion, garlic powder, salt, and pepper in a small mixing bowl. Stir in the water and set aside to allow the flavors to blend.

Place the oil in a large frying pan over medium heat. Add the onion and celery and cook, stirring frequently, until the vegetables have begun to sweat their liquid and the onion is translucent, about 10 minutes. Remove from the heat and set aside.

Place the bread cubes in a large mixing bowl. If using, add the apple, cranberries, and nuts, tossing to blend. Scrape the reserved onion-celery mixture over the top. Add the reserved seasoned water and the chicken stock, tossing until the mixture is completely blended and the bread is nicely moistened.

Scrape the mixture into the prepared casserole. Transfer to the preheated oven and bake until golden brown and crispy on the top and cooked through, about 45 minutes. (Alternatively, use as a stuffing for chicken, turkey, or a rolled pork roast.)

Serve hot.

ACKNOWLEDGMENTS

I would like to sincerely thank the following, without whose efforts this book would not have been possible: my incredible wife, Missy, for her tireless support of me, La Farm Bakery, and the world of artisan bread; my beautiful daughters, Léa and Emilie, may they never know a bad loaf of bread; our wonderful writer, Judith Choate, for finding the essence of my pilgrimage and passion for bread and bringing it to life in words; café designer, menu consultant, and dear friend Gary Wood, whose direction shows in every brick and *tartine* of the café; David Kuhn and the incredible agent team at Kuhn Projects; editor Michael Sand, for the guidance and support, and the entire team at Little, Brown and Company; our recipe testers, Connie and Donn Hay, Belinda Ellis, and Fred Thompson, as well as Ginger Zucchino and her fearless team of home testers who valiantly marched into the world of bread; the photographer, Gordon Munro, for his gorgeous work; Tamara Lackey and David Sciabarasi for their supporting photographs; my amazing press agent, Jennifer Noble Kelly; and the wonderful staffs at Williams-Sonoma Southpoint, Southern Season, and Pottery Barn Southpoint for their generosity in loaning some of the beautiful props you see in this book.

To every baker who ever taught me, and to every student I ever worked with—from whom I learned so much more; to Michel Suas, author of *Advanced Bread and Pastry: A Professional Approach,* for bringing me to this wonderful country and allowing me the platform to teach and consult on my passion for bread; to Didier Rosada, a great baker and friend who helped review the book, since he is better at English than me; and, finally, to the La Farm Bakery staff and customers and the professional teams of bakers I still get to work for around the world—thank you for allowing and appreciating my passion for bread.

SOURCES

Southern Season (specialty foods, cheeses, wines, and kitchen equipment)
(866) 253-5317
www.southernseason.com

Williams-Sonoma (gourmet foods, professional kitchen equipment, and supplies)
(877) 812-6235
www.williams-sonoma.com

Sur la Table (fine cookware, cutlery, kitchen equipment, and supplies)
(800)-243-0852
www.surlatable.com

Pottery Barn (tableware and some cookware)
(888) 779-5176
www.potterybarn.com

Crate & Barrel (tableware, kitchen equipment, and supplies)
(800) 967-6696
www.crateandbarrel.com

Sassafras Enterprises (La Cloche baker and other specialty baking supplies)
(800) 537-4941
www.sassafrasstore.com

Mora (kitchen equipment and supplies)
01-45-08-1924 (France)
www.mora.fr

King Arthur Flour (specialty baking supplies)
(800) 827-6836
www.kingarthurflour.com

Whole Foods Market (natural and organic food market)
Contact local store for telephone number
www.wholefoodsmarket.com

INDEX

ABOUT THE AUTHOR

Lionel Vatinet is a distinguished Master Baker and one of the most sought-after bread consultants in America. Educated as a baker's apprentice in France, Lionel remains true to the pledge he gave when inducted as a guild member in Les Compagnons du Devoir to educate others in the art of baking. He was the founding instructor at the San Francisco Baking Institute, where he educated bakers from such respected bakeries as La Brea Bakery, Zabar's, Terra Breads in Vancover, Cottage Lane in New Zealand, and Panera Bread, and in 1999 he coached the American team to their first-ever First Place win in the World Cup of Baking tournament. Lionel opened La Farm Bakery in the same year, a modern bakery that continues to respect and honor the centuries-old baking traditions and techniques Vatinet learned in his native France. He lives in Cary, North Carolina, with his wife and business partner, Missy Vatinet, and their two children.